WAR NOIR

WAR NOIR

Raymond Chandler and the Hard-Boiled Detective as Veteran in American Fiction

Sarah Trott

UNIVERSITY PRESS OF MISSISSIPPI • JACKSON

www.upress.state.ms.us

Designed by Peter D. Halverson

The University Press of Mississippi is a member of the Association of American University Presses.

First printing 2016
∞
Library of Congress Cataloging-in-Publication Data

Names: Trott, Sarah, 1982– author.
Title: War noir : Raymond Chandler and the hard-boiled detective as veteran in American fiction / Sarah Trott.
Other titles: Raymond Chandler and the hard-boiled detective as veteran in American fiction | Hard-boiled detective as veteran in American fiction
Description: Jackson : University Press of Mississippi, 2016. | Includes bibliographical references and index.
Identifiers: LCCN 2016019967 (print) | LCCN 2016033878 (ebook) | ISBN 9781496808646 (hardback) | ISBN 9781496808653 (epub single) | ISBN 9781496808660 (epub institutional) | ISBN 9781496808677 (pdf single) | ISBN 9781496808684 (pdf institutional)
Subjects: LCSH: Chandler, Raymond, 1888–1959—Criticism and interpretation. | Chandler, Raymond, 1888–1959—Characters—Philip Marlowe. | Marlowe, Philip (Fictitious character) | World War, 1939–1945—Influence. | Post-traumatic stress disorder in literature. | Noir fiction, American—History and criticism. | Detective and mystery stories, American—History and criticism. | BISAC: LITERARY CRITICISM / American / General. | LITERARY CRITICISM / Mystery & Detective.
Classification: LCC PS3505.H3224 Z87 2016 (print) | LCC PS3505.H3224 (ebook) | DDC 813/.52—dc23
LC record available at https://lccn.loc.gov/2016019967

British Library Cataloging-in-Publication Data available

CONTENTS

ACKNOWLEDGMENTS

Raymond Chandler once noted that "whatever you set out to do, you have to do as well as you know how," and this work would not have been completed to such a standard without the support of a few special people, to whom I would like to extend my gratitude.

I would first and foremost like to thank Swansea University for providing the financial assistance necessary for me to pursue the research for this work. I would like to thank the Department of Political and Cultural Studies at Swansea University and in particular my very good friend and colleague Stephen McVeigh. Our long discussions on the finer details of Chandler's life and works proved incredibly useful and helped to shape many of the ideas in this project. His continued assistance and guidance have made it possible to realize everything I set out to achieve in this work; to Steve I owe so much and am unequivocally grateful for his constant enthusiasm and unfaltering support. Additionally, to Rachel Farebrother at Swansea University and Andrew Pepper at Queen's College Belfast I extend huge thanks not only for providing continued support, but also for offering advice on structure and style, and acting as sounding boards for my ideas.

I would like to extend thanks to Tamsen Harward at Chorion, the company monitoring the literary rights for the Raymond Chandler Estate. Through our correspondence I received not only sustained interest and support but also the assistance of the estate. Graham Greene, the executor of Chandler's estate, generously provided permission to use any material uncovered at both Oxford's New Bodleian Library and the Charles E. Young Research Library, University of California Los Angeles. To Ms. Harward, Mr. Greene, and the Special Collections Departments at both the Bodleian and at UCLA I give very sincere thanks for all their assistance.

I also wish to acknowledge Yves Tremblay, Bill Rawling, and the archival team at the Directorate of History and Heritage in Ottawa, Canada. The

DHH kindly supplied copies of Raymond Chandler's original military and medical file and surpassed my expectations by offering helpful guidance on documents and resources. Additionally, Calista Lucy, the keeper of the archives at Dulwich College, England, assisted me in developing many of my ideas surrounding Philip Marlowe's classical origins.

Last but not least, I want to thank my friends and family who have supported me in so many ways during the course of this project. Thanks to Anne-Marie, Chris, and Mike for having complete faith in me and supporting me during the early dark days; Esther for keeping me grounded; and Sarah for the regular cake infusions. To Suzanne and David, who kept me going with regular coffee breaks, stimulating intellectual discussion, and reading drafts of various chapters, I extend the biggest of thanks. In your individual ways you have each kept me going throughout this process and have provided me with support whenever I asked.

Finally, thanks to my parents. This work has been eight years in the making, and I genuinely could not have completed it without them. They have been my rock, and I am more grateful to them than they will ever know. Since there are simply no words to fully express the extent of my love and appreciation, I dedicate this book to them as a gesture of my heartfelt gratitude for their unwavering support.

PREFACE

I have lived my whole life on the edge of nothing. Once you have had to lead a platoon into direct machine-gun fire, nothing is ever the same again.

—CHANDLER, "THE RAYMOND CHANDLER PAPERS," BODLEIAN LIBRARY

First, I should preface this book by stating that I am not the first to write an interpretation of the works of and life of the American author Raymond Chandler. Over the years prominent scholars have produced a number of insightful studies on Chandler's life, and writers such as Frank MacShane, Jerry Speir, Tom Hiney, and Tom Williams have each examined a variety of biographical, literary, or social aspects. However, unlike many of the previous examinations, which have considered Chandler throughout his life, the central emphasis of this particular work has been to focus on the writer at particular moments during his life and, crucially, to reexamine the existing research concerning Chandler's experiences during the First World War, which are ambiguous at best. While MacShane, Hiney, and Williams offer interpretations of his experience during the war, much of their information only intermittently contemplates the bearing that the war had upon Chandler's later life and work. This book is an attempt to address that deficit by creating a biographical and psychological framework in an attempt to understand the inner motivation that stimulated Chandler to behave the way he did and that became incorporated within his unique writing style.

The second point I need to make is that I have endeavored to pinpoint the precise position that Chandler's work occupies in the literary and biographical studies of war and its consequential trauma by utilizing a style of literature generally categorized as "popular" or "lowbrow." The phrase "hard-boiled"—a term unquestionably associated with the crime genre to describe its unique style—has been in popular usage since the First World

War as an adjective applied to the tough drill sergeants who made men out of boys and soldiers out of civilians. When the war ended, the soldiers who had been molded by the horror and brutality of war once again returned to civilian life, popularizing the term "hard-boiled" as a reference that reflected a tough, hard-hitting, and cynical form of behavior, but that, nonetheless, had been associated with and shaped by war. As Peter Tamony points out, in the postwar era "the word developed [. . .] to [mean] hard, shrewd, keen" (258). It is this meaning that carries over into the hard-boiled fiction of the 1920s and 1930s, yet war is rarely acknowledged as an influence upon this style of writing.

Raymond Chandler always admitted that he was a poor plotter, and Philip Marlowe is perhaps the greatest mystery Chandler created. Yet, to my mind, it is impossible to read *The Big Sleep* and *The Long Goodbye*—witnessing the Marlowe/Sternwood and Marlowe/Lennox relationships—and *not* come to the opinion that the detective is a veteran of war. Having said that, however, it is valuable to delineate the clues that Chandler deploys *across* the limited series of just seven Marlowe novels and which in their entirety reveal the detective's veteran status. I acknowledge that some may argue that "small signs" by themselves do not *prove* that Chandler suffered from any war-related trauma or posttraumatic stress disorder (PTSD), and admittedly, many of the peculiarities and foibles examined in this book could be interpreted as simply the qualities of an old, eccentric writer. However, my aim with the research conducted for this book is to emphasize that by aggregating all those "small signs," the theory that Chandler created Marlowe as a war-troubled veteran of the Great War starts to become a real possibility. When examined collectively what becomes visible are the broader symptoms of traumatic wounding. While this work examines Chandler's biography in detail, it will be subsequently demonstrated that the writer's peculiarities and character traits are vital in recognizing the transference of symptoms onto his detective protagonist. By acknowledging the symptoms suffered by Chandler himself, it is thus feasible to recognize Philip Marlowe as a traumatized veteran of war.

And so, the quote that prefaces this introduction is a fitting way to begin an examination of a war-traumatized protagonist because it alludes to the horrors of the First World War and the extent to which Chandler was affected. This small but nevertheless telling insight is the only occasion that Chandler wrote candidly about how acutely his experiences on the front line in France had changed him, openly expressing how his encounters while fighting had left him feeling as though he had lived "on the edge of nothing."

This provocative quote, by perhaps the most distinguished American crime writer of the twentieth century, poses a valuable vantage point to illuminate and critically reevaluate the frequently neglected impact of war upon the hard-boiled style of crime writing.

One line of particular inquiry in this work has been to scrutinize Chandler's existing biographical material. The two prominent biographies used for this work, *The Life of Raymond Chandler* (1978), by Frank MacShane, and *Raymond Chandler: A Biography* (1997), by Tom Hiney, approach their subject from different viewpoints and have placed their own distinctive emphases upon differing aspects of Chandler's character and experiences. MacShane, who was approached by Chandler's heir and executrix, Helga Greene, to write his biography, concentrates on Chandler's life in great detail and wrote what is generally considered to be the most exhaustive examination of the author to date. Utilizing original sources, MacShane accessed Chandler's letters, papers, and manuscripts from various agents, publishing houses, and acquaintances. His analysis of Chandler's war experience relied upon documentary evidence from the Ministry of Defence in London, the Air Historical Branch (later the Royal Air Force), the Ministry of Defence in Ottawa, and the Public Archives of Canada. But despite this wealth of data, an examination of this collected material shows that MacShane's biography nonetheless contains a number of significant inconsistencies that will be discussed later in this work.

Tom Hiney focused on creating a cultural and social framework through which to examine Chandler's life and work. He notes interesting connections between Chandler's experiences during the First World War and the depiction of violence in his novels in addition to drawing attention to the psychological and behavioral difficulties that Chandler suffered later in life. But Hiney's biography does not improve upon MacShane's account of Chandler's life, and it also contains irregularities in the description of the writer's experiences on the French front line during the war.

In addition to the two principal biographies, Jerry Speir's unique and important contribution to understanding Philip Marlowe's character highlights fascinating recurring themes that appear in the author's works. In *Raymond Chandler* (1981) Speir examines each of the novels within its own individual context, providing a persuasive and intelligent argument of how each story should be read and understood. He explains that by examining Marlowe in this way many of the arguments posited by critics regarding the detective's temperament should be either reevaluated or dismissed. By placing particular emphasis on Marlowe's reactions while investigating individual scenarios, the detective appears a far more authentic and sympathetic character than previously acknowledged. And so by generating a further literary examination of the writer's works, my contribution more naturally resembles the scholarly approach taken by Speir.

This monograph, therefore, establishes a case for a style of hard-boiled crime fiction that I have characterized as "war noir"; a description that seems reasonable given it is a style that merges two complimentary genres—the hard-boiled and war genres—into a single entity.

In the field of hard-boiled crime fiction the influence of war has traditionally been marginalized in favor of tackling more "pressing" issues such as race, gender, class, economics, and politics. Considering the prevailing presence of warfare in twentieth-century American culture it is reasonable to assume that crime fiction, like any other literary style, could be profoundly influenced by these historical events. Culture, after all, takes its lead from the established social environment and the meaning that we assign to various historical or personal events.

Nevertheless, we must remember that war has also had a significant influence in a different area of contemporary culture. The Second World War is extremely important in understanding the style of 1940s–1950s cinema referred to as "film noir." In Edward Dmytryk's film *Crossfire* (1947), for example, a minor character, soon to be murdered by Robert Ryan's sadistic and anti-Semitic army sergeant, Montgomery, compares the war with an uneaten peanut: while it is before you, desired but uneaten, the peanut is the focus of your complete attention; once the peanut is eaten it is no longer the object of your attention. This rather crude analogy sums up how the war had dominated the lives and mentality of Americans for a long time. All of a sudden, however, the war was over and no longer the dominant influence upon individual lives. For the veteran in society, the significance lies in the postwar disorientation at returning home: instead of relief and celebration there is confusion, uncertainty, and a seriously changed world to come to terms with. Several noir films are explicitly concerned with this, and many implicitly invoke the wartime and postwar American world. Raymond Chandler's own screenplay *The Blue Dahlia* (1946), discussed later in this work, depicts Alan Ladd's distinguished fighter pilot, Johnny Morrisson, who returns from the war with two comrades only to find a world that they scarcely recognize. Soldiers do not return necessarily as wartime heroes; instead they become confused inhabitants of a socially and morally ambiguous world.

Many noir films are quite obvious about the dark side of American society they seek to portray, a society which became even darker during these years and afterwards. Even the phrase itself—"film noir"—signifies a "blackening" of film, a comment made by French film critic Nino Frank in 1946 to describe the darkened, shadowy, and isolated atmosphere of many films at the time.

Ultimately film noir is very much a "postwar" style representative of the postwar male whose problems suggested the breakdown of established notions of social functioning within society, including the historical trauma of the war itself. Experienced in film noir is the acute fear of a loss of stability, identity, and security on the part of the male. Men have returned from combat to find a social order that is no longer familiar to them and an apprehension that women are overstepping their traditional roles in postwar America.

The point to be made, then, is that this "philosophy" seems to be an appropriate summation of American society during the immediate postwar years: America had survived the war but was, to many, inexplicably "darkening," just as Weimar Germany had in the years following the First World War. During this time philosophers and sociologists, such as Siegfried Kracauer, saw that many people, including young people in Germany, were becoming nihilistic; they were somehow hollow and directionless, living blameless but bland lives. Many of the best film noir directors of the 1940s were of German descent, escaping the rise of the Nazis by escaping to America. These post–World War I immigrant directors, such as Billy Wilder (who collaborated with Chandler on the screenplay for *Double Indemnity*), Edgar Ulmer, and Robert Siodmak, came from that "darkening" world and saw a resemblance between it and the America they emigrated to during and after the Second World War. It is out of these dark beginnings and the careful and skillful incorporation of German expressionism that the complex and violent world of *noir* would arise in 1940s America.

And so Chandler's assertion that after experiencing war nothing is ever the same goes to the very core of how we should understand and interpret "war noir." It is my assertion that Chandler transposed representations of war into his work, creating an urban location that smacks of corruption, vice, and postwar disillusionment. To complement the sordid surroundings, Chandler created a protagonist who suffers the torment of returning to a society that does not acknowledge his sacrifice and loyalty. But this is not the only difficulty confronting Chandler's protagonist, since, as this book will show, while Chandler never explicitly identified Marlowe as a veteran of war, revealing signs demonstrate that Marlowe was psychologically ill-equipped to cope adequately with his surroundings. By closely examining Marlowe's behavior in certain situations, it does not take an enormous leap of faith to interpret him as a combat veteran suffering under the weight of his experiences and returning to an alien landscape, an urban Los Angles that has become a no-man's land, a ruin of its former self, now in the grip of gangsters, femme fatales, brutish police, and sleazy politicians.

Yet while Chandler is crucial in establishing the foundation and parameters of war noir, he is by no means the sole purveyor of the style. Numerous writers have, since the Second World War sought to include a war veteran protagonist or draw upon war-influenced themes to "darken" the mood and tone of their work. Writers such as Elmore Leonard, Charles Willeford, Robert B. Parker, James Crumley, Robert Stone, Newton Thornburg, James Lee Burke, Jeremiah Healy, Robert Crais, Benjamin M. Shutz, Robert Ray, Geoffrey Norman, Walter Mosley, and James Ellroy have all sought to include a veteran protagonist into their work, suggesting that American hard-boiled crime fiction is the perfect vehicle for representing any era's social concerns, disillusionment, and postwar tension. This book, then, is, on the one hand an attempt to correct certain misconceptions about Raymond Chandler, and on the other hand an attempt to highlight the importance of war as a major influence upon the style by taking Chandler as the originator of war noir.

Because no other writer in the genre experienced the First World War, including Dashiell Hammett, who was an army ambulance driver in Baltimore for the duration of his military experience, not only are Chandler and his work the ideal prism through which to examine the close stylistic connection between the crime fiction and other significant literary movements in the early twentieth century, but they also provide an opportunity to highlight the significance of the veteran in American fiction. What will be argued in this book is that Chandler demonstrates the crucial interaction between crime and war literatures. Both of these styles capture the essence of society; encapsulate the zeitgeist of the period; and not infrequently reveal soldiers, veterans, and traumatized participants of American war. Both genres produce literary figures that have provided American literature with an intersecting style of fiction; a legacy that has remained a subliminal aspect of hard-boiled fiction, while nevertheless holding a significant place in the American canon.

War noir becomes a far more observable literary style in the wake of the Vietnam War in particular. Woody Haut's assertion that post-Vietnam crime fiction writers became obsessed with verisimilitude, which therefore requires us to "reappraise the genre's relationship to the culture" (*Neon Noir* 2), lays the groundwork for reassessing the significance of hard-boiled fiction in light of war's traumatic impact. Following the war in Southeast Asia, a literature that was obsessed with telling the truth, questioning leaders, exposing lies, and, above all, gaining recognition for those who, some argued, had sacrificed themselves for a so-called "just" American cause, unashamedly emerged with cynical enthusiasm. Writers such as Crumley, Willeford, Thornburg, Stone, Ellroy, Leonard, and, later, Crais, Burke, Parker, and Mosley represent merely a small selection of the era's crime writers whose work owes itself to the impact of war and/or military experience. From Crumley's almost apocalyptic vision of post-Vietnam American society to Ellroy's deeply disturbed and conflicted characters to Mosley's witnesses to history, all of the writers have woven war trauma so successfully into their works that they openly question and examine the relationship between the private "I" and public crimes.

Though groundbreaking in style, we must acknowledge that many of the greatest crime novelists and critics of the contemporary era give credit to an earlier school of writers, and eminent among them is Raymond Chandler. Demonstrating his respect for his predecessor, Crumley coarsely noted, "I always introduce my work by explaining that I am a bastard child of Raymond Chandler—without his books, my books would be completely different" (*Contemporary Authors* 67). In the years since Chandler's death various writers have attempted to emulate Chandler's work and style, picking up on the subliminal indicators that have hinted at something appreciably more complex than the traditional (and rather simplistic) concept of Philip Marlowe as the embodiment of chivalric honor. With the resurgence of interest in the crime genre in the 1970s, writers since the Vietnam War have bypassed the long-established perceptions of Chandler's protagonist in favor of a multifaceted interpretation of Marlowe as something more than simply a knight. Instead, Marlowe is reinterpreted in this book as a warrior, a soldier, a remnant of something far more complex than Malory's tales of *Le Morte d'Arthur*.

And so, while contemporary writers have used the hard-boiled genre to formulate a crime *literature* that incorporates war-traumatized protagonists forcefully into the disillusionment of the era, we should not forget that their initial inspiration is rooted in the style of an earlier generation. As we see from the cinematic style of film noir, American society in the 1940s and 50s had little appetite for representations of disenchanted veterans, war trauma, and bitterness; instead mystery, crime, cynicism, wit, and sexual motivations were popular choices. Yet, like film noir, hard-boiled fiction—and war noir in particular—focuses upon the diminished masculinity of the male protagonist and the dark side of human nature. War is the subliminal psychological crisis troubling the protagonists of both film noir and war noir. The major difference in hard-boiled crime fiction, especially in the post-Vietnam era, is the extent to which the protagonists *recognize* that war is the underlying factor affecting their ability to function socially and emotionally.

As Chandler himself noted, the psychological foundation for the popularity of the murder and crime novel was a topic that had never been fully considered. In 1943 he hypothesized, "There is a lot more to this subject than most people realize . . . [I]t is just possible that the tensions in a novel of murder are the simplest and yet most complete pattern of the tensions in which we live in this generation" (qtd. in Hiney and MacShane 95). Considering America's propensity for foreign intervention throughout the twentieth century, it is not too simplistic to assume that Chandler was making reference to the damaging impact of war upon American society. The genre, as he observed, merely recreates and reiterates the simplest tensions of a particular generation, something that becomes extremely explicit in the work of later writers: the crimes are those of government and state, and the unwarranted deaths are those of soldiers and veterans who are serving some obscure political end. While Marlowe's psychological symptoms of war's experience are subconscious, contemporary detectives openly display their postcombat trauma and war experience; it is both a badge of honor and a nightmare to forget. The crimes of the state are neither easily forgotten nor forgiven. Post-Vietnam crime novels, therefore, represent, as Haut suggests, a reinterpretation of the national narrative (*Neon Noir* 2). However, it is my contention that war noir, as a narrative, opens up the American canon and owes much to Raymond Chandler, whose novels synthesize the key components of detective fiction and the war genre by integrating a war-damaged and traumatized protagonist into the complexity of postwar American society: his veteran detective Philip Marlowe.

In order to develop this argument, chapter 1 will examine Chandler's biography to question the established view of the author's life and experiences. By employing a psychological sketch of Chandler's experience during the First World War, fresh new insights into his writing and characterization can be gleaned. The primary research undertaken recognizes Chandler as a psychologically scarred veteran who projected his own psychological frailties into his writing. Accordingly his detective fiction appears less like the narrative of a selfless and idealized hero and more that of a traumatized individual attempting to find meaning for his war experience in a society that is indifferent toward his sacrifices. It appears increasingly evident that Chandler used his fictional detective as an attempt to bridge a gap between the noble ideals for which war was fought and the indifference of contemporary society. Marlowe strives to ameliorate society's ills against seemingly overwhelming odds because if he does not he feels his sacrifices will have been in vain. After reconsidering the effects of Chandler's own war trauma, this work proposes that his detective fiction is a literature of traumatic war experience.

Chandler's experiences during the First World War were instrumental in forming the psychological flaws that would later emerge from his detective, Philip Marlowe. Thus, chapter 2 discusses the version of Chandler's experiences presented by his biographers, Frank MacShane and Tom Hiney, before conducting a new and original investigation into the accuracy of their survey. MacShane and Hiney used Chandler's own correspondence to formulate a narrative version of his experiences in France.[1] In pursuance of this objective, Chandler's letters, which are held at the Bodleian Library in Oxford and at the University of California, Los Angeles, were reexamined, paying particular attention to the author's state of mind at the time of writing. To fully appreciate the nature of the trauma suffered during the war, Chandler's war records were obtained from the Canadian Archives in Ottawa, and research was conducted into the precise circumstances of his wounding and subsequent reassignment in 1918. This aspect of Chandler's life is an area that has not previously been examined in great detail, and obtaining the relevant material was achieved by consulting the Directorate of History and Heritage in Ottawa, Canada, to gain vital documentary evidence and troop movements on the front line. The evidence contained in Chandler's military records and medical files provides a far more tangible version of his wartime experience, ascertaining as it does, the precise location of his battalion on the front and the circumstances surrounding his return to England in June 1918.

Chapter 3 considers the relationship between detective fiction and war fiction and the impact of one style upon the other. Taking examples from renowned First World War novels it will demonstrate that the same disillusionment and despair prevalent in the work of the renowned Lost Generation are equally prevalent in Chandler's novels. When reconsidered in this light, Chandler's works, like the Lost Generation, represent the angst and trauma of a specific moment in American history. Reading his novels as a convergence of the war novel and crime fiction, Chandler's work can be reconsidered as a legitimate representation of society and the trauma of war. Significantly then, Chandler's work shifts from the realms of "popular culture" to the "high culture" of the wider "Lost" Generation of the First World War.

In a similar way that the first three chapters focus on the peculiar idiosyncrasies of Chandler as a person, chapters 4 and 5 explore how these characteristics have been projected onto his protagonist Philip Marlowe. In the first of these chapters Marlowe's character traits will be closely examined by considering certain notable features such as the detective's origins, characterization, disillusionment, and chivalric code of honor. A careful examination of Chandler's work, including his short stories, highlights the differences between Marlowe's generally accepted character and his war-weary persona, demonstrating that his personality and motivation are far more complex than the stereotypical hard-boiled detective. Instead, like Chandler, it becomes possible to identify the small but distinctive aspects of Marlowe's character that suggest that he is a psychologically damaged war veteran fighting new battles on a different front.

Chapter 5 reconsiders Chandler's own war experience to show that Marlowe, like his creator, displayed symptoms of combat-related posttraumatic stress disorder. Examining the novels for these manifestations, Marlowe's symptoms appear to fall into the three separate symptom-related categorizations of PTSD. Over the course of the novels Marlowe reveals many physical and psychological indicators that are attributable to the harrowing experience of warfare, all of which have been overlooked by previous critics.

In this chapter also, I discuss Marlowe's love of chess and the symbolic meaning that it has within the detective stories themselves. According to the conventional view Marlowe suffers rejection and disillusionment with every case he solves and appears to take comfort in the chivalric values of the game. But while Marlowe appears to possess a certain chivalrous quality, it will be argued that Chandler did not originally intend Marlowe to be interpreted as a knight in shining armor. Instead, the chapter will demonstrate how the game of chess becomes a metaphor for the city of Los Angeles that enables the troubled detective to locate himself within a structured and orderly environment. It also allows Marlowe to reassess and review his own case-related actions and dealings by evaluating his movements on the board. The chessboard becomes a metaphorical device conveying Marlowe and Chandler's opinions of the society in which they reside.

In addition to Marlowe, his other veteran characters also unwittingly suffer posttraumatic symptoms, and the focus of chapter 6 will be an exploration of the most significant of Chandler's novels and the work that best represents his protagonist as a veteran, *The Long Goodbye* (1953). Examining Marlowe's behavior around, and attitude towards, the two veterans identified in the novel, Roger Wade and Terry Lennox, it is argued that Marlowe becomes part of a "band of brothers," an intimate group of veterans in whose company the detective displays the undeniable evidence of his past experiences and trauma.

The final chapter will consider how Chandler's novels have created a lasting legacy in contemporary fiction. The Vietnam War and the revival of the "traditional" hard-boiled detective during the 1970s signaled a considerable change in the image of the detective and the crime genre in general. In the aftermath of Vietnam, renewed interest in Chandler's novels brought with it a revival of the character of the veteran detective, with contemporary writers taking Chandler and Marlowe as their models. Just like these war veteran detectives, psychologists Roy Grinker and John Speigel note that soldiers returning from battle, "particularly those suffering from war neuroses[,] show much more aggressiveness and hostility in their verbalizations and behaviour [. . .] They are resentful and openly angry [. . .] and are freely and destructively critical of what they see and hear at home" (308). Rather than concealing their trauma like Marlowe, contemporary detectives instead wore their trauma on their sleeves. Characters became hard-hitting, hard-drinking, drug-taking, embittered characters that were unafraid to voice their aversion to society and the government. They developed an almost psychopathic personality that swung between aggressiveness and submission. Grinker and Speigel state that the "psychopathic personality vacillate[s] between an aggressive hostility, overcompensated independence and a passive drive, which [is] always frustrated [. . .] The result [is] a dangerous character, who [is] likely to commit either suicide or homicide" (342).

Within the framework of a war veteran detective, this book aims to challenge the conventional interpretation of crime fiction as "pop culture" and the description of Raymond Chandler as simply an eccentric old man. Just as contemporary Hemingway biographer Kenneth Lynn used original documents and testimony to challenge and expose the shortcomings in Carlos Baker's decades-old accepted view of the writer, this monograph aims to go beyond the commonly accepted interpretation to uncover the "genuine" Chandler.[2] The trauma Chandler suffered in combat affected the writer to such a degree that it became impossible to avoid the transference of traumatic symptoms into his work. The troubled life he led and the symptoms he suffered after his war-time experience are testimony to the fact that his trauma was real. But through his trauma came creativity and originality, and Chandler came to view Marlowe as far more than a protagonist in his novels. The detective became a major source of comfort and a cathartic device from which Chandler could evade, but never fully escape, his troubling symptoms.

Like the Lost Generation, Chandler's work became a platform capable of depicting the emotional consequences of war and its brutal impact upon the individual. Chandler's lasting legacy remains his creation of a vehicle for the representation of veterans, their trauma, and their dislocation from the wider society. These significant similarities with the themes of the Lost Generation present a strong argument for his inclusion. Chandler incorporated his own psychological trauma into his work, creating in the process a character that epitomized the disillusionment of an entire generation sent to war and propelled him and his work into a maelstrom of emotional trauma, social change, and human indifference.

WAR NOIR

1

WAR'S TRAUMATIC IMPACT

I should guess that all in all he has had a lonely life . . . He's a lonely old eagle.
—CHANDLER, QTD. IN MACSHANE, *LIFE*

The impact of war upon American hard-boiled fiction is a topic that is rarely discussed. While many works in the crime genre touch upon the more disagreeable aspects of peacetime society—corporate greed, political dishonesty, a corrupt police force—the psychological and emotional impact of war upon the genre has remained relatively unappreciated. Utilizing the crime genre to express their disillusionment arising from war and the subsequent treatment of American veterans, many contemporary writers expose a society ignorant of their characters' traumas. They focus their discontent upon a government that routinely abandons its soldiers after their return from combat. While in combat they are hailed as heroes, but on their return they are quietly forgotten and left to survive on their own. As a form of protest, many embittered writers who belonged to the generations "lost" to conflict consciously incorporated a new, more extreme vision into their work. By embedding a war-traumatized protagonist, an unforgiving portrayal of violence, a seething undercurrent of frustration and resentment, and the insensitivity of an uncaring society into the story-line, the hard-boiled novel and the war genre became inextricably fused to produce a unique hybrid. This distinctive "war noir" absorbed the anger, discontent, and brutality of both genres and came to symbolize the bitter criticism directed against an unsympathetic American culture and a cynical and corrupted state.

Yet while the impact of war upon crime fiction, particularly since the Vietnam War, has received some consideration, the influence of war upon the writers themselves has received less attention. American hard-boiled crime writers were directly involved in the numerous wars that have occurred throughout the twentieth century, including Dashiell Hammett, Raymond Chandler, Charles Willeford, Robert B. Parker, Elmore Leonard, and James Crumley. As well as those directly involved in war, many other writers have been exposed to war's destabilizing influence upon society, especially during and immediately after Vietnam. As a result of this destabilization, biographical studies of many of these writers reveal a new and greater forcefulness in their work that, in many cases, necessitates a reevaluation of the complexity of the literature produced in the crime genre.

As one of the principal proponents of the advancement of American hard-boiled fiction, an examination of Raymond Chandler's life is especially relevant to the task of establishing the impact of war—in this case, the First World War—not only on the author's life and work, but more importantly on the origins of the distinctive subtleties in Chandler's style. It is these subtleties, this book argues, that would inspire later generations of crime writers to establish more nuanced and multifaceted characters that resonate with the era's wartime generations. Understanding the nuances and idiosyncrasies of Chandler's life is important because they reveal not only the impact of war upon the intimate construction of his work, but also how he achieved his place within the American literary landscape as a writer of traumatic literature.

While many of the peculiarities and character traits described in this chapter may be interpreted as simply the qualities of an eccentric personality, when considered collectively and placed within the psychological framework of Chandler's biography, something more significant starts to emerge, demonstrative of the symptoms of severe emotional stress. In light of the damaging aftermath of the First World War, Chandler's own behavior and symptoms become a fundamental factor in creating the potential for the veteran status of his detective protagonist. By recognizing the symptoms of trauma in Chandler himself it becomes plausible to see how these same symptoms became a central facet of the idiosyncrasies bestowed upon Philip Marlowe.

Two years before he died Chandler gave an illuminating summation of his troubled life in a letter to his London solicitor, Michael Gilbert. Writing, "I have lived on the edge of nothing" (qtd. in Hiney and MacShane 242), Chandler described a life marred by torment and lacking lasting contentment. He lived, as Frank MacShane says, "a tortured and lonely life only temporarily relieved by moments of happiness," when he would, like his fictional detective Philip Marlowe, become an "effective Galahad" (*Life* 268, 246). Like many war veterans Chandler was never able to fully erase the memory of his wartime experience, which troubled him throughout his life. To fully understand the theory that Philip Marlowe is a character born from the traumatizing impact of war it is essential to recognize the intensity of Chandler's own experiences in France. Only by doing so can we appreciate how his trauma seeped into cultural representations, thereby creating war noir.

Judith Lewis Herman makes the assertion that while the normal response to atrocities is to "banish them from [the] consciousness," quite often these horrors "refuse to be buried," and in time "the story of the traumatic events surface not as verbal narrative but as a symptom" (1). Chandler's postwar life is a catalogue of unpredictable behavior, mood swings, alcoholism, oscillating swings between intimacy and loneliness, attempted suicide and recklessness, all of which are symptomatic of psychological neurosis. Although not recognized institutionally as a medical condition at the time, it now seems plausible that Chandler suffered combat-related PTSD, the debilitating psychological condition prevalent in veterans of war. For Chandler, this neurosis would reemerge during times of stress throughout the rest of his life.

▾ ▾ ▾

Born in Chicago on 23 July 1888, Raymond Thornton Chandler was the only son of Maurice and Florence Chandler. Living in England for his most informative years after his parents' divorce, he quickly became accustomed to the dominance of his female relatives, social isolation, and an extreme sense of loneliness. Tom Hiney notes, "In both suburban South London and Quaker Waterford, Chandler was an anomaly—an American-sounding boy with a pretty Irish mother about whom people, including her own family, gossiped [. . .] In late Victorian England, he was without a clear social class, nationality or male role model" (11). The solitude and seclusion of his early life caused Chandler to develop "an extraordinary sense of loyalty [. . .] and a sense of justice that became a central part of his character and gave him the attitudes he was to express later through his character Philip Marlowe" (MacShane, *Life* 5).

Chandler attended Dulwich College from the age of twelve, where he was educated until 1905 under the tutelage of Arthur Herman Gilkes, a published novelist. Under his guidance Chandler developed a passion for literature and language, and acquired the belief that a man of honor was one who was "capable of understanding that which was good" (qtd. in MacShane, *Life* 9). It was a quality that Chandler eagerly embraced and which would later become the thread that links all of his fictional detectives. Intent on a literary career, Chandler began writing poetry and articles for London newspapers and magazines, such as *Academy* and the *Westminster Gazette*. His poetry was highly romanticized and conventional, and invariably explored the theme of knights and ladies, nobility and honorable sacrifice. Although MacShane believes "The less said of Chandler's poetry the better" (*Life* 16), these verses were the first expression of the individualistic code of chivalry that would later develop into an important facet of Philip Marlowe's character.

In the five years that followed, Chandler wrote twenty-seven poems, seven essays, and numerous reviews. But despite this achievement he felt restless and unfulfilled; yearning to return to the land of his birth, declaring that, "America seemed to call to me in some mysterious way" (qtd. in Gardiner and Walker, 25). Initially, however, his experience of America was a disappointment that precipitated a rude awakening when he quickly realized that contrary to his expectation he "had no feeling of identity with the United States" and no feeling of identity for England either. Chandler felt as though he had become "a man without a country" (qtd. in Gardiner and Walker, 24, 25) and would later proclaim that "to be homesick for a home you haven't got is rather poignant" (qtd. in Hiney and MacShane 206). Unsurprisingly, this acute sensation of a lack of identity later emerged as a prominent feature of the personality that Chandler gave to Marlowe, and although Chandler always denied any direct autobiographical connection, years later he would admit, "there's a lot of him in me," especially "his loneliness" (qtd. in MacShane, *Life* 253).

By 1916 Chandler's mother joined him in California, but the tranquility of their new life together was cut short when a year later Chandler decided to return to Europe following America's entrance into the First World War. Choosing to enlist with the Canadian Army, he traveled to Victoria, British Columbia, where he joined the Fiftieth Regiment of the Canadian Army, declaring that "it was still natural for me to prefer a British uniform" (qtd. in MacShane, *Life* 27). He received a brief induction before sailing to Liverpool on 7 November 1917. After training in Seaford, Sussex, Chandler was assigned to the Seventh Battalion of the Canadian Expeditionary Force, which was ordered to the French front line in March 1918. It was a shocking experience. For the young Chandler, "as for most soldiers brought so quickly to the front, his experiences were too overwhelming to digest" (MacShane, *Life* 28–9) and the carnage around him would have soon shattered "the illusion of manly honour and glory in battle" (Herman 20). This reaction was, however, not unusual among new recruits. According to psychiatrists J. W. Appel and G. W. Bebbe, "There is no such thing as 'getting used to combat.' [. . .] Each moment of combat imposes a strain so great that men will break down" (1470). It is incredible to think, that "in every war in which American soldiers have fought in [the twentieth century], the chances of becoming a psychiatric casualty—of being debilitated for some period of time as a consequence of the stresses of military life—were greater than the chances of being killed by enemy fire" (qtd. in Grossman 43). Similarly, in a study conducted by R. L. Swank and W. E. Marchand on the psychological effects of World War Two, it was found that at least 98 percent of soldiers suffered some form of psychological breakdown. They noted that when it came to combat, "One thing alone seems certain: Practically all infantry soldiers suffer from a neurotic reaction eventually if they are subjected to the stress of modern combat continuously enough" (21).

Throughout the First World War and for most of the twentieth century the political and military establishment denied the connection between psychological disorder and combat, and the complaint remained undiagnosed and unaccepted as a legitimate injury. Viewed by the military as the male counterpart of female hysteria, it became regarded as a sign of weakness and cowardice, treated with a brief rest period, or in more severe instances a so-called treatment "based on shaming, threats, and punishment" (Herman 21). In 1941, Abram Kardiner and Herbert Spiegel published a comprehensive clinical and theoretical study of "war neuroses," in which they protested: "The subject of neurotic disturbances consequent upon war has, in the past twenty-five years, been submitted to a good deal of capriciousness in public interest and psychiatric whims. But the public does not sustain its interest . . . and neither does psychiatry. Hence these conditions are not subject to continuous study . . . but only to periodic efforts which cannot be described as very diligent" (1). They further maintained that to incorrectly diagnose patients suffering from war neuroses as "hysterical" could be extremely injurious in its own right, essentially feminizing sufferers and impeding recovery. Furthermore, they also asserted that when the word is used, "its social meaning is that the subject is a predatory individual, trying to get something for nothing. The victim of such a neurosis is, therefore, without sympathy in court, and . . . without sympathy from his physicians, who often take . . . 'hysterical' to mean that the individual is suffering from some persistent form of wickedness, perversity, or weakness of will" (406).

It was not until the years following the Vietnam War that it finally became institutionally acceptable to recognize posttraumatic injury and psychological trauma as a permanent and unavoidable legacy of war (Herman 27). In 1980, psychological trauma became a "real" diagnosis when the American Psychiatric Association incorporated a new category, called "post-traumatic stress disorder" in its official manual of medical disorders (Herman 28).

This of course was too late for many veterans of the First World War who were aware of their psychological illness but unable to obtain help, and subsequently articulated their predicament in their work. Writers such as Chandler and also Ernest Hemingway, who committed suicide in 1961, would die before the causal relationship between combat and psychological trauma could be established, and before PTSD would gain social recognition as an injury equally as damaging as the severest of physical injuries.

According to the biographies by MacShane and Hiney, Chandler's military service came to an end in June 1918. MacShane states that "Chandler's service in France ended abruptly when an artillery barrage of eleven-inch German shells blew up everyone in his outfit, leaving him the sole survivor" (MacShane, Life 29). And Hiney notes that "Chandler was knocked unconscious [. . .] He was concussed and taken behind lines. The bombardment so depleted his outfit that it was disbanded and survivors, including Chandler, were transferred back to England" (43). They both note that Chandler was evacuated to Britain concussed and "shell-shocked" (Hiney 43) where he began drinking heavily. In all likelihood Chandler's experience of war caused the author psychological injury, yet because the existing biographical material is vague it does not allow us to comprehend the gravity of Chandler's war experiences. As such, the biographers' account will be reexamined in the next chapter.

The First World War was a pivotal moment for the twenty-eight-year-old Chandler. While MacShane believes that the psychological impact of war's brutality would make Chandler block out the memory of it (*Life* 29), many have overlooked the experience as a key influence upon Chandler's formulation of Philip Marlowe. MacShane, Hiney, Jerry Speir and more recently Tom Williams, have all confined their attention to dissecting his complex personality, believing Chandler's eccentricity to stem either from his upbringing, his education, his relationship with women, or his belief that he lacked a definite sense of identity. Chandler's only overt depiction of warfare, a short piece of prose titled "Trench Raid," has generally been cited as the writer's *only* attempt to exorcise his demons. Written between June and December 1918 while supposedly recuperating in England, "Trench Raid" is the only work in which Chandler explicitly attempted to recount his war experiences.

The piece, which is only 352 words long, is direct and displays the first signs of the detachment he employed to manage unpleasant realities. This short section combines the opening and ending of the piece:

> As he pushed aside the dirty blanket that served for a gas curtain the force of the bombardment hit him like the blow of a club to the base of the brain. He grovelled against the wall of the trench, nauseated by the din. He seemed to be alone in a universe of incredibly brutal noise . . . Time to move on. Mustn't stay too long in one place. He groped round the corner of the bay to the Lewis gun post. On the firing step the Number One of the gun crew was standing to with half of his body silhouetted above the parapet, motionless against the glare of the lights except that his hand was playing scales on the butt of his gun. (Qtd. in Moss 33)

This detached but precise writing style would later be used to great effect in the Philip Marlowe stories.

Because the story is incomplete, MacShane believes that Chandler never felt the need to finish "Trench Raid" or attempt further work in this style because suffering "bombardment was not as unbearable a memory as leading other men to their deaths in an infantry attack" (*Life* 29). By drawing this conclusion, however, MacShane demonstrates the failure of 1970s society to comprehend the variety of experiences that affect soldiers in wartime, and did not have the benefit of more recent scientific and medical evidence concerning the causal relationship between combat and PTSD. It is therefore likely that MacShane did not understand just how devastating warfare could be, whatever a soldier's location or experience of conflict. With this in mind, Chandler's failure to complete "Trench Raid" was not simply a matter of *choosing* to leave it unfinished, but, as contemporary medical evidence suggests, more likely a conscious decision not to revisit painful memories so soon after the event. As will be shown later in this chapter, it matters little whether a soldier is involved in an infantry attack or an artillery bombardment since each can result in some form of traumatic neuroses. Herman explains, "No two people have identical reactions [to a traumatic incident], even to the same event [. . . a] traumatic syndrome, despite its many constant features is not the same for everyone" (58). It is therefore likely that Chandler (together with countless thousands of soldiers from the Great War) emerged from combat suffering some form of emotional distress. Although MacShane's biography was published before PTSD became widely accepted as a legitimate injury, critics since have continued to overlook the crucial role that war experience played in the psychological development of his fictional characters, and the style and realism of his work. Such an oversight not only fails to appreciate the intensity of Chandler's own psychological suffering but fails to discern the motivation for in creating Philip Marlowe as a character who, like himself, was troubled by psychological wounds.

Further insight may be gained from Herbert Hendin and Ann Pollinger Haas's study, *Wounds of War: The Psychological Aftermath of Combat in Vietnam* (1984). Discussing a study conducted after World War Two to determine the variables for a person's susceptibility to PTSD, Hendin and Haas cite various analysts' discoveries of increased levels of trauma among those who had endured a troublesome childhood. In a study of combat veterans with PTSD, it was argued that each man's main pattern of symptoms was related to his individual childhood history, previous emotional conflicts, and his method of adaptation (Hendin and Haas 34). It is quite feasible, then, that Chandler's war experience may have been exacerbated by the tensions and insecurities of his early childhood. Exaggerated moral imperatives and an introverted demeanor had been etched on Chandler's character as a child, and it is plausible that after his war experiences that these personality traits may well have transformed themselves into periods of extreme depression, despair, and emotional instability.

This altered behavior, which was previously regarded as simple eccentricities, is a symptom consistent with PTSD. However, Hendin and Haas also note in their study that this theory has not been definitively proven, and some analysts have argued that childhood history plays less of a role in the development of trauma than does the severity of the traumatic event itself (34). Kardiner and Spiegel, for example, argued simply that with sufficient stress, "war neuroses" could affect anyone exposed to combat, no matter what war they fought in, the methods used, or the location of battle (2–7).

Nonetheless, the difficulty in diagnosing PTSD is that "[w]ith the passage of time . . . negative symptoms become the most prominent feature of the post-traumatic disorder, [and] the diagnosis becomes increasingly easy to overlook" (Herman 49). Herman continues, "Because post-traumatic symptoms are so persistent and so wide-ranging, they may be mistaken for enduring characteristics of the victim's personality" (49). However, simply dismissing these symptoms as merely the peculiarities or eccentricities of an individual's character can be extremely destructive for the sufferer. Disregarding a sufferer's symptoms can be "a costly error," because, "the person with unrecognized post-traumatic stress disorder is condemned to a diminished life, tormented by memory and bounded by helplessness and fear" (Herman 49).

In his later years Chandler acknowledged the lasting effects of his war experience. In 1957 he wrote, "Once you have led a platoon into direct machine gun fire, nothing is ever the same again" (qtd. in Moss 32). In this extremely rare insight Chandler acknowledged that his experience of combat had fundamentally changed him. Enduring horrifying events will, therefore, predictably lead to some form of psychological harm.

Likewise, an extreme heightening of cognition and the physiological senses can cause a profound inexpressibility, or as Elaine Scarry observes, it can "actively destroy" (4) the function of basic human expression. To put it a different way, a person can literally become "scared *senseless*" by certain events that are triggered by an amplification of the central nervous system. Roy Grinker and John Spiegel maintain that the effect of combat "is not like the writing on a slate that can be erased, leaving the slate as it was before. Combat leaves a lasting impression on men's minds, changing them as radically as any crucial experience through which they live" (371). The horror that Chandler observed inflicted psychological scarring that molded his subsequent behavior and profoundly influenced his self-expression.

Officially discharged from the Canadian Army on 20 February 1919, Chandler returned to America, but quickly became restless as he realized that he had progressed little from where he had been in 1913. He traveled the Pacific Coast, becoming particularly familiar with Washington State, a familiarity that he would later use in his short story "Goldfish" (1936).

Disenchanted with life, it is highly likely that by this time he was suffering the symptoms of PTSD, a condition that was almost certainly aggravated by his introspection and withdrawal from social interaction. Despite his troubles he was considered an eligible bachelor, and his so-called "natural shyness" (MacShane, *Life* 31) made him an attractive prospect to the women in his circle. Upon his arrival back in Los Angeles, Chandler renewed and deepened his relationship with Pearl Eugenie "Cissy" Pascal, the stepmother of Chandler's friend Gordon Pascal. Their friendship had developed while Chandler had been stationed in France, sharing news of Gordon, with whom Chandler had enlisted. Although Cissy was eighteen years his senior, the pair quickly fell in love and Cissy's husband, Julian, granted her a divorce in 1920. Chandler's mother, Florence, disapproved of the match and in compliance with her wishes the couple postponed their wedding. They eventually married on 6 February 1924, two weeks after Florence's death.

Chandler's relationship with a woman nearly twenty years his senior has always attracted supposition and speculation. Jerry Speir noted, "Inevitably, pseudo-psychological commentaries on Chandler make much of the age discrepancy. The impulse is to say something like 'Chandler married his mother' and then to use that idea to try to explain the mind of the novelist" (8). Both Speir and MacShane believe that this line of reasoning contains little merit because Cissy was a lively, intelligent, mature, and youthful-looking woman who provided a stable and grounded environment for the troubled Chandler, and was therefore an ideal companion. While there is no doubt that Chandler loved Cissy deeply, we should not entirely dismiss the theory, as Speir noted that, Chandler symbolically married his mother. It is quite conceivable that Chandler's insecurities may have impelled him to seek out a maternal figure, and certainly adds credence to the belief that he viewed Cissy as someone to "protect" in much the same way as he had protected and provided for his mother.

At the time of his marriage, Chandler had been employed at the Dabney Oil Syndicate for two years and had risen quickly to the position of company vice-president. Outwardly he seemed relatively contented; he was married, had a good job with an excellent salary, and was enjoying the vitality of the Los Angeles sprawl that he would later describe in his stories. It quickly became apparent, however, that his marriage and newfound stability had seemingly done very little to alleviate the tensions that haunted him. At work colleagues regarded him as "a lonely man who did little consulting before he acted and who was always on guard" (MacShane, *Life* 36). His behavior suggests a man who was ill at ease when he was required to interact with others in social situations, and this uneasiness would certainly have heightened his mood swings.

Herman and Dave Grossman have both noted that fluctuating emotions and character disorders can manifest themselves as a result of combat-related trauma and are symptoms commonly associated with PTSD.[1] For most sufferers these emotional "swings" generally present themselves in more intimate relationships, but may also surface in relationships of a professional and social nature where close interaction with others is required (Herman 56). As an adolescent Chandler had suffered from shyness and a lack of confidence, and even though he grew up surrounded by women he always felt uneasy in female company. As a result he was often frustrated in love, once confessing, "When I was about sixteen . . . I had an infatuation for a girl, but was too shy even to speak to her about it" (qtd. in Macshane, *Life* 11). His poem

"Nocturne from Nowhere," written as he was beginning to write his successful short stories in 1932, took thwarted love as its theme, and interestingly introduced the image of an unattainable blond with "cornflower-blue" eyes whom Marlowe frequently encounters but never wins:

> *There are no women as tender as this woman*
> *Whose cornflower-blue eyes look at me*
> *With the magic of frustration*
> *And the promise of an impossible paradise.* (Qtd. in Macshane, *Life* 21)

Chandler routinely felt uncomfortable and would invariably avoid drawing attention to himself. "I'm strictly the background type" he once said, "and my character is an unbecoming mixture of outer diffidence and inward arrogance" (qtd. in Macshane, *Life* 2). As Chandler grew older his shyness became so severe that he started to become antisocial and even hostile. Those who knew him described him as someone who "detested loneliness yet found it difficult to be at ease with strangers" (qtd. in Macshane, *Life* 231). This internal conflict reveals an emotional duality that explains Chandler's obsession for letter writing, an activity which, notably, satisfied his need for social interaction (thereby relieving his loneliness), and also allowed him to minimize direct personal contact (thus allowing him to keep people at a distance). In later years, even his close friends such as Willis Todhunter Ballard claimed Chandler "was a very retiring person who would sit at the dinners after the table had been cleared, sucking on his pipe and offering very little comment. Most writers like to talk about their own work . . . Ray seldom did" (qtd. in MacShane, *Life* 74). Chandler's fellow *Black Mask* writer Dwight Babcock noted of the writer: "I could never get close to him," and even when dining with other couples he "always remained somewhat apart . . . [he] was not intimate with anyone" (qtd. in MacShane, *Life* 74–75). Although this may simply have been Chandler's personality, Herman suggests that emotional trauma of any kind can accentuate such feelings; someone who already had an inhibited predisposition prior to a traumatic event may become increasingly reclusive and introverted afterwards. There is a specific duality to this type of trauma which "impels people both to withdraw from close relationships and to seek them desperately" (Herman 56). She says: "The profound disruption in basic trust, the common feelings of shame, guilt, and inferiority, and the need to avoid reminders of the trauma that might be found in social life, all foster withdrawal from close relationships. But the terror of the traumatic event intensifies the need for protective attachments. The traumatised person therefore frequently alternates between isolation and anxious clinging to others" (Herman 56).

Chandler's unpredictable behavior may have been aggravated further by a growing recognition of the age difference between him and his wife, Cissy. By the late 1920s she was approaching sixty while he was not yet forty. Cissy's illnesses were becoming more persistent, and their marriage went through one of its most troubled periods. Chandler began to drink heavily, something he had not done since the war. When he drank—usually too much—he would become glum and melancholy. His excessive drinking soon began to jeopardize his position at Dabney's, and he would sometimes disappear for days on end. MacShane says: "The drinking, brought on initially by a nervous shyness with other people, which he believed whiskey would diminish, plunged him into a black Irish depression. Sometimes he would go off for days at a time, without telling Cissy or anybody else where he was" (39).

It is evident that by this point in his life Chandler was far from content; his reliance upon alcohol "gave him energy and a self-assurance that he could achieve in no other way" (qtd. in Moss 131). While it is plausible that Chandler had become an alcoholic because of his own frustrations, we cannot discount the view that this type of behavior is not uncommon among veterans. A majority of veterans have a predilection for alcohol or narcotics, which develops into a severe dependency when removed from the combat environment. This behavior is understandable: the act of simply trying to stay alive during battle causes "a person [to become] completely powerless [. . . ; they] go into a state of surrender. The system of self-defence shuts down completely. The helpless person escapes from [. . . their] situation not by action in the real world but rather by altering [. . . their] state of consciousness" (Herman 42). Herman notes, traumatized people "who cannot spontaneously dissociate may attempt to produce similar numbing effects by using alcohol or narcotics." She continues by explaining that "the soldiers' use of alcohol appear[s] to be an attempt to obliterate their growing sense of helplessness and terror. It seems clear that traumatised people run a high risk of compounding their difficulties by developing a dependence on alcohol or drugs" (44).

Furthermore, as well as sharing this predilection for alcohol, Chandler's emotional troubles, which are suggestive of psychological injury, also appear to have manifested themselves in his frequent threats to take his own life. While still an executive at Dabney's, his excessive drinking aggravated his moods to the point where he would "phone up the office and say he was about to jump out of the window of a room in the Mayfair Hotel on West Seventh Street in Los Angeles. These suicide threats became so frequent that after a while his friends began ignoring them, believing that he was just calling attention to himself in a childish way" (MacShane, *Life* 39). Psychiatrists have noted that an increased level of suicidal tendencies exists among those who suffer from combat-related trauma, which suggests that Chandler's depression and threats of suicide stemmed from his wartime experience. Although estimates of actual suicide following a severe traumatic experience are controversial, Herman argues that the statistics nevertheless suggest that "combat trauma may indeed increase the risk of suicide" (50). Likewise, in their article "Suicide and Guilt as Manifestations of PTSD in Vietnam Combat Veterans" (1991), Hendin and Haas noted that in a postcombat-related study of suicide rates among veterans, those who had endured heavy combat exposure all suffered from permanent unresolved wartime guilt and severe unremitting anxiety, depression, and posttraumatic symptoms (586–91).

While I am not suggesting here that all combat veterans attempt suicide, it has been established that the propensity of actual or attempted suicide is far greater among sufferers of psychological trauma or PTSD than for the population as a whole. And the single biggest factor provoking suicidal thoughts and tendencies among war veterans is survivor guilt. As Herman notes: "Feelings of guilt are especially severe when the survivor has been a witness to the suffering or death of other people. To be spared oneself in the knowledge that others have met a worse fate, creates a severe burden of conscience . . . In combat, witnessing the death of a buddy places the soldier at particularly high risk for developing post-traumatic stress disorder" (54). In the aftermath of traumatic events, veterans doubt themselves and those around them to such an extent that they must continually seek reassurance and recognition for their sacrifices. This deep psychological need, however, is completely alien to the rest of society because "[w]ar and victims are something the community wants to forget; a veil of oblivion drawn over everything painful and unpleasant" (Herman 8). This antipathy is sensed by veterans as they "look for tangible evidence of public recognition[, . . . fearful] their sacrifices will be quickly forgotten" (Herman 70). A caring community encourages the reintegration of soldiers into civilian life, while a community that excludes and rejects the veteran may invariably drive him or her into solitude and deepen the sense of isolation. Without assistance veterans are forced to relive the memory of their trauma alone. Herman notes the example of the First World War poet Siegfried Sassoon who, because of shell-shock, was "condemned to relive [his experiences] for the rest of his life [. . .] devot[ing] himself to writing and rewriting his war memoirs, to preserve the memory of the fallen" (22–23).

In 1932 Chandler was dismissed from his job at Dabney's as the direct consequence of his alcohol dependency and unpredictable behavior. Although not entirely unexpected, it undoubtedly intensified his sense of rejection and exacerbated his misery and isolation. MacShane notes, "The dismissal was a terrible blow, for it destroyed his sense of identity. Exactly twenty years after his return to America he was back where he began, except that he had a bad reputation, fewer possibilities, and less energy than before" (40). Chandler's dismissal from Dabney's invoked dramatic mood swings which his friend Natasha Spender noted, "alternated quite wildly between exuberance and depression" (qtd. in MacShane, *Life* 234). According to MacShane this indicates that he "was undergoing considerable strain [. . . and] was subject to a wild feeling of despair" (*Life* 39).

His erratic behavior, especially after drinking, also prompted him to take extraordinary risks. After service in the Royal Flying Corps, Chandler found flying an exhilarating experience that appealed to his sense of recklessness. On one occasion while flying, Chandler undid his seatbelt and stood up in the cockpit, refusing to return to his seat and only doing so when the pilot threatened to soak him with the contents of a fire extinguisher (MacShane, *Life* 38). This kind of thrill-seeking behavior has its corresponding parallel in a soldier's wartime experiences. For example, Malcolm Cowley remarked that during conflict the threat of death became "something to be courted like a woman" (7). He explained that "the risk of death exerts a magnetic attraction on young men," and even the pacifist John Dos Passos declared that "the winey thought of death sings in the spring blood" (13). Later, Dos Passos wrote that the immediate threat of death "sharpened the senses. The sweetness of white roses, the shape and striping of a snail shell, the taste of an omelet, the most casual sight or sound appeared desperately intense against the background of the great massacres" (qtd. in Cowley 13).

The turning point in Chandler's life occurred when he resolved to rekindle his dream of becoming a full-time writer, and he began studying the work of such writers as Dashiell Hammett and Ernest Hemingway for inspiration. Chandler's first story, "Blackmailers Don't Shoot," took five months to write and was finished in December 1933. *Black Mask* magazine, specializing in detective stories, welcomed his contributions, and he finally began to feel the degree of acceptance that psychiatrists contend is vital for recovery from trauma. For the next six years Chandler's stories were regularly published in *Black Mask* and he became something of a celebrity, regarded as a "genius" among his contemporaries who envied the realism of his writing. Chandler intertwined his own cynicism with his detectives' unique code of ethics and chivalrous nature. This became a constant thread that ran throughout his stories and finally reached maturity in his novels. Yet despite the acceptance of his contemporaries, the absence of a regular income played heavily on his mind, and his moods ebbed and flowed with each successive story. Nevertheless, Chandler's determination finally paid off. During the 1930s he completed seventeen stories for various magazines, and as his work improved he felt sufficiently confident, at the age of fifty, to attempt his first novel.

In hindsight MacShane believes that Chandler's novels were successful because of "his decision to use Philip Marlowe as his first-person narrator." He says: "Marlowe was an ordinary *Black Mask* character: tough, strong, attractive to women, an honest man in a crooked trade. This kind of hero is common in American literature and seems to represent a faith in the incorruptibility of at least part of the population" (*Life* 69). Although his character is damaged, Marlowe represented a feeling of lone morality in an America that had become too decayed for many to comprehend. In a letter to Edgar Carter in 1957, Chandler expressed: "[T]o me Marlowe is a character of some nobility, of scorching wit, sad but not defeated, lonely but never really sure of himself. He will at any time, because he is that sort of man, meet any danger, since he thinks that is what he was created for, and because he knows the corruption of his country can only be cured by men who are determined if necessary to sacrifice themselves to cure it. He doesn't talk or behave like an idealist, but I think that he is one at heart [. . .]" (UCLA 9:15, p. 2). Chandler's words are suggestive of a warrior mentality. Like a soldier, Chandler notes that Marlowe will meet any danger because that is what he was created for, and he is willing to sacrifice himself in order to bring about a sense of honorable balance. Marlowe not only becomes the embodiment of Chandler's grave misgivings about society, but he is also, like many of the Lost Generation, a product of the author's personal trauma and disillusionment; he is a fictional embodiment of Chandler's own character. As the *London Daily Express* journalist Merrick Winn wrote in an article titled "A Confession by Raymond Chandler" (1956): "What kind of man is Raymond Chandler? Well, what kind of man is Philip Marlowe? For these two are head and tail of the same coin." During the same interview, after years of denying that his detective was a representation of himself, Chandler confessed, "I suppose Marlowe really is a sort of secret me . . . I wouldn't see it as clearly as other people, but I can see quite a lot of me in him. We're both lonely, sentimental, cynical—and we're both incorruptible" (Winn 4). While this view may be true of Marlowe, whether Chandler was incorruptible is open to argument. According to Hiney and MacShane, numerous accounts exist of the author's infidelities, occurrences that although Chandler denied, seemed to be supported by his conscious and continuous flirtations with women later in life.

Critical of many of his contemporaries for their characterization of their detectives, Chandler claimed that their depictions "[do] not and could not exist [. . . The detective] is the personification of an attitude, the exaggeration of a possibility" (qtd. in MacShane, *Life* 70). When creating Marlowe, Chandler consciously avoided these caricatures and tried to create an authentic individual, seeking to bridge the gap between detective fiction and regular fiction by developing a believable and convincing individual who just happened to earn his living as a detective. The detective, Chandler asserted, "must be a complete man, and a common man, and yet an unusual man. He must be, to use a rather weathered phrase, a man of honour—by instinct, by inevitability, without thought of it, and certainly without saying it" (*Simple Art of Murder* 18).

Chandler's first novel, *The Big Sleep,* was "cannibalized" from his short stories "Killer in the Rain" and "The Curtain" and published in 1939. The novel was generally well received but its "gritty" realism also attracted some critical reviews, including accusations that it was "nasty and perverted" (qtd. in Macshane, *Life* 73). The tone of this criticism surprised and upset Chandler, undermining his fragile confidence. The novel had taken three months to complete, and though he felt pressured to produce a second in a similar time frame, he was hesitant to do so. The mixed reviews compelled him to reexamine his style of writing, fearing what further reviews of this kind might do to his reputation, declaring, "I do not want to write depraved books" (qtd. in Hiney and MacShane 15). However, despite undermining his confidence, the success of the book also had another, more positive, result; it gave him the recognition he craved. And yet, in reality Chandler was trying to live a contradiction, for although he sought recognition and social acceptance through his writing, the fame that accompanied the book's publication reduced his solitude and anonymity. It is significant that in the same year that *The Big Sleep* was published Chandler also wrote a fantasy tale entitled "The Bronze Door" (1939). In this short story a man installs an antique bronze door in his house only to discover that anyone who passes through it vanishes. Again, in 1951, Chandler would write a story with a similar theme, "Professor Bingo's Snuff," in which a man is capable of making himself invisible by taking magic snuff. For a man sensitive to criticism and intrusion into his personal life, Chandler's own desire to literally "disappear" during both of these periods must have been strong, and it is tempting to make a connection between the author's state of mind and his desperate need to escape.

By mid-1939 work on his next two novels, *The Lady in the Lake* and *Farewell, My Lovely* (originally intended to be published in this order), was well underway when the prospect of war in Europe stirred up unwelcomed memories. Chandler became so distracted for much of this period that he lost the ability to write coherently. As he watched Adolf Hitler occupy one European country after another, Chandler remarked in August 1939 that the "effort to keep my mind off the war has reduced me to the mental age of seven [. . .] I know how to write, but I have momentarily mislaid the urge" (qtd. in Gardiner and Walker 210). As Herman has explained, although some posttraumatic symptoms may fade over time, "they can be revived, years after the event, by reminders of the original trauma" (48). The thirties were an anxious time for the writer, who moved nine times during the decade. His incessant desire to relocate was driven by varying causes. As Roy Meador notes, "At one place the children were noisy, at another the traffic distracted. Sometimes the neighbours were difficult or the climate was inhospitable" (146). Such sensitivity suggests that Chandler was unsettled and insecure in his surroundings and was beginning to suffer from the lack of peace and quiet that he desperately craved. As Robert J. Lifton has noted, a "restless shifting of jobs and living arrangements" as well as "degrees of bitterness, distrust, and suspicion" may all be associated with combat trauma, and in varying degrees are symptoms that are common among veterans (35). However, one advantage (if it may be labeled so) of relocating so frequently was that Chandler "absorbed the whole of Los Angeles through his pores. He added to his already substantial knowledge of the city until his familiarity with the area was encyclopedic, covering the mood, look, temper, moral attitudes, and social realities of the place" (Meador 146).

Widespread coverage of the terrible events in Europe appears to have unsettled Chandler and could suggest signs of a growing reemergence of his troubling war experience. During this period of global turmoil Chandler suffered severe insomnia and extreme melancholy, and by 1946 he regularly complained of exhaustion. In a note to Charles Morton, the associate editor of *Atlantic Monthly*, he wrote, "Can't sleep, can't eat, can't make a decision, can hardly get out of a chair," and he even contemplated admitting himself to a clinic where, he joked, "they take in decayed personalities and try to find out if it is any use letting them live" (qtd. in MacShane, *Life* 128). Chandler's inability to work during the duration of the Second World War is clearly evidenced in the draft of a letter written in conjunction with a tax refund claim that he was pursuing. In it he writes that "the year 1940, partly from reasons of health and still more from the state of the world, seems to have contained an abnormal amount of vacillation" (qtd. in Gardiner and Walker 26).

Notwithstanding his worsening psychological health, Chandler had accomplished an extraordinary amount by the end of the Second World War. He had published five short stories and three novels—*Farewell My Lovely* (1940), *The High Window* (1942), and *The Lady in the Lake* (1943)—all of which received cautious but satisfactory reviews. But by this time Chandler had also grown disenchanted with Los Angeles, and his growing frustration with the city is palpable in his novels. The war had almost certainly taken its toll; he yearned to escape the impropriety of Los Angeles, and in 1946 he and Cissy moved to La Jolla, a community within San Diego, in Southern California.

The war years also proved fruitful in other ways. Hollywood had beckoned, and by 1943 film studios had bought the rights to *The Big Sleep*, *Farewell, My Lovely*, and *The High Window*. Paramount Studios quickly recognized Chandler's writing talent and repeatedly requested his assistance in adapting screenplays. He finally acquiesced in mid-1943 to collaborate with Billy Wilder on an adaptation of James Cain's *Double Indemnity*. In an acknowledgment to the ongoing war in Europe, the screenplay included on its opening page the words, "Save Film! Win the war!" (UCLA 9:1). But Chandler was still discontented. While appreciating the regular income, he was initially ill at ease in Hollywood and had difficulty working with other writers. Gradually, however, he overcame his apprehension, and his time at the studio appears to have done "him a great deal of good. For the first time in a decade, apart from conversations with his wife and rare meetings with pulp writers, he was involved in intellectual conversations as a normal part of his daily life. He belonged to a society of fellow writers, and their company brought him out" (MacShane, *Life* 110). His recognition and acceptance into a group of professional people on his own intellectual plane stimulated him sufficiently to regain a degree of self-confidence. According to Herman, acceptance and positive judgment from others are of great psychological importance in repairing "the sense of connection between the combat veteran and those closest to him" (66). Herman continues, "The veteran is isolated . . . [and too] often, this view of the veteran as a man apart is shared by civilians, who are content to idealise or disparage his military service while avoiding detailed knowledge of what that service entailed" (66).

Unfortunately, things were about to change. As the studios applied tighter deadlines, Chandler's sense of stability began to waver to such an extent that Billy Wilder, his one-time screen-writing partner, was prompted to later describe him as "bad tempered—kind of acid, sour, grouchy" (qtd. in Speir 12). These emotions are most explicitly exhibited in Chandler's fourth novel, *The Lady in the Lake* (1943). Furthermore, his unpredictable state of mind was clearly visible in his second screenplay *The Blue Dahlia* (1945), a film that contains aspects of psychological injuries inflicted by warfare. The film's plot revolves around the character of Johnny Morrison, a US Navy sailor played by Alan Ladd, who returns from war to find that his wife has been having an affair. When she is murdered, he becomes the main suspect. In Chandler's original version of *The Blue Dahlia* the murderer was to have been the shell-shocked character Buzz, one of Johnny's two naval friends. Buzz was supposed to have committed the murder during a blackout, the consequence of a head wound suffered during the war. The US Navy, however, insisted that the plot be changed, arguing that having a psychologically traumatized naval officer commit a murder would be a devastating blow to morale in the armed forces. Consequently, in the redrafted final version of the film a hotel detective is instead exposed as the real murderer.

The script changes forced upon *The Blue Dahlia* upset Chandler immensely. Angry at being forced to rewrite the film's ending, he remarked sardonically, "What the Navy department did to The Blue Dahlia was a little thing like making me change the murderer and hence make a routine whodunit out of a fairly original idea" (UCLA 10:2, p. 90). The "fairly original idea" to which Chandler refers was the idea that a man suffering from the traumatic effects of "shell shock" could unknowingly do something during a flashback or blackout. The original screenplay was one of the first attempts to broaden the public discussion of psychiatric illness, and specifically the psychological effects of war.

The strain involved in writing *The Blue Dahlia* had an extremely destructive effect upon Chandler's physical and psychological well-being, and it is no exaggeration to suggest that its completion nearly cost him his life. Further pressure was placed on him when it emerged that the star of the film, Alan Ladd, was to be drafted into the army for almost immediate deployment to Europe. The production managers at Paramount offered Chandler a five-thousand-dollar "bonus" to complete the script as soon as possible. However, as Chandler's friend and fellow public school colleague John Houseman recalled, what they succeeded in doing was causing more distress to an already fragile personality. Houseman believed that the inducement destroyed

Chandler's own self-confidence that he could complete the project on time. Chandler felt insulted by the idea that the only way he would complete the script on time was through bribery, and viewing it as dishonorable, he refused to accept the bonus. The actions of those at Paramount severely wounded Chandler's sense of honor and responsibility, and the incident left him in such a state of nervous despair and humiliation that he immediately resigned.

Chandler, however, was not completely crestfallen and told Houseman in a private meeting that he *could* complete the screenplay on the condition that he be allowed to do so in his own home, drunk. Although Cissy bitterly opposed the idea, Chandler convinced her that, in Houseman's words, "duty came before safety and that his honor was deeply engaged [. . .] in *The Blue Dahlia*" (qtd. in Moss 131). For eight days "Chandler did not draw a sober breath" (qtd. in Moss 132). The script was completed with two days to spare, and Houseman was forced to acknowledge that "Ray had not exaggerated when he said that he was risking his life for *The Blue Dahlia*." The effects of Chandler's "sacrifice" "seriously weakened him" Houseman said, "and it took him almost a month to recover[.] . . . [He] acknowledged my expressions of gratitude with the modest smile of a gravely wounded hero who has shown courage far beyond the call of duty" (qtd. in Moss 133). Chandler's "sacrifice" for his art would later be recognized when he received Academy Award nominations for the screenplays of both *Double Indemnity* in 1945 and *The Blue Dahlia* in 1947.

Nonetheless, it was Chandler's articles that routinely provided the evidence of his deep frustration and darkened moods. The best example of this long-suffering pattern was his celebrated article for *Atlantic Monthly* titled "The Simple Art of Murder." Published in 1944, the article mocked the traditional British style of detective and clue puzzle stories of authors such as Arthur Conan Doyle, Agatha Christie, and Dorothy Sayers and praised the new hard-boiled form of Dashiell Hammett. Although Chandler still considered himself an Englishman at heart, he had no qualms about ridiculing the British style of writing. Applauding the new American style for its realism, he proclaimed in his own inimitable manner that Hammett and American detective writers had taken "murder out of the Venetian vase and dropped it into the alley" (*Simple Art of Murder* 14). Chandler's fundamental condemnation, however, was that writing should not be mass produced as a money-making endeavor but as something far more worthwhile.

However, while "The Simple Art of Murder" has a solid argument—that "good" literature could be written in any style and should not be written for profit—his example of Hammett seems very much out of place when we consider how Hammett cynically viewed his writing solely as a money-making venture. Shortly after his death in 1961, the writer's friend Nunnally Johnson said that Hammett "saw no more reason to write when he not only had all the money he needed but was assured of all that he would even need for the remainder of his life." Johnson continues: "Apparently there was nothing in writing that interested [Hammett] but the money. He had none of the usual incentives that keep writers at their typewriters for as long as they have the strength to hit the keys. He had no impulse to tell any more stories, no ambition to accomplish more as a writer, no interest in keeping his name alive [. . . O]nce he had made his pile, that was all there was to it" (qtd. in Symons, *Hammett* 120–21). In contrast, commenting on the writers who appeared to "churn" out novels, Chandler would later write, "The Gardners and the Christies can go on for ever, but Chandler has to believe in something. To me writing is not a business or a racket, it is an art" (UCLA 9:13, p. 9).

The exertion of completing three novels, two screenplays, two articles, and four short stories during the war years, in addition to managing his insecurities, drained Chandler, and it took him four years to recover sufficiently to complete his next novel. Despite his absence from the literary scene, Chandler was still a writer in demand. In 1947 Universal Studios, in a huge leap of faith, asked Chandler to write his own screenplay. Disenchanted by the seedy streets of Los Angeles, he set *Playback* in Vancouver, a location approximately sixty-two miles from Victoria, where he had enlisted with the Canadian Army in 1917. It took only eight months to complete the screenplay, but due to an alleged lack of funding the studio eventually shelved the project. Although this was setback, an undeterred Chandler would later resurrect the *Playback* screenplay and rework it to become his seventh and final Southern California–based Marlowe novel.

After years of anticipation, Chandler's fifth novel, *The Little Sister,* was published in 1949. The dispiriting effect that Hollywood had left on Chandler is apparent throughout the novel as Marlowe gradually becomes "depressed by the restless emptiness of everything, the lack of human communication, the indifference and the ugliness" (MacShane, *Life* 151) of the world about him. *The Little Sister* received muted acclaim as well as some negative criticism mainly because the actual "detecting" in the story was minimal. Chandler deflected this criticism with a defense that allowed him to pretend "his book [was] being criticised because it [was] too good" (MacShane, *Life* 156). Inwardly, however, his confidence again slumped because "he knew the faults of *The Little Sister* . . . [and] what upset him was the doubt these reviews created that he would be able to do what he wanted to do with the mystery story" (MacShane, *Life* 156–57). He wrote to his publisher: "I am very uneasy in mind. I seem to have lost ambition and have no ideas any more. I don't really want to do anything, or rather one part of me does and the other doesn't. One of the penalties of even a mild success is an indifference to it, and the effort to do something that will attract interest and praise is really something it is a pity to lose" (qtd. in Hiney and MacShane 118). At the same time, Chandler seemingly began to feel increasingly protective toward his detective and came to rely on him more and more. In a letter to Charles Morton in 1948 Chandler said that "the trouble with the Marlowe character is he has been written and talked about too much. He's getting self-conscious, trying to live up to his reputation among the quasi-intellectuals. The boy is bothered" (qtd. in Gardiner and Walker 220). What is interesting here is how Chandler gives Marlowe real human qualities and refers to the detective as though he were a friend, a real person. Yet Chandler's words were not just applicable to Marlowe; they were equally valid as a self-description , for as he admitted to Hamish Hamilton in the same year, "I have a very, very tired mind" (qtd. in Gardiner and Walker 220). Even later, after complaining to the creators of the Philip Marlowe television series in 1959, Chandler justified his interference by arguing, "If I am critical of any writer of the show, it is only because I know my character so well, so very much better than anyone else could" (qtd. in Gardiner and Walker 144). Chandler's defense of Marlowe ran deep, not only from a literary point of view, but also from a personal perspective, suggesting that Chandler regarded Marlowe as much more than simply a fictional character. It seems as though Chandler's detective became a catharsis to the troubled writer, who went as far as to admit, "It begins to look as though I were tied to this fellow for life. I simply cannot function without him" (qtd. in Hiney and MacShane 166).

By 1949 Chandler's physical health had begun to deteriorate, and he suffered from bronchitis, sore throats, skin allergies, and painful rashes for which he was prescribed morphine. The psychological effects of these complaints left him "nervous, tired, discouraged, sick [, . . .] bored [, . . .] disgusted," and he remarked, "I seem to be crumbling slowly" (qtd. in MacShane, *Life* 159). His weakened psychological state left him feeling vulnerable and fragile, and according to MacShane, after agreeing to undertake the film adaptation of *Strangers on a Train* in 1950, Chandler became fascinated by "the theme of hidden guilt that lies at the heart of Patricia Highsmith's novel" (*Life* 170).

In 1951 Chandler wrote a story, which for the first time explicitly examined the mental condition of a veteran. The story, "A Couple of Writers," which is discussed in detail in chapter 3, is the tale of a married couple who are both struggling writers. The notable difference between this story and the Marlowe novels is that Chandler openly made the protagonist, Hank Bruton, a war veteran who suffers from combat-related injuries. Hank suffers deep insecurities; he is confused by the uncaring and indifferent attitude of his wife, Marion, and by his own inability to make her understand his state of mind. Marion's lack of support appears to be in total contrast to the stalwart support provided by Chandler's own wife, Cissy. McShane notes that Cissy's "willingness to endure hardships spurred him on," and his strength as a writer was stimulated "through the knowledge that his wife believed in him. There was a passion that encompassed the thing itself and the artist who created it, working with the help of his wife" (qtd. in MacShane, *Life* 60). Rather than represent his wife in the role of Marion, Chandler appears to have created the character as an illustration of the general attitude of society and the isolation felt by veterans once they have returned home. Comparing the veteran Hank before and after he went to war, Marion shouts hysterically: "I thought you were quite a fellow then . . . You had wit and imagination and a sort of buccaneering gaiety [. . . But now you] get drunk every night and every morning [you] start to get drunk again [. . .] And then comes that day when everything happens all at once that ought with a normal person to happen slowly, over the months and years, reasonable steps in reasonable time. One minute you're looking at a healthy man and then next you're looking at a shrivelled up horror that reeks of whiskey. Do you expect me to wait for that?" (qtd. in Gardiner and Walker 105–6). Hank's response is numbed silence. Marion's feelings are of annoyance, contempt, and ignorance. She epitomizes the attitude of a society that has turned its back on returning veterans; a distain that leaves them feeling unappreciated and unwelcome in society. Her reaction is to simply overlook and disregard Hank's underlying psychological problems, which serves as a metaphor for the cynicism of the era and its seeming inability to understand how to respond to a generation irrevocably changed by their experiences of war.

By this time in Chandler's life Cissy's health also started to deteriorate as her degenerative lung disease worsened, once again putting both immense physical and psychological strain on the tired and troubled writer. Yet Chandler refused to complain. In the last years of Cissy's life Chandler took over the domestic chores and provided around-the-clock care for his ailing wife. Cissy's failing health was acutely detrimental to his work. In 1952 while writing his penultimate novel, *The Long Goodbye*, he wrote to Bernice Baumgarten, an associate of his agent Carl Brandt, confessing that he was severely fraught: "My kind of writing demands a certain amount of dash and high spirits—the word is gusto . . . and you could not know the bitter struggle I have had in the past year even to achieve enough cheerfulness to live on, much less to put into a book" (qtd. in Hiney and MacShane 183).

While his wife became progressively worse, Chandler's short story "A Couple of Writers" was circulated to and rejected by various magazines. Although he recognized that the story had "no commercial value whatever," he considered it a "fancy piece of writing all the same" (qtd. in Gardiner and Walker 99). Disappointed, Chandler told Baumgarten that "if a thing is well written and penetrating and at the same time as lightly handled as cannot find a home, why go on trying?" Replying that magazines had found the story too depressing, she suggested altering the story to give it a happier ending, a proposal that enraged Chandler. He had only one reply: "How the hell would you put a happy ending on that story? What is 'happy'? [. . .] The trouble is you don't care enough for the characters to worry about what happens to them. They are in a trap they have created for themselves and have no alternatives" (qtd. in MacShane, *Life* 178–79). Chandler's stinging rebuke of Baumgarten's suggestion stems from the story's suggestive depiction of both the physical and psychological troubles endured by the veteran writer protagonist. Although not intended to be autobiographical, the story certainly does attempt to depict the lack of social understanding and tolerance for veterans. And the fact that Chandler refused to alter "A Couple of Writers" shows he had an emotional stake in the work, since for the author the story was realistic, and altering it would have nullified the intimate emotions Chandler was trying to evoke. Just as he had tried to do in *The Blue Dahlia*, Chandler's reply to Baumgarten indicates that his purpose was to evoke some consideration of the soldiers' experience of war and how veterans are received back into society. Chanler pointed out to her that "you don't care enough for the characters to worry about what happens to them." Baumgarten's suggested alterations to the story, combined with the story's rejection by various magazines, would have strengthened Chandler's empathy with the suffering of Hank Bruton and provoked his explosive emotional condition. Taking ownership of "A Couple of Writers" and the themes it portrayed, Chandler, showing his personal connection to his works, believed: "I am a writer, and there comes a time when that which I write has to belong to me, has to be written alone and in silence with no one looking over my shoulder, no one telling me a better way to write it. It doesn't have to be great writing, it doesn't have to be terribly good. It just has to be mine" (qtd. in MacShane, *Life* 192).

While Chandler was denied the opportunity to publish a piece of work that was of personal importance, his temper was nonetheless easily provoked by what he believed to be dishonest descriptions of soldiering, or even ignorance of what war was really like. In a letter to Jamie Hamilton discussing Armistice Day in 1949 he described it as "a sort of mixed holiday . . . Big parade of troops and marines and sailors, none of them have any idea what the first world war was like. It was a damn sight worse than they think [. . .]" (qtd. in Hiney and MacShane 127). This is an extremely significant and rare example of Chandler not only making a specific reference to the war, but also acknowledging that the experience itself was far more terrible than people could imagine. It also appears that the literary language used in war novels came under Chandler's scrutiny. In a letter to Hamish Hamilton in May 1950 for example, Chandler discusses in great detail the work of New Zealand lexicographer Eric Partridge, who had served in the Australian infantry during the First World War. Chandler described his work as "interesting" but criticized him for "overlook[ing] some of the most commonly used words of soldier-slang . . . e.g 'bomb-proofer,' 'cushy-job,' 'bivvy,' and above all 'napoo,' 'strafe,' long a, for bombardment (the morning strafe), 'street cars' or 'tram cars' for heavy long range shells, 'whizzbangs' for rapid small shells, and the inimitable American 'goldbrick' which is as superior to English 'lead-swinger' as 'milk run' (from the last war) is to 'piece of cake'" (qtd. in Gardiner and Walker 88). It would seem that even though Partridge was a veteran of the First and Second World Wars, his diluted and often inappropriate vocabulary made Chandler "uneasy" and the story unrealistic. This was mainly down to his grievance that "these scholarly excursions into the language of the underworld, so to speak [. . .] smell of the dictionary. The so-called experts in this line have their ear to the library, very seldom to the ground" (ibid.). These "scholarly excursions" as he called them, rarely used a realistic vernacular, and Chandler was adamant that whatever an author chose to write about, "it must be about real people in a real world" (qtd. in Gardiner and Walker 63). He believed that "no amount of editing or polishing will have any appreciable effect on the flavour of how a man writes" (ibid.).

Chandler's lifelong emotional despair, disillusionment, loneliness, and recurring physical illness peaked in 1954. It is hard to imagine a more destructive psychological combination of problems than those that beset Chandler as he wrote his most acclaimed novel, *The Long Goodbye.* His concern for Cissy, who was now in her eighties and terminally ill, and the anxiety over her illness seriously threatened to completely undermine Chandler's self-confidence in his work. In an effort to set aside his disintegrating psychological state, he lightheartedly wrote, "I'm caught talking to myself quite a lot lately. They say that is not too bad unless you answer back. I not only answer back, I argue and get mad" (qtd. in Hiney and MacShane 197). But he was unable to sustain this outlook on his life and in a letter to his publisher he disclosed the full extent of his misgivings when he confessed: "In bad moods, which are not too infrequent, I feel the icy touch of despair" (qtd. in Macshane 192). The agony of watching his wife's slow and painful decline was undoubtedly extremely distressing and yet he was able to produce a novel that commentators argue is his finest piece of writing: *The Long Goodbye*; a novel that can be interpreted as Marlowe's drawn-out farewell to his war veteran friend Terry Lennox. Furthermore, the novel also suggests that it was Chandler's attempt to rid himself of the psychological symptoms of his own postcombat stress, something that is examined further in chapter 6. Despite this valiant attempt, neither objective was actually achieved since the novel ends with Marlowe more disillusioned than ever, being both deceived by Lennox and still beset with an overwhelming sense of desolation.

Chandler received his biggest blow in December 1954 when, after long periods of hospitalization, Cissy finally died. Her death drove Chandler into deep despair and he again turned to drink in an attempt to cope with his loss. Excessive alcohol abuse worsened his already erratic behavior and in the weeks that followed he threatened suicide on a number of occasions. At first these cries for help from a man lonely and distressed were not treated with any degree of seriousness and were ignored. It was not until his fourth suicide attempt on 22 February 1955, when Chandler attempted to shoot himself in a drunken stupor, that those closest to him actively responded to his plight. Sympathetic police officers in attendance concluded that Chandler should be committed to the psychiatric ward of the county hospital for his own safety, and later Chandler candidly admitted that he wasn't sure whether he had intended to shoot himself or whether his subconscious was "putting on a cheap dramatic performance" (qtd. in MacShane, *Life* 226) that was simply a cry for help.

Whatever his thoughts at the time, judging by his actions it is certain that his wife's death was one of the most devastating events of his later life and undoubtedly tipped him over the edge. Under the influence of such an enormous stressor, it is highly likely that the trauma Chandler had suffered jumped from his subconscious to his conscious, bringing to the surface emotions that had lain dormant for years. Grossman has noted that, "Often you can keep things out of your mind when you are young and active, but they came back to haunt your nights in your old age" (75). Cissy had been Chandler's only companion and the major stabilizing influence on his troubled life. With her death his depression and suffering came flooding back with devastating effect.

The remaining five years of Chandler's life proved to be his most destructive and a period in which he suffered profound psychological stress. The overwhelming feeling of despair and loneliness reached the point where, "life was empty in every respect, and the future seemed completely without purpose" (MacShane, *Life* 227). As Jerry Speir has noted, Chandler's last lonely years "serve as an indicator of the depths of the frustration of this man" (17). Chandler confessed, "I don't sleep more than four hours a night. Often not at all. There are ghosts. Memories that keep me awake [. . .] Life has lost something" (qtd. in MacShane, *Life* 232). After Cissy's death he was often incredibly open and honest in interviews. As Patrick Doncaster of the *Daily Mail* recounted when he prompted Chandler to discuss Cissy in a 1955 interview:

> "Mrs. Chandler," I said gently [. . .]
>
> "What about Mrs. Chandler?" Chandler said edgily. "She's dead. Died last year." He looked away across the bar. He twitched a little, jumpy. Then something choked in his throat.
>
> "I've not got over it yet," he said quietly. And a big tear rolled down his cheek. (ibid.)

It was about this time that Chandler may have finally begun to understand the "therapeutic value of talk" (MacShane, *Life* 232). Whether a public or private trauma, Herman maintains that talking can be a "prerequisite both for the restoration of the social order and for the healing of [the] individual" (1). But this respite was only temporary, and although Chandler's sense of loss was never completely erased, frequent visits to London kept him occupied during his final few years.

Chandler frequently threatened suicide while in London, and his female friends in the city felt compelled to organize what they described as a "shuttle service" to make certain he was not neglected. His friend Jocelyn Richards reasoned that the "shuttle service" was an effort "to keep him socially engaged" (qtd. in Macshane, *Life* 234). Natasha Spender hoped that their attention would "see him through to a point where he would want to go on living [. . . and] reverse the process of slowly killing himself with drink" (ibid.). Alison Hooper, another friend, recalls how they would "take turns to keep him company at crucial hours—such as mealtimes when the idea was to get him to eat at least something, since like many alcoholics he tended to starve. There was a lunch hour patrol, a drinks-and-dinner shift—even on occasions a dawn watch" (ibid.). The women he entertained and dined with were painfully aware of his loneliness and suffering. Their companionship was greatly appreciated by Chandler as it very much appealed to the gentlemanly side of his character and enabled him to act out the role of the mythic "Galahad" of his poetry for his female friends.

Herman states that the response of those around a trauma sufferer "has a powerful influence on the ultimate resolution of the trauma" (70). However, Chandler's female friends realized that "the oscillation of his mood between exuberance and despair" was that of a "concealed nervous breakdown, concealed in that he could put up a good superficial show on social occasions, but in private he was resolutely and scornfully impervious to our suggestions that he consult medical advice for these extreme episodes" (qtd. in Gross 130). Spender noted that Chandler's friends admired the courage and humor with which he fought through "alarming roller-coaster changes of mood, the plunging into loneliness and illness, the zooming up into deliciously irresistible sagas of outrageous nonsense; the bullying contentiousness swivelling suddenly to the disarming repartee, and all as if it was happening to him entirely outside of his control" (qtd. in Gross 136). Yet however valiant his efforts at keeping his demons at bay, she notes how in "both despairing and exuberant phases he seemed propelled by anxiety" (qtd. in Gross 130).

While Chandler's social interaction may have outwardly eased his traumatic symptoms, his worsening addiction to alcohol, which had made him irritable and forgetful, also did irreparable damage to his health. Shortly after returning to New York in 1956 he was again hospitalized, and after being discharged he returned to California but was almost immediately forced to seek help for his alcoholism and extreme depression at the Las Encinas Sanatorium in Pasadena. He later said, "What was the matter with me—and has been for some time, was a total mental, physical and emotional exhaustion masked by my drinking enough whiskey to keep me on my feet, and then a severe malnutrition" (qtd. in Gardiner and Walker 40). His physician, Whitelaw Birss, told him that he was "one of the most highly-strung and emotional people he ever met, that alcohol can never give me any real relaxation because my mind operates mostly on the subconscious level, which alcohol can't reach, while it merely irritates the emotions it can reach" (qtd. in MacShane, *Life* 250).

At this point, Chandler appears to have started to accept his emotional shortcomings and acknowledged the extent of his own suffering. In 1956 he admitted, "I used, like most people, to dramatize myself in all sorts of heroic situations. As a great athlete or war hero. Now I've come to terms with the real me" (qtd. in Moss 245).

The fatigue, anxiety, and character disorder that Chandler suffered during this time are further indicators of his persistent combat-related PTSD, for which the only cure is total rest if a complete psychological collapse and a permanent alteration of the personality were to be avoided. The effects of warfare can be so severe that "there can be no erasure because the experience acts profoundly on the individual's personality, causing significant alteration" (Grinker and Speigel 371). Evelyn Hooker, a close friend of Natasha Spender and a trained psychologist, "could immediately detect how close Chandler had become to insanity . . . and was convinced that he needed professional help" (Hiney 246). It is probable that Chandler was able to avoid a complete and permanent breakdown, however, because he held onto two things: first, the diversion and companionship that came from his frequent visits to London after Cissy's death; and second, his work. By reworking his final novel, *Playback,* during this time, it became "clear to him . . . that he was far more stable when he was writing" (Hiney 245). In this period Chandler also toyed with the idea of writing a novel situated in England called *English Summer*, which, interestingly, would feature a protagonist that "feels lost in a society he doesn't quite understand, and among people he will never understand, but he nevertheless can't just walk out. He has to do something. He has, according to his code and mine, incurred an obligation . . . when we have that feeling we are willing to destroy ourselves rather than let someone down" (qtd. in Gardiner and Walker 240). The individual he described was both symbolically and characteristically identical to Philip Marlowe. Evidently, the motif of the gallant antihero was one that Chandler was unwilling to discard, striking, as it did, a chord with the author's own sense of righteousness and honor. This notion of laying one's life down for the greater good is characteristically and intrinsically indicative of a warrior mentality.

In his final years, Chandler became a person tormented by contradiction, being both hopeful that he might find someone with whom to share his life and saddened by the thought of replacing Cissy. As Speir says, "whatever conflicts and difficulties he and Cissy may have shared, she was for him the force that made his life worth the effort" (17). With Cissy gone, Chandler's life seemed to lose all sense of direction and purpose. He returned to California where he cultivated friendships with a number of women but which always ended in disappointment and became a further source of psychological pain. It was during this period that Chandler admitted, "I don't miss alcohol physically at all [. . . but] I do miss it mentally and spiritually" (qtd. in Gardiner and Walker 248). By 1959 his health had greatly deteriorated, and many of his friends became worried that he had all but lost the will to live. His English agent, Helga Greene, worried over Chandler's psychological state, stayed with him during his last months, helping to restore a degree of stability to his life, and it was she who encouraged him to fly to New York to accept the presidency of the Mystery Writers of America in 1959. While in New York Chandler met Helga's father and asked for her hand in marriage, but when he was refused he returned to California utterly broken and dejected.

This was to be Chandler's final rejection. On 23 March, after yet another heavy bout of drinking, he was admitted to La Jolla Convalescent Hospital suffering from pneumonia. Two days later he was transferred to the Scripps Clinic where he died on 26 March 1959. After a funeral service that was attended by just seventeen people, he was buried in a small plot in Mount Hope Cemetery in San Diego.

Chandler's lonely existence was echoed in his death. While an individual showing *some* of the behavioral traits Chandler displayed may not necessarily be said to be suffering from a severe psychological disorder, to display *all* of these symptoms would suggest that the sufferer *had* endured some significant trauma. Physiologists and experts in the field have demonstrated that postcombat trauma is not uncommon among soldiers, even when the soldier has not been involved in battle. The question to be considered, then, is this: Could Chandler have acquired his idiosyncratic behavior without ever experiencing a trauma that turned his world up-side-down, left his behavior full of contradictions, and eventually produced a unique style of writing culminating in the character of Philip Marlowe? It is highly unlikely. Without such an intimate connection to the effects of trauma it is extremely doubtful that Chandler could, or would, have bestowed these specific symptoms onto Marlowe unless they were some unconscious—almost subliminal—projection of the writer's own disability.

Consequently, traumatized by his experiences in the war, Chandler used his writing as a way to achieve a sense of catharsis and acceptance. Like many other members of the post–First World War literary cohort, his demons could not be completely laid to rest, and they continued to torment him throughout his life. Although Chandler is remembered "as a premier detective novelist," the main force of his novels, as Speir observed, owes something to the experiences that blighted his existence, and from this disability, the way he was able to entwine his own trauma into "his persistent struggle to get beyond the severe limitations of [crime fiction's generic] form" (17). As Hiney and MacShane have noted, "The qualities and attributes he held are often found on the boundaries of sanity, and Chandler held those in spades." They believe, "The payback for a life of odd ends was the sort of raw wit that appears in print only once or twice a century. The sort of eye that can see straight through what people say to what they mean. Few writers of his own generation have dated so little" (Hiney and MacShane xi). Thus, as the creator of a unique detective, the following chapters will demonstrate that Chandler's undoubted genius owes much to the transference of his tormented self, his trauma, his cynicism, and his despair, onto his veteran protagonist Philip Marlowe.

2

A NEW VIEW: CHANDLER AND WAR

[Y]ou have to hurt like hell before you can write seriously.

—HEMINGWAY, QTD. IN MEYERS, *HEMINGWAY*

When Frank MacShane and Tom Hiney researched their biographical accounts of Raymond Chandler's war experience, neither took into account how this traumatic episode might have altered the author's psychological state or how it might have subsequently influenced the development and characterization of his detective, Philip Marlowe. Both biographers focused on the belief that the war acted as the source of the stark realism that served to make Chandler's descriptions of crime scenes shockingly realistic. Chandler's combat experience, therefore, was not viewed in the context of distress and psychological suffering, but instead as an occurrence that created a rich reserve of imagery from which the author could later draw for his novels. While this is almost certainly true, the biographers missed an opportunity to consider the devastating psychological effects that the war had upon Chandler's life and work. Furthermore, when recounting the experience of war, MacShane and Hiney both appear to have placed their absolute confidence in the frankness of Chandler's firsthand testimony. However, this chapter will demonstrate that in light of further examination Chandler's correspondence may not be quite as straightforward as it originally appears and may include ambiguities and misleading statements.

It is widely known that Ernest Hemingway exaggerated and magnified his own wartime exploits in order to portray himself as a masculine veteran. Chandler, on the other hand, did not refer to his wartime experiences until later in his life, and only then, seemingly, as a means of attracting the attentions of supposedly impressionable women. MacShane and Hiney placed their knowledge of Chandler's war experience upon his letters to one particular correspondent, an Australian student named Deirdre Gartrell. In this correspondence Chandler briefly describes his experiences in a manner intended to impress, and as such, we must reexamine the accuracy and circumstances in which these original letters were written. Therefore, chapter 2 will pick apart previous accounts of Chandler's time in France in order to resolve the ambiguity surrounding his location, encounters, and supposed wounding on the front line. This chapter raises important questions concerning the authenticity of the original biographical interpretation and the degree of confidence that may be placed on the accuracy of Chandler's account. In light of historical and documentary evidence regarding Chandler's precise location on the front line, the intensity of battle that he actually witnessed, and his alleged wounding during an artillery barrage in June 1918, the original accounts appear to be based on slender evidence.

Chandler's most recent biographer, Tom Williams, has attempted to fill the gaps regarding Chandler's wartime experience in *A Mysterious Something in the Light: Raymond Chandler, A Life* (2012) and has created a plausible account of the writer's time in France. However, a thorough examination of the primary sources has made it possible to accomplish something that MacShane, Hiney, and Williams did not achieve in their research: to trace the movement and location of the First Canadian Division on the Western Front and thereby pinpoint Chandler's precise deployments during his time in France. By reexamining Chandler's military records and cross-referencing with his medical file, it is possible to understand how and why Chandler returned to England and develop an accurate account of his later transfer to the Royal Air Force (RAF), none of which was examined in any great detail by previous biographers. Although Williams believes that the account of Chandler's war experience rendered by MacShane is "a typical Ray story" (67) (implying that MacShane utilized Chandler's own words in order to construct the account), Williams nevertheless does draw attention to the flaws that exist in both MacShane and Hiney's accounts, which will be examined further in this chapter. The evidence therefore suggests that the version of events provided by MacShane and Hiney is ambiguous and that both biographers' accounts of the war were mistaken on points of fundamental importance.

Evidence suggests that unlike Hemingway, who was wounded as the result of an *active* traumatic event arising from an artillery explosion, Chandler may have suffered a far more *passive* trauma arising from the dangerous and hostile environment. First World War soldiers often complained that the incessant inactivity of trench warfare greatly heightened their fear of imminent death, and in this terrifying situation a soldier often psychologically experiences "intense fear, helplessness, loss of control, and [the] threat of annihilation" (Herman 33). The sensation of overpowering apprehension is highly psychologically corrosive and a significant contributor to the development of traumatic neuroses. "Traumatic events," says Herman "produce profound and lasting changes in psychological arousal, emotion, cognition, and memory. Moreover, traumatic events may sever these normally integrated functions from one another . . . This kind of fragmentation, whereby trauma tears apart a complex system of self-protection that normally functions in an integrated fashion is central to the historic observations of post-traumatic stress disorder" (34). There is no doubt that a soldier's experience of war, however short, can be life changing. Chandler's experiences in France undoubtedly played a major role in the derivation and progressive decline of his psychological state, including the erratic behavior that came to define his later life.

The style and voice of countless writers have been shaped and defined by the experience of war, and in the United States the most renowned of these became known as the writers of the Lost Generation. Not only do they represent a generation that went to war and returned either physically or psychologically injured, but they also captured the plight of a generation that felt dislocated from the modernized America they encountered upon their return from war. As well as this outpouring of disillusionment, confusion, and loss of direction was the overriding belief that "they were an oppressed minority, orphans and strangers in their own country" (Cowley 13). In 1915 Sigmund Freud posited the view that the "most potent factors in the mental distress felt by non-combatants" was "the disillusionment which this war has evoked; and the altered attitude towards death" (qtd. in Rickman 2). As far as combat itself was concerned, Freud affirmed that "never has any event been destructive of so much that is valuable in the common wealth of humanity, nor so misleading to many of the clearest intelligences, nor so debasing to the highest that we know" (qtd. in Rickman 1). Although some of the Lost Generation writers did not actually experience warfare firsthand, after the war they were all able to tap into the discontent and frustration felt by many that had.

However, for the few, the decadence of the jazz age, the rise of consumerism, and the general air of exuberance following the war did not signal a time of disillusionment. But this perception of the 1920s was not one that was uniformly shared. The Lost Generation, for example, fixed their attention instead on the overpowering sensation of "no longer belonging" in what for many was the carefree abandon of postwar American society. This contrasting image of the "Roaring 20s" and the disillusionment of veterans is summed up by F. Scott Fitzgerald's *The Great Gatsby.* Remarkably, Fitzgerald was able to combine both of these prevailing social moods in his novel, which he wrote without any explicit reference to the subject of war or its aftermath. In a manner similar to Chandler's detective, Gatsby is a disillusioned veteran surrounded by decadence. But unlike Marlowe, the decadence surrounding Gatsby is of his own making. His desperate attempt to hold on to Daisy Buchanan has forced him "steadily upwards" to become "a 'success'—but as a bootlegger and possibly as a swindler" (Prigozy 83). Daisy represents the one "good" thing from Gatsby's prewar existence, and it is his determination to keep her in his life which leaves him resigned to adopt the decadence of the 1920s and exploit the era's consumption needs. Gatsby uses the very decadence that Marlowe considers phony in order to cling on to the only remnant of his prewar past that he considers worthwhile, his love for Daisy.

The Great Gatsby can be considered a postwar novel because it combines the story of two veterans, the protagonist Jay Gatsby and the narrator Nick Carraway, through the all-pervading postwar social indifference toward those who fought. Gatsby and Carraway strike up a friendship based on their service in the same infantry division of the American army. They have a shared experience and as such, appear to have a bond of empathetic understanding, demonstrated by Carraway's declaration at Gatsby's funeral: "I began to have a feeling of defiance, of scornful solidarity between Gatsby and me against them all" (Fitzgerald, *Great Gatsby* 157). This outlook is very similar to the persona of Chandler's Philip Marlowe. Although Marlowe has no real friends, his recognition of another character's war experience immediately evokes empathy and bonding with fellow veterans, a feature particularly striking in the cases of Roger Wade and Terry Lennox in *The Long Goodbye.*

If Fitzgerald wrote *The Great Gatsby* as a novel about the effects of war, then Chandler may be thought of as having done something very similar in his own writing. The major difference between Fitzgerald and Chandler is that while Fitzgerald did not experience combat, Chandler did, and he was therefore able to draw, as Hiney has noted, from a deeper well of personal and emotional experience. The use of a remarkably descriptive first-person narrative smoldering with discontentment connects Chandler's work more closely to that of Fitzgerald and the Lost Generation than to the works of Hammett and the early crime genre in general.

A number of Lost Generation writers such as John Dos Passos and Ernest Hemingway chose to experience the war by serving as ambulance drivers because "rescue work offered a splendid way to get close to the fighting without actually being a foot soldier" (Lynn 73). Yet even being on the periphery of the actual combat was dangerous, as Hemingway discovered in July 1918 when he was injured delivering chocolate to frontline troops. Although Hemingway candidly admitted that he had been terrified by his wounding on the Italian front, he believed that "serious injuries purified men who endured them, enabling them to transcend the brutal and destructive side of war" (Meyers, *Hemingway* 35). Hemingway was convinced that by incorporating such terrifying experiences and emotions into his work he could produce a form of literature that was far more honest and realistic.

Although he had enlisted in the Canadian infantry and saw action first-hand, unlike Hemingway Chandler rarely discussed his wartime experiences, doing so only "obliquely" (MacShane, *Life* 29) in letters towards the end of his life. The following section will examine the implications of these brief glimpses of emotions and more specifically, how much credence we should draw from them.

CHANDLER'S CORRESPONDENCE

Many of Chandler's key allusions to the war appear briefly in letters written to one correspondent in particular in the three years prior to his death. His correspondence with the Australian student Deirdre Gartrell was initiated in 1956 as a dialogue that initially revolved around the personal significance of Chandler's novels to her as she struggled with her own depression and anxiety. Gartrell's vulnerability appealed to Chandler's sense of honor and bolstered by his desire to comfort and protect her, a flirtatious correspondence began (at least from Chandler's perspective) which lasted until the end of his life. Chandler's letters are both introspective and sentimental, and as such their content and factual accuracy should be treated with a measure of caution.

Failing to recognize the significance of Chandler's letters as a means of understanding the writer's deteriorating emotional state, the correspondence has remained psychologically uncharted by his biographers. Despite recognizing that letter writing was "an important outlet for a writer who [. . .] had restricted himself to detective stories" (MacShane, *Letters* xvi), Frank MacShane, Tom Hiney, and Tom Williams failed to comprehend the irregular circumstances in which the letters were written or the anomalous nature of the dialogue contained in the letters. Yet the importance of the letters is considerable; as Chandler himself noted, "I suppose in my letters I more or less revealed those facets of my mind which had to be obscured or distorted in what I wrote for publication" (qtd. in ibid.). Although MacShane and Hiney draw upon the content of Chandler's letters to Gartrell to explain the writer's war experience, they do not consider the unusual nature of their relationship and the influence that it may have had on the content of the correspondence. As a result, the credibility and reliability of the content as an accurate description of what may have taken place on the front line in France have remained largely unchallenged.

Acknowledging that Chandler was a romantic and a flirt during his final years, MacShane would have understood Chandler's propensity for embellishing stories with touches of fantasy. However, the principal setback to MacShane's account of Chandler's war experience is that he accepted the letters as truth. Even more surprising is that MacShane and Hiney cite the content of Chandler's letters to Gartrell as fact without considering the exceptional circumstances in which they were written.

Despite this, on the surface Chandler's letters certainly provide a fascinating insight into his perceived experience of battle. In a letter to Gartrell in March 1957 Chandler included a brief reflection on his wartime experiences. He wrote:

> Courage is a strange thing: one can never be sure of it. As a platoon commander very many years ago, I never seemed to be afraid, and yet I have been afraid of the most insignificant risks. If you had to go over the top somehow all you seemed to think of was trying to keep the men spaced, in order to reduce casualties. It was always very difficult, especially if you had replacements or men who had been wounded. It's only human to want to bunch for companionship in the face of heavy fire. Nowadays war is very different. In some ways it's much worse, but the casualties don't compare with those in trench warfare. My battalion (Canadian) had a normal strength of 1200 men and it had over 14,000 casualties. (Qtd. in MacShane, *Life* 29)

This passage provides us with not simply an insight into Chandler's character but also a sense of the emotional stimulation he gained from the episode. We learn that Chandler was a platoon commander with the responsibility of taking roughly thirty men into action. He notes that he has been "over the top," and in all likelihood this is accurate since entries in the Seventh Battalion war diaries recorded the constant activity of scouting and raiding parties during the time Chandler spent in the battalion. Chandler also displays his awareness of the normal human response during traumatizing situations by noting the futility of telling soldiers to space themselves apart to avoid unnecessary casualties, going against the natural human instinct to cluster together when frightened or under stress.

One inconsistency in Chandler's account above, however, appears to be in his recollection of the 14,000 casualties suffered by the Seventh Battalion Canadian Expeditionary Force (CEF). According to Major T. V. Scudamore in *A Short History of the 7th Battalion C.E.F.,* there were approximately 1,380 soldiers either killed or declared missing from the Seventh Battalion between 1915 and 1918 (*History* appendix). A possible explanation for this discrepancy is that when he rounded up the total number of casualties to 1,400, Chandler made a typing error and added an extra digit to the figure. Another possibility is that he may have confused the battalion casualty figure with the casualty figure for the entire First Division.

Nevertheless, it is clear that Chandler's correspondence with Gartrell offers a valuable insight into the author's state of mind in later life. The letters are important because, although they were written almost forty years after the event, they offer Chandler's perceived recollections of his wartime experiences. He divulges information that enables us to understand how these events changed his personality and his postwar life and displays his emotional state at the time of writing. In short, the letters show that Chandler's mind had become fragile and erratic as he became increasingly infatuated with his female correspondents. They also make it clear he had become lonely, unpredictable, and capable of self-contradiction. Chandler appears to have been reaching out to those around him for more meaningful connections. Showing his increased desperation, Chandler noted in a letter from 1948, "Friends are too scarce these days" (Bodleian 57:5), and by 1952 he believed that in years to come "Letters are going to be my greatest burden" (Bodleian 41:100).

Chandler's grief and sense of loss following Cissy's death aroused conflicting emotions that caused him to behave unpredictably, especially toward women. According to theories first offered by Sigmund Freud in 1920, this type of erratic behavior may have been exacerbated by Chandler's war experience. Freud believed that in the wake of a traumatic event, notions of love and death could become conflicted, triggering extreme psychological behavior. Placed in a context of war, his theory, which he named "The Pleasure Principle," argued that love and death maintain a symbiotic relationship. Freud's theory, which is now considered as a legitimate traumatic response to war, is complex. As Edward Tick has explained: "War brings us into the most intense engagement with other human beings. It demands that we love some of our neighbours and destroy others. And it asks us to align ourselves—to love and hate thus—in the most uncompromising terms" (119). In an environment where the forces of love and death connect so completely, warfare radically transforms not only combatants' relationships with others, but also their enduring attitudes toward love and sex. Developing an abnormal sex drive is a common example of how war can transform a soldier's understanding of love and passion, and the primeval instinct awakened by war transfers to a combatant's sexuality when the combatant returns home (Tick 123). As a result, increased sexual appetite and promiscuity are not uncommon as veterans develop a "hunger for the restoration of life that only the intensity of erotic arousal could promise to fulfill" (Tick 124). "The Pleasure Principle" suggests that engaging the sex drive can be the primary means by which a trauma victim is able to feel alive while suffering a fear of death.

This theory certainly sheds light upon Chandler's attitude toward women. Hiney and MacShane both note that after only three years of marriage to Cissy, Chandler became restless, and while pretending to be Cissy's chivalric knight, he allegedly began extramarital affairs with the secretaries at the Dabney Oil Company. A colleague of Chandler at Dabney's, John Abrams, commented that during many company banquets he became "a shadowy figure, stinko drunk and hovering in the wings with a bevy of showgirls, a nuisance" (qtd. in MacShane, *Life* 39). His drinking and womanizing became so excessive that he moved out of the home he shared with Cissy and into a hotel, visiting his secretary on weekends to binge drink in an apartment he had rented for her. At this point in his life, Chandler appeared to have hit rock bottom, and yet it seems to have been his concern for his wife's failing health and his writing that pulled him back from the brink of submitting to conflicting and destructive forces.

Chandler's excessive reaction to other women after Cissy's death in 1954 may also be explained by Freud's theory. On a trip to London in 1955 he exclaimed,

> But the women! [. . .] I've seen glamour girls at parties that would stun Hollywood. And they are so damn honest they won't even let you pay their taxi fares [. . .] If you want them to go to bed with you, you have to say "please" five times [. . .] Americans are not as a rule successful with the best type of English girls and women. They move too fast and too roughly. There is far too much of this "Come on, baby, let's hit they hay" motif. They don't like it. They expect to be treated as ladies. They

> are perfectly willing to sleep with you if they like you and if you treat them with deference, because [. . .] they don't want to be treated like easy lays. They want you to work up to it slowly and fastidiously, and I certainly think they are right. (Qtd. in MacShane, *Letters* 390–91)

Chandler would often briefly indulge his sexual fantasies. After meeting the writer Marcel Duhamel and his wife in New York in 1956, Chandler wrote to Helga Greene, "His wife is charming. I'd like to sleep with her. Right now I'd like to sleep with almost any pretty soft gentle woman," yet, the overly romantic Chandler admitted, "but of course I shan't do it (even if I had the chance) because there has to be love. Without that it is nothing" (qtd. in MacShane, *Letters* 401). And curiously, although he lusted after women, he insisted to Greene that there was "nothing predatory" (qtd. in MacShane, *Letters* 402) about his feelings and behavior.

With Cissy's death his sole stabilizing influence disappeared. A lonely Chandler admitted as much in a letter to Jessica Tyndale in 1956 while he was recovering from a nervous breakdown. He said, "I had been married so long and so happily that after the slow torture of my wife's death it seemed at first treason to look at another woman, and then suddenly I seemed to be in love with all women" (qtd. in MacShane, *Letters* 408). His impulsive sexual desire, whether real or a fantasy, emerged in numerous letters to female friends. Again, to Tyndale he divulges views that portray him as a philanderer, but also, curiously, as a romantic:

> I had no idea what I had to give them that they gave so much to me, that the most strict and puritanical woman I had ever met had been in bed with me a week after I met her. That the strange thing was that such affairs as I had had never ended. There was never any bitterness or boredom. I loved them all still and they seemed to love me. But I could not live alone. It destroyed me. Therefore I could not be completely faithful to any woman who could not share my life, but that I didn't regard this as infidelity, because after all sex is only a rather minor part of love, delicious as it is when it is right. I said I really didn't want to get married again because my heart was in too many places and a wife would never have more than a part of me. (Qtd. in MacShane, *Letters* 408–9)

What is striking about Chandler's dialogue in his letters, and especially with Gartrell, is how quickly and fluidly he moves between subjects and how he manages to manipulate the feelings of his correspondent. He also manages to insert references to war in the most simple of conversations. In July 1957, for example, Chandler wrote to Gartrell regarding his health, but he ended up comparing it to his war experience: "It seems that I have a serious anaemic condition. Not fatal, but quite serious. These diagnoses never make much impression on me, since I have lived my whole life on the edge of nothing. Once you have had to lead a platoon into direct machine-gun fire, nothing is ever the same again."[1] In this small insightful passage Chandler shows just how much of an impact his war experience had on his life. This is the only time that he admits how deeply his experiences had changed him. Yet while confessing his troubled feelings about his life-altering experience of warfare and his melancholia, he appears to be trying to manipulate Gartrell's feelings by hinting to the seriousness of his condition. It offers a unique insight not only into Chandler's feelings toward the war but also his growing emotional attachment to his correspondent.

Although Chandler's accounts of his war experience appear earnest and sincere, upon closer examination these allusions become decidedly less credible and trustworthy. His letters sway between commonsense advice for Gartrell, subtle flirtation, and the roguish exploitation of her reverence. It appears as though he is playing for her sympathies by endeavoring to present himself in the role of a hero. Like many of the women he socialized with on his frequent visits to London in his later years, it is as though Chandler looked upon Gartrell as a person to be "saved." As with many other women, his sympathetic advice soon began to carry definite sexual connotations, with Chandler later confessing, "I don't quite know why you are so close to my heart, but you are. In some mysterious way you have put me inside of you, so that I have to lie awake at night and worry about you—you a girl I have not ever seen" (qtd. in Hiney and MacShane 243).

Chandler's desire to meet Gartrell was almost perfectly counterbalanced by his need to keep her at a distance; she became an object to be worshiped from afar. He said in March 1957: "[W]e may never meet. I rather hope we shall, unless it destroys an illusion. You need the illusion" (qtd. in MacShane, *Letters* 430). Deirdre Gartrell, a woman less than half his age whom he had never met, became the privileged confidant to Chandler's casual comments. His letters to her demonstrate his desperation for admiration and a need to impress, and as such the disclosure of Chandler's war experience in these uncertain circumstances becomes problematic, making his motives ambiguous. It is likely that Chandler's propensity for acting out the role of knight and hero meant that he felt the same impulse when describing his war deeds. Hemingway admitted in his Spanish War dispatches that he and other soldiers had often exaggerated the severity of their injuries, in all likelihood to augment their belief in their own bravery and masculinity. In his dispatch "The Spanish War" in July 1938 Hemingway said, "In the war that I had known, men often lied about the manner of their wounding. Not at first; but later. I'd lied a little myself in my time" (qtd. in Meyers, *Hemingway* 33). And certainly, as Hemingway's biographer Jeffrey Meyers concedes, the writer's later versions of his experiences have been "exaggerated into myth" (*Hemingway* 33).

In the same way that critics and the public took Hemingway's depiction of his war experience and wounding as the truth (until the publication of Lynn's biography in 1987), it is likely that the accounts of Chandler's exploits by MacShane and Hiney are flawed in a similar way. Lynn revealed that the level of myth constructed around Hemingway originated from sources that had remained unquestioned for almost two decades. Most astonishingly, the account of Hemingway's wounding emanated from the author himself while recovering in a hospital in Italy, and Carlos Baker's 1969 biography, *Hemingway: A Life Story*, kept alive the perception of his "heroic" wounding at Fossalta di Piave on 8 July 1918.[2] It is quite possible that in his last few years Chandler assumed a similar stance in order to win the sympathies and admiration of the opposite sex. Just as he chose to play the role of the knight to his female friends in London and Los Angeles, Chandler may have seen an opportunity to impress Gartrell—his damsel in distress—by dramatizing his exploits during the war.

And so, although it was Gartrell that initiated their correspondence, Chandler's words of comfort quickly served to take advantage of her adoration and became increasingly intimate. His letters reveal his oscillating emotions, subtle flirtation, and a noticeable sexual dimension. Although wanting to adhere to his noble ideals of virtue, Chandler routinely portrays himself as quite the opposite, as a manipulative philanderer. In a letter from 1957, in which he comments upon Gartrell's proposed trip to Germany, Chandler said, "If you really do go to Germany while I am in England, I hope you will fly over to London to visit me, as my guest in every sense of course" (Bodleian 58:183–44, p. 183). These suggestive comments show a striking departure from the common image we have of a person who has generally been considered as a timid, reserved, and detached character. We only have to look at accounts from Chandler's early Hollywood days to realize how shy and introverted he was, and yet in his letter to Gartrell in March 1957 Chandler says,

> I am more than twice your age and it may be out of place for me to be saying these things to you, but it is nevertheless a simple fact that I could never hurt, cheapen or demean a woman, and often, when I was young and unmarried, I had to think for the girl too, to prevent her sometimes from doing something which I know would shame her later. . . . I don't go too far with this, because after all I am writing to a well-bred young lady, and I don't want to offend her. I could go much farther, but would it be right? (Qtd. in MacShane, *Letters* 430)

Chandler's sexual overture to Gartrell is made all the more observable by his admission that his comments "may be out of place," embarrassing, or even offensive. Curiously, the letters demonstrate that he created a dual persona of himself: on the one hand as a young bachelor with a penchant for flirting, and on the other as a noble protector of female virtue. This sexual uncertainty is a theme that recurs in many of his later letters, and his overtly sexual allusions would have certainly been enough to make the recipient wonder about Chandler's intentions. For example, in a relatively innocent letter from April 1957 Chandler describes his blissful marriage, saying, "I can't, as I think back, find any reason why I should have been so favoured." But what is immediately startling is the explanation he gives for this conviction: he did not deserve such a happy marriage, because "as a young man I was anything but virginal" (Bodleian 75:42). The imagery of his knightly courtship of his wife is in harsh contrast to his description of himself as a promiscuous youth. And again, just eight months later in December 1957, contrary to his previous statement, Chandler wrote to Gartrell: "I was pretty tame at your age, almost afraid to speak to a girl. But I made up for it later" (Bodleian 58:183). It would appear that Chandler genuinely believed he had "a strange sort of instinct for understanding people, especially women" (Bodleian 75:35–62, p. 41). What is so startling is that despite his age—at this point Chandler was sixty-nine and two years from death—he appears to have relished the idea of being sexually provocative with his female correspondents while at the same time endeavoring to portray himself as someone wise and pure.

In an attempt to discern whether Chandler embellished or even fabricated events from his past, it is also pertinent to consider the letters that he wrote to his British literary agent, Helga Greene. In these letters too, Chandler not only inflates his sexual prowess while displaying his chivalric ideals, but he also envisages scenarios of a sexual nature that were a complete fiction. Yet, Chandler simply does not divulge enough information to garner an accurate or adequately informative picture of his wartime exploits.

In contrast to the correspondence with Gartrell, then, Chandler's tone is notably different in his letters to Helga Greene. Instead of the overtly sexual manner he used with Gartrell, when conversing with Greene he routinely adopts a chaste and innocent manner. In July 1956 Chandler had written to Greene describing,

> When I was a young man and very innocent, I lived in a pension on the Boul' Miche [in Paris] and was very happy wandering around, with very little money, but a sort of starry-eyed love of everything I saw. The only thing that upset me was the whores at the door of the apartment building if I happened to be out a little late. And I was so innocent that I didn't realise that there were two girls at the pension that couldn't keep their feet off mine and were offering themselves to my innocence and I never knew it. (Qtd. in MacShane, *Life* 13)

The differing tones of the correspondence to Gartrell and Greene show how Chandler's demeanor and degree of elaboration depended not only on whom he was conversing with but also on his particular frame of mind. While he certainly enjoyed his flirtatious correspondence with a number of women, his tone is noticeably more understated and gentle when writing to Greene, making it plain that he carried a genuine affection for her. His letters to her show a softer side of his character, the side that few of his correspondents ever saw. It is possible that with Greene he allowed his bravado to slip and was disposed to lay bare the sincere and vulnerable side of his character.

In view of the eagerness in his later years to overstate his own sexual prowess, it is a little surprising that Chandler did not disclose more about his war experience. This is where the major difference between Chandler and Hemingway lies. While Hemingway completely transformed the story of his wounding in order to play the role of the gallant war hero, Chandler revealed very little of his exploits during the war, which are limited to small slivers of information in his correspondence. While MacShane and Hiney used Chandler's statement that he had led a platoon under fire and other concise remarks to theorize that Chandler was the sole survivor of an explosion that killed his entire platoon, his words actually reveal nothing more than that he endured the experience of commanding a group of men into battle. In the letter from which this comment was taken Chandler says nothing of surviving an artillery attack, nor is it mentioned in any of his other correspondence. If this had in fact happened, it certainly might have provided Chandler with an occurrence to elaborate. His letters, however, provide insufficient information to enable us to satisfactorily piece together a full biographical account of Chandler's wartime experiences. The only thing that we conclude with some certainty from the letters is that Chandler emerged from the war emotionally troubled.

At about the same time that Chandler was writing his letters to Gartrell and Greene, he had also begun writing short stories that represented a major departure from any of his previous work. In a letter to Neil Morgan, a columnist at the San Diego *Tribune*, Chandler admitted that "lately I have been indulging in a form of polite pornography . . . and I am, therefore enclosing a couple of samples" (qtd. in MacShane, *Letters* 389). In the summer of 1957 he wrote a series of stories which he titled "A Routine to Shock the Neighbours." Natasha Spender recounted that these sketches evolved from rude anecdotal "improvisations" that Chandler would loudly discuss with his guests while lunching at the Connaught Hotel in London, improvisations that were designed to "titillate those at neighbouring tables" (MacShane, *Life* 248). Chandler claimed that they had been written to test his ear for English dialogue and were comprised of numerous suggestive stories that he nicknamed his "Pornographic Sketches." In a letter to his San Diego lawyer, Leroy Wright, in March 1957, Chandler acknowledged that they "were mildly pornographic" but reasoned that it "was only to make them fun to write" (qtd. in MacShane, *Letters* 437). He explained that "the basic motif behind [the stories] is an attempt to spoof the upper-middle class sort of talk" (qtd. in MacShane, *Letters* 389). He sent many of these stories to some of his closest friends, mainly female, and invited them to make comments and offer advice. In one such story, which he called "Faster, Slower, Neither," the theme is subtly suggestive: "Well, really, much as one hates to interrupt at a time like this, isn't the tempo—well, one might possibly say a bit adagio?" (qtd. in MacShane, *Life* 248–49). Even if, as Chandler insisted, these stories had been written for amusement, it is not difficult to imagine the emotional state that prompted him to write an assessment of English dialogue in such a format.[3]

Interestingly Hiney and MacShane view Chandler's letters to Gartrell—and Gartrell herself—in very different ways. MacShane does not specifically acknowledge or reference any of Chandler's letters to her, except to piece together a vague picture of Chandler's war experience. Hiney acknowledges the relationship between Chandler and Gartrell and acknowledges that in the letters "Chandler's mood swings were transparent" (261). But he misleadingly depicts her as a distressed and obsessive fan that fueled Chandler's "knightly" advances.

However, in her own account of her relationship with Chandler, Gartrell notes that Chandler's psychological state in the last years of his life was far from stable. In reality he was a far more melancholic character, bordering on a breakdown and suffering the effects of losing his wife. In 1960 Gartrell shed some light on Chandler's emotional state in his final years. Corresponding with Helga Greene after Chandler's death, Gartrell confirmed that, despite her huge respect for the author, in her opinion he possessed an overly active imagination. She revealingly said, "I never knew how much to believe . . . [H] is words sometimes ran away with him" (Bodleian 71:146–48, p. 148). As with most of his other female friends, Gartrell's relationship with Chandler had been complex. "Ray wrote to me more as a father to daughter, than writer to writer," she said. "He used to worry about my developmental problems, . . . give me advice, sometimes by cable, or even telephone, when I appeared on the brink of some madcap scheme, and sigh with relief when I recovered from my foolishness" (Bodleian 71:146–48, p. 146). One of these "madcap schemes" in which he tried to intervene was Gartrell's marriage to Walter Stube, a Danish German building contractor she had met while corresponding with Chandler. He wanted her to end the relationship because, as Gartrell disclosed to Greene, "Germans don't make understanding mates!" (ibid.), an assessment which might be indicative of a deep-seated suspicion and mistrust of Germans emanating from his wartime experiences.

It appears the attachment between Gartrell and Chandler was far more one-sided than Hiney and others recognized. In 1957, the increasingly troubled Chandler confessed to Gartrell that in his mind their friendship had become something more. He admitted, "In some strange way you have become a part of me, so that I wake in the night and wonder what is Deirdre thinking or doing" (qtd. in Hiney 261). But Gartrell's intentions toward the author seem to have been far more conventional and straightforward. In her letter to Helga Greene, Gartrell states that her sole aim was friendship. She said, "I [only] wanted an anonymous outlet for my writer[']s thoughts" (Bodleian 71:146–47, p. 147).

But as Chandler's tone changed, so did the nature of their friendship. She continued, "First flattered and then incredulous, then irritated [. . .] at losing my iceberg confidante, [. . .] gradually we changed; Ray realized I had shown him only one aspect of myself, and so he felt a little cheated and disillusioned. So [. . . we] drifted apart, letters fizzled out" (ibid.). It seems Chandler had become addicted to filling the role of hero. He cherished the attention he received from women and was drawn to those who revered him; the adoration excited him and encouraged him to further embellish his correspondence.

But by the time his correspondence with Gartrell diminished, Chandler had already provided the recollections about his war experience that today we recognize as the basis for his exploits during the First World War.

While reliable indicators of Chandler's state of mind during his final years, his letters to Gartrell are problematic if they are considered as an *accurate* source of information concerning his wartime experiences. Furthermore, because they were written so long after the events—almost forty years—in addition to the limited amount of information that they divulge, it is not unreasonable to question whether they can be deemed a source of legitimate historical data. Nonetheless, the letters *are* significant as an insight into the *emotional intensity* of Chandler's experiences and as a measure of the effects that stayed with him for the rest of his life. The experience of being so close to the sights, sounds, and action of the battlefield etched a deep scar in Chandler's psyche which not only molded his personality, but also encouraged the author to create a character who not only survived his war experiences but emerged a hero, the very quality Chandler longed to possess.

Beyond reflections taken from correspondence of dubious substance forty years after the event, one further short-fall in MacShane and Hiney's biographies is an accurate account of Chandler's time in France; neither biographer attempted to plot the course of the First Canadian Division or examine Chandler's assumed wounding. This omission leaves the critical events that were to shape and influence the unique character of Philip Marlowe, untold.

MAPPING CHANDLER'S WAR

To facilitate an understanding of the transference of combat motifs and symptoms into Chandler's work, it is vital to explore the wartime events which influenced such an incidence. While Frank MacShane makes some effort to plot the First Division's location in France, his contribution is very vague. He notes that the Seventh Battalion of the First Canadian Division, the battalion to which Chandler would be assigned, had successfully defended Vimy Ridge in April 1917 and had also emerged triumphant after the battle of Passchendaele in November 1917. However, by the time of Chandler's arrival in France, MacShane merely described the location of the First Division as situated "on either side of the road that linked Arras with Cambrai" (MacShane, *Life* 28). This description of his location is simply too vague to be of meaningful value, identifying one of many deployment sites between

March and June 1918. Although attempting to ascertain the exact position of Chandler's battalion from such scant detail is not without its difficulties, it is nonetheless quite possible not only to pinpoint the location of Chandler's division but also to follow its course as it was dispatched to various positions along the Western Front. These movements are catalogued and readily accessible in the official war diaries of the Seventh Infantry Battalion. Even though Chandler's battalion was said to occupy a "reserve" position, previous biographies have failed to observe the extraordinary amount of heavy fighting and artillery bombardments that Chandler's battalion experienced. As will be shown, the biographers did not emphasize the proximity of the Canadian forces to the German front line during these last few months of the war and consequently underestimated the dangers inherent in occupying such a precarious position.

Although the factual detail provided by Chandler's biographers has proved ambiguous, Hiney does largely make some attempt to provide a cogent picture of Chandler's experiences in the First World War and attempts to describe what Chandler witnessed. Acknowledging his frontline role, Hiney describes how Chandler was involved in "sporadic trench warfare" (43). Peter Leese has observed that during the First World War even low-level combat, like that experienced by soldiers in reserve, was potentially just as traumatic as the all-out trench warfare witnessed in other areas of the Western Front, and those involved in combat conditions for short periods of time were just as susceptible to suffer its traumatic effects (26). During any experience of war Richard Gabriel has noted that "almost everybody exposed to combat will, within a comparatively short period of time, be killed, wounded, or driven mad" (qtd. in Tick 102).

Psychological injury does not only occur to those engaged in active combat situations. In fact, it is just as likely to occur with noncombat troops who can do nothing but endure the unrelenting inactivity and live with the unremitting expectation of death. In his article "Beyond the Pleasure Principle" Freud argued that in cases of "war neuroses," as it was called at the time, "symptoms sometimes came about without the intervention of any gross mechanical force" (qtd. in Gay 598). To put it simply, in war a trauma-inducing event does not necessarily have to be a consequence of an active combat-related incident in order to inflict serious psychological damage. In his view "the chief weight" in the onset of war neuroses "rest[s] upon the factor of surprise, of fright" (ibid.). Freud believed "'Fright,' 'fear,' and 'anxiety' are in fact capable of clear distinction in their relation to danger." He noted, "'Anxiety' describes a particular state of expecting the danger or preparing for it, even though it may be an unknown one. 'Fear' requires a definite object of which to be afraid. 'Fright' [. . .] emphasizes the factor of surprise" (ibid.). Freud also suggested that the human ego possesses a defensive barrier that controls the amount of stimulation absorbed by the brain; a proposition suggesting now that different people would be affected in different ways, the conclusion reached by many contemporary psychologists.[4] Even Chandler appears to have been aware of the effects of "active" versus "passive" trauma. In 1947, while discussing the psychological trauma featured in his film *The Blue Dahlia*, he explained, "The real point at issue [in the film] is whether physical violence is worse than psychological violence" (qtd. in MacShane, *Letters* 97). Chandler recognized not only that psychological trauma existed, but also that it should be considered just as damaging as physical war trauma.

While Freud did not believe "anxiety" could cause war neuroses, it would be proved decades later that unlike physical trauma, the combination of anxiety and fear—where events are beyond a person's control—are in fact the two largest contributors to the development of PTSD. Patrick Bracken has noted that it is now "acknowledged that being a *witness* to a distressing event can be traumatizing, even in the absence of direct threat to self" (Bracken 48). The 1994 edition of the American Psychiatric Association's *Diagnostic and Statistical Manual of Mental Disorders* (DSM) therefore recognized that a posttraumatic reaction could be triggered if

> [t]he person has been exposed to a traumatic event in which both the following were present:
> (1) The person experienced, witnessed, or was confronted with an event or events that involved actual or threatened death or serious injury, or a threat to the physical integrity of self or others.
> (2) The person's response involved fear, helplessness, or horror. (Qtd. in Bracken 48)

Bracken concludes that the threat of annihilation could induce sufficient terror to cause PTSD, and that placed in an environment such as the Western Front it is highly likely that soldiers would have been extremely susceptible to developing severe psychological trauma.

In accounts of Chandler's time in France, Hiney provides a reasonably accurate picture of life in the battalion by drawing attention to the particularly high turnover rate among commanders, an indication of the enormously high casualty rate suffered by the Canadians. As a result of this Hiney asserts that by the time Chandler reached England in June 1918 he had been awarded a "battlefield promotion" (MacShane, *Life* 30) to acting sergeant and that his increased pay rate substantiates this conclusion. Although Hiney's account of Chandler's experience is somewhat more detailed than MacShane's, it nonetheless still lacks the crucial information to fully understand the extent of the conditions endured by the Canadian soldiers. The quantity of consistent factual information concerning Chandler's war experience is disappointing for biographers who have paved the way for studies of the author. Neither MacShane nor Hiney provides primary evidence of Chandler's actual experience of war, which can be gleaned by tracking the First Division in its campaign across northern France. Nor do the biographers offer any contextual information concerning the circumstances of Chandler's transfer back to England, instead basing their accounts solely on assumptions that were contradicted by the official military documents.

Although the Canadian forces played a central role in the British Commonwealth forces from 1914, very little has been published about the progress and fate of the Canadians during the First World War. One of the few existing accounts of their experience in the war is Colonel G. W. L. Nicholson's *Canadian Expeditionary Force 1914–1919*. Published in 1962, it is a detailed account of every Canadian division that fought in the war and itemizes their particular geographical location at important moments in the overall campaign. Nicholson's work provides a comprehensive analysis of the day-to-day activity that is manifestly at odds with the version of events espoused by both MacShane and Hiney. By utilizing Nicholson's work it is quite possible to precisely follow the movements of the Seventh Battalion, and hence establish an accurate picture of the conditions that Chandler would have experienced in France.

Although the four divisions of the CEF were officially in reserve, they were actually on the front line of Allied defense for much of the time Chandler was in France. By the beginning of 1918 the location occupied by the Canadian Corps around Arras had become precarious due to events occurring on the Eastern Front. The Russian Revolution of October 1917 and the subsequent signing of the German-Bolshevik peace treaty on 3 March 1918 released vast numbers of German troops and artillery pieces for transportation to the Western Front (Evans 68). Between November 1917 and the end of March 1918 the number of German divisions along the Western Front had risen from 150 to 192. In the early months of 1918 the Canadian divisions intensified their efforts to repair damaged defenses in preparation for a German offensive that, according to intelligence, would occur at the end of March. When the offensive finally began on 21 March, the Canadian Corps had three divisions on the front line "from the north to south the 1st Division opposite Hill 70, the 4th in front of Lens, and the 3rd Division in the Avion-Mericourt sector. The 2nd Division was in the Corps training area at Auchel, eight miles west of Bethune" (Nicholson 378). Once the German offensive began, the Second Division was ordered forward into GHQ reserve in the Mont St. Aloi area while Chandler's First Division was taken out of the line and placed in First Army reserve. The Fourth Division extended northward to cover the area vacated by the First opposite Hill 70, and the Third Division was called upon to extend southward to cover a British division in the Vimy region. By 25 March, the Canadian Corps held a seventeen-thousand-yard (9.6 miles) front with only two divisions.

On 26 March 1918 the First Division was stationed "astride the Arras-Cambrai road," while the Second Division was located "on its immediate right in the Neuville-Vitasse sector," both under Lieutenant General Sir Julian Byng's British Third Army (Nicholson 379). The Canadian forces were severely stretched, and Lieutenant General Sir Arthur Currie, commander of the Canadian Corps, pointed out: "We are holding a 10 mile front with two divisions" (Nicholson 382). By mid-April 1918 the position became even more acute as the Canadian Corps—without support—was ordered to hold a defensive front of more than sixteen miles.

A few weeks later there was a possibility that Chandler and the Canadian divisions would be ordered to participate in a counterattack as part of a larger Allied offensive. Planned for late April, Operation Delta was designed "to forestall a renewal of the enemy's offensive on the Bailleul-Ypres front. The proposed operation, to be launched on a ten-mile front [. . .] was a northward thrust against the left" (ibid.). Difficulties arose, however, when it proved unfeasible to release the Canadian divisions for the operation due to the shortage of reserves. As a result Operation Delta was suspended, and Chandler, probably to his great relief, was denied the opportunity of frontline combat as part of a Canadian division.

Although the action was suspended, the preparation required to mount it brought certain benefits, since preparing for the anticipated attack proved to be a useful exercise for the Canadian divisions. It had, said General Currie, exerted "a most vivifying influence on the training of the Canadian Corps" (ibid.). But during the same period, the Canadian Corps had been pushed almost to "breaking point and [were] under the continued threat of an overwhelming attack" (ibid.). The sheer scale of the front line now being defended was "altogether too much," said Currie, "but owing to a lack of men in the British Army it cannot be helped" (ibid.).

With the Battle of the Lys raging to their north and ever-decreasing reserves upon which to draw, the Canadians along the ten-mile front outside Arras prepared for the German offensive. As the German offensive progressed, and as Nicholson harrowingly describes, "the Canadians found themselves in a dangerously deepening salient. To deceive the enemy regarding the frugality of their dispositions they 'adopted a very aggressive attitude'" (ibid.). During April and May, "[t]he artillery maintained a vigorous programme of harassing fire, supplemented by the gas shells, while infantry carried out numerous raids and patrols" (ibid). The Seventh Battalion war diaries show that the Canadians were aware of their weak situation, noting on 9 April 1918 that "retaliation is not strong enough. Our artillery now firing 3 rounds per minute per gun" (Directorate of Heritage and History, "War Diary," 9–13 April 1918).

Although Chandler had not been involved in what Hiney described as "the attritional carnage that had characterized the worst battles" (Hiney 43), it is certain that conditions were extremely stressful for the Canadian troops. Despite the false display of military might through vigorous aggression, many soldiers ordered to defend the line were under unrelenting pressure, suffering from the constant barrage that would have exacerbated their physical and psychological exhaustion and their sense of utter helplessness.

On 7 May, Chandler's First Division, as well as the Third and Fourth Divisions of the Canadian Corps were ordered into reserve and were replaced by five divisions of British soldiers. Their respite, taken out of potential range of the German heavy artillery was, however, short-lived as the Canadian divisions were soon ordered to reorganize. They were subsequently ordered south to Amiens to prepare for the final push against the Germans, which would eventually end the war.

The precise details of what happened after May 1918, while Chandler's platoon was in reserve, present another area in which MacShane's and Hiney's accounts are open to question. Ever since the publication of MacShane's biography in 1976, critics have accepted without question the circumstances that surrounded Chandler's departure from the Western Front. MacShane explains how in June 1918 a German artillery barrage killed Chandler's platoon of men, leaving him the only survivor. He believes this event left Chandler sufficiently concussed for him to be transferred out of the front line before being shipped back to the English depot at Seaford. Given that the outcome of this incident is commonly regarded as being responsible for preventing Chandler from further duty in France, it is extremely puzzling that neither

MacShane nor Hiney felt it necessary to explore more closely the circumstances and consequences of this event.

Interestingly, Hiney offers his own contrasting theory about Chandler's return to England, suggesting that he was not alone in surviving the explosion. In contrast to MacShane's claim that Chandler was the only survivor, Hiney notes, "The bombardment had so depleted his own outfit that it was disbanded and *survivors*, including Chandler, were transferred back to England" (Hiney 43. Emphasis added). The obvious disparity here requires further investigation.

Despite its distance from the front line in a so-called reserve position, Chandler's division was still vulnerable to both air attacks and long-range enemy bombardment. The pivotal "strategic arm" of the German forces was the artillery, which by spring 1918 had "gathered in unprecedented strength" (Evans 69) along the entire the Western Front. This dramatic increase of German heavy artillery pieces brought the prospect of bombardment to a much greater depth behind the Allied lines. "Since the beginning of the German offensive in March," the time when Chandler arrived in France, the Canadian divisions "had suffered upwards of 9000 casualties." However, of these only "5690 had been sustained *up to* the time when the Corps withdrew into reserve" (Nicholson 385. Emphasis added). This would indicate that after the beginning of May a further 3,310 soldiers had been killed while *in reserve*, demonstrating that even being away from the front line brought no guarantee of safety.

Putting to one side the explanations provided by Hiney and MacShane, and instead utilizing the mortality rates cited by Nicholson, a far more accurate picture of the circumstances that confronted Chandler in 1918 emerges.

Almost one-third of Canadian soldiers killed between 7 May and the end of July 1918 had been in reserve, with the possibility that Chandler's platoon of thirty men was among them. If Chandler escaped the explosion with only a concussion when so many others lost their lives around him, it is reasonable to assume that such a defining moment may well have returned to haunt him later in life. In the case of Hemingway, for example, Meyers has documented how "[t]he main psychological effects of his concussion did not occur until he returned home, when he suffered long nights of insomnia and could not bear to have the lights out" (Meyers, *Hemingway* 36). Hemingway incorporated his trauma into his short story "Now I Lay Me," where Nick Adams felt, "if I ever shut my eyes in the dark and let myself go, my soul would go out of my body. I had been that way for a long time, ever since I had been blown up at night and felt it go out me and off and then come back" (*First Forty-Nine Stories* 340). Insomnia is a symptom that both Hemingway and Chandler suffered in the aftermath of the First World War and is clearly represented in their later fictional writing.

There is, however, one major impediment with MacShane and Hiney's account of Chandler's supposed wounding in an artillery barrage that killed his platoon: there is no evidence to support the claim that such an event ever occurred. The official documents plotting the movements of the Seventh Battalion simply do not support the biographical account of the circumstances that precipitated Chandler's early return to England in June 1918. Here, the Canadian Archives—which retains Chandler's original military record, his medical file, and the entire Seventh Battalion war diaries—provides the evidence to underpin a very different description of the events that led to Chandler's return to England. While the information gleaned from Nicholson's *Canadian Expeditionary Force 1914–1919* provides an invaluable starting point, it by no means provides the level of detail essential for examining and tracing the smaller individual battalions within the Canadian Corps. By contrast, the Seventh Battalion war diaries are specific to Chandler's battalion and plot the daily events as well as recording the companies to which reinforcements were assigned.

The documents indicate that having arrived in the battalion on 16 March, Raymond Thornton Chandler was officially posted to Number 1 Company of the Seventh Battalion on 23 March 1918. With the commencement of the German Offensive on 21 March, Chandler arrived in the Seventh Battalion at a time which marked the deepest advances by either side since 1914. Between March and May 1918 Chandler's battalion was positioned in various locations behind the front line and to the west of Arras in northern France. On three separate occasions he and his battalion were rotated into the front line, where several soldiers were either killed or wounded. After this period of rotation, the order was given for the Seventh Battalion to be sent into reserve (Directorate of Heritage and History, "War Diary," 30 April–7 May 1918). On 6 May the battalion officially began a month of training in the Nord-Pas-de-Calais regions of Lignereuil (approximately fourteen miles west of Arras) and Cambligneul (approximately nine miles northwest of Arras) to prepare for an advance in August from a new position to the south at Amiens; a drive that would eventually end the war (Directorate of Heritage and History, "War Diary," March–May 1918).

The war diaries state that the Seventh Battalion was encamped at Cambligneul 1 and 2 June 1918 and at Anzin (approximately forty-three miles east of Arras) for the remainder of that week. During this short period the battalion came under fire from artillery and shrapnel bursts on three separate occasions. The first was on 2 June while the battalion was passing through the locality of Villers Au Bois and Mont St. Aloy on its way to Anzin; the second occurred in Anzin on the afternoon of 3 June; and the third was on 7 June, while fortification work was being undertaken. The dispatches show that in none of these bombardments were any casualties sustained. Furthermore, there is no documentary evidence that any soldiers from Chandler's Seventh Battalion were killed for a period of approximately two months, a revelation that directly contradicts the accounts provided by MacShane and Hiney regarding Chandler's wounding and the annihilation of his platoon.

The war diaries for June also offer an insight into Chandler's transfer back to England. In his biography MacShane noted, "*By June 11* Chandler was back at the depot of the British Columbia Regiment in Seaford" (MacShane, *Life* 30. Emphasis added). Yet the battalion's orders, where strength increases, decreases, appointments, punishments, and honors were recorded, show that Chandler actually left France *on* that very day. As reported in the orders on 12 June 1918: "2025271 Pte. Chandler, R.T., No. 1 Coy.—Proceeded to England 11–6–18 to report to R.A.F H.Q., England" (Directorate of History and Heritage, "Battalion Orders"). MacShane's version of events is therefore slightly flawed; Chandler left the Seventh Battalion in Anzin on 11 June, arriving back in England sometime thereafter to report to the RAF. More revealingly, these orders show that Chandler was not injured at the time of his transfer since it would have been denoted on the battalion orders in the format "To Hosp." For example, in the same battalion orders that show Chandler's transfer out of the division there *is* a record of three soldiers who are indeed listed as being transferred "To Hosp." But without any mention of Chandler himself, it appears that the unscathed young writer was simply transferred or reassigned to the RAF and returned to England in accordance with the battalion's orders.

In *A Short History of the 7th Battalion C.E.F* (1930), the only historical account written by a First World War veteran that specifically provided firsthand data about the activities of the Seventh Battalion, Major T. V. Scudamore notes, "The first six months of the last year of the war were quiet ones for the battle-scarred battalion, and we were occupied in holding the trenches around Loos and Vimy Ridge . . . The great German offensive, their last despairing effort in the war, was expanding its force on others whilst we held our line" (20). As well as providing an invaluable insight into daily activities, Scudamore's pamphlet also contains a meticulously recorded index of casualties suffered by the Seventh Battalion during the war. While MacShane and Hiney claim that Chandler's platoon was killed in the first week of June, Scudamore's appendix clearly shows there were no recorded casualties in the battalion during this period. In fact, this full and detailed index of names shows that no Seventh Battalion soldiers were killed in action or died of their wounds between 3 May and 25 July 1918.

The Seventh Battalion war diaries and Scudamore's pamphlet, however, do record numerous other dates on which small groups of soldiers were reported killed in action in April and May. On several of these occasions small groups of soldiers were killed while undertaking probing raids on the enemy's positions. If Chandler had commanded a platoon and led soldiers into direct machine-gun fire, as he wrote in his letters, it may well have occurred during this brief period of skirmishing activity. The records show that between one and five men were killed on 8, 9, 21, 29 April, and 3 May 1918, adding credence to the suggestion that if Chandler *had* been in command of a platoon facing machine-gun fire it is likely to have occurred on one of these dates. Yet it is also entirely possible that despite leading men into "direct machine gun fire," as Chandler claimed, none of his platoon were killed or injured.

It is further likely that MacShane and Hiney are mistaken in their accounts since Chandler's medical records show that he suffered no physical injuries while in France. Furthermore, if Chandler had been wounded, a transfer back to England would not have been considered until he was able to pass a medical examination, and given that antibiotics had not yet been developed, and that even sulfa drugs were decades in the future, convalescence from wounds could have taken months. With the exception of regular vaccinations and injections, Chandler's records show that he experienced only two six-day hospital convalescence periods in July and October 1918 respectively, and each of these was necessitated by bouts of influenza and *not* combat-related injury ("Casualty Form"). Therefore, without any verification to support a claim for Chandler's wounding, it would appear that MacShane and Hiney mistakenly recounted the circumstances of Chandler's transfer.

Taking these facts into consideration, three possible explanations emerge to explain why Chandler was transferred back to England, all of which are significantly less remarkable than the versions of events presented by MacShane or Hiney.

The first possibility is that the biographers were incorrect about the time frame of the supposed shell attack and that it actually happened earlier than they described. The Seventh Battalion war diaries clearly show that the unit endured much shelling in the period Chandler was at the front, and on many occasions his battalion was caught in the center of the action. If Chandler had commanded a platoon that suffered casualties, it is likely that it occurred sometime during April or May 1918.

The second possible explanation for the inconsistencies concerning Chandler's return to England is that he might have been seconded to another military unit, and any casualties sustained by the other platoon would not therefore be recorded as sustained by the Seventh Battalion. This would certainly have been possible as many Canadian divisions were put under the command of the British Army. Nevertheless, despite being under a different command the Canadians would still have fought as a unit and retained their national status. This explanation is also insufficient, however, because had Chandler transferred out of the Seventh Battalion and into another Canadian division it would be recorded in his active service record as "TOS," meaning he had been "taken on strength" to another unit. There is no such notation. Significantly, this fact all but quashes Hiney's contention that Chandler's departure was due to a depleted outfit. The only TOS that appears on Chandler's record is dated 8 July 1918, *after* Chandler arrived back in England. The record shows that Chandler was TOS at the British Columbia Regiment Depot in Seaford, Sussex, before being sent as a command cadet to the Distribution Depot for the RAF in London ("Statement of Service in the Canadian Armed Forces").

The final explanation is by far the simplest and probably the most likely given that there is no evidence to suggest that Chandler was injured while he was stationed in France. Since the Seventh Battalion did not suffer any casualties during the period between May and June 1918, it must surely indicate that Chandler simply transferred from the Seventh Battalion to the RAF in England, as did so many other officers during the First World War. Although we must acknowledge that the Seventh Battalion was under almost continuous barrage, without evidence to prove that any fatalities actually occurred we must conclude that the simplest account is the most likely; and credible documentary evidence regarding the actual circumstances of Chandler's departure from France appears to support this.

Contrary to the version described by his two biographers, Chandler's "Casualty Form for Active Service" makes no mention of an injury severe enough to warrant field treatment or convalescence or offer any explanation of an incident that reputedly killed an entire platoon. The lynchpin, however, is documentary proof of battalion orders given on 6 June 1918 which explicitly direct Chandler back to England, "for the purpose of obtaining a commission in the R.A.F." (Directorate of History and Heritage, "Battalion Orders, March 23rd 1918"). The evidence drawn from the original documents at the Canadian Archives is unequivocal and explains that Chandler's reason for leaving the front was far more pedestrian than either biographer acknowledged. Their two biographies, drawn largely from Chandler's own accounts, allowed the myth surrounding Chandler's war experience to be preserved and perpetuated in much the same way that Carlos Baker's biography of Hemingway allowed his subject's real war experiences to be overstated and severely embellished.

Instead of fighting in the trenches of France it seems plausible that Chandler simply took the opportunity to escape the carnage of the Western Front. Possibly as a result of corresponding with his friend Gordon Pasqual (the son of Cissy, Chandler's future wife)—who had joined the Royal Flying Corps soon after his enlistment in Vancouver—Chandler may have been persuaded to transfer to the newly formed Royal Air Force. Chandler may have had dreams of sharing in the glory of the Canadian aviators who had a reputation for being the best flyers of the war. "Canadians made wonderful fighters," wrote Colonel George Nasmith in 1919, "and the majority of the greatest fighters in the R.A.F were Canadians" (qtd. in MacShane, *Life* 30). The prowess and mythology surrounding these early aviators may also have appealed to Chandler's sense of chivalry. Frank Freidel says, "The aviators themselves were knights, the cavalrymen of the war, bringing to it what little chivalry could be rescued from the bygone day when making war was the favorite occupation of the high born, operating in keeping with a gentleman's code" (109).

Shortly after Chandler left France, the Canadian divisions he left behind were reorganized in readiness for the final offensive that would eventually lead to the Armistice. While he was safely back on British soil, his old division, the First Canadian, had had the glory of pushing back the Germans at Amiens and then marching over the Rhine in December 1918. As Nicholson explains, the First and Second Canadian Divisions were then "disposed in depth for the defense of the southern sector of the Cologne-Bonn bridgehead, where their area of responsibility encompassed ground on the east or right bank of the Rhine, including the city of Bonn itself" (527). The Canadian occupation lasted into 1919, when on 18 January it was withdrawn and assigned to garrison duty in Belgium. Chandler accordingly missed the division's finest moment and undoubtedly would have had mixed emotions about his own departure from this distinguished fighting force. Although it is impossible to know for sure, it is feasible that Chandler held decidedly conflicting emotions of relief at having survived the war, disappointment that he could not share the honor of pushing back the German army, and guilt at having left his battalion just as it was preparing for the final bloody push against the German position.

▼▼▼

Recounting the motives that prompted F. Scott Fitzgerald to enlist in the American army, Jeffrey Meyers notes that the writer had "imagined himself as a war hero" (Meyers, *Fitzgerald* 34). He had "wanted to prove his courage, gain glory and win the acceptance of his comrades," yet he "never even got close to making the fatal sacrifice of [those . . .] who were killed in the war" (Meyers, *Fitzgerald* 39). Fitzgerald "always considered his lack of combat experience one of the deepest disappointments in his life" (ibid.). Noting the emotions that beset Fitzgerald upon learning of the Armistice and the end of his military service, Malcolm Cowley summed up the feeling of guilt and frustration that infused a generation of soldiers at the end of the war:

> The war ended too soon for many Americans—not for those who had fought at Bellau Wood or in the Argonne, but for others who had only marched and countermarched behind the lines; now they would never know whether or not they were brave men. Some were ashamed of being unmedaled and unwounded. Others, especially the airmen, had lived more intensely than they would ever live again and began to feel vaguely, at intervals, that something in them had died on the eleventh of November 1918. *All the young men had been exposed to a variety of strong emotions.* Their individualities had been affirmed, even in the anonymous disguise of a uniform, and *they had dreamed of peacetime careers in which they would play the part of heroes.* Now the war had ended without giving them a chance, as Fitzgerald was to say, of expending all that accumulated nervous energy. Many of them—with Hemingway the most conspicuous example among writers—were to spend the next ten years *looking for another stage on which they could re-enact the dangers and recapture the winey taste of war.* (12. Emphasis added)

Despite highlighting the fact that these men would never know whether they were brave soldiers or not, it is worth bearing in mind that involvement in such a destructive event was in itself an act of bravery. However, together with the sense of pure intoxicating relief at having survived the war, these upsetting and confusing feelings would have undoubtedly troubled Chandler as the Armistice was declared. He had missed the final and decisive push with his comrades of the Seventh Battalion and had also narrowly missed out on dueling with his German counterparts in the skies over Europe. He was, like Fitzgerald, Hemingway, and many others Lost Generation soldiers, unable to claim that he had been involved in any genuinely heroic action and may instead have dwelt upon the guilt at leaving his fellow soldiers behind at such a crucial moment in world history.

And so, while Los Angeles became the "stage," as Meyers noted, upon which Chandler sought to re-create in some small way the dangers he had encountered on the French front line, Philip Marlowe became the persona—or alter ego—upon which Chandler set out to highlight his own frustration and the ills that beset society. Chandler was unable to prevent the feelings of disappointment and lost opportunity from flowing over into his illustration of the detective. Marlowe became everything Chandler would like to have been, but he instinctively retains the trauma that was imprinted onto him by his creator; the detective embodies the thousands of men who went to war expecting to find glory, but instead returned frustrated and traumatized by their experiences. Marlowe became the prism through which we can view the trauma that tormented Chandler.

By considering Marlowe in this way, we see Chandler's views of the First World War—that many misguidedly believed would be a gentlemanly and honorable affair—being reflected back though the detective's own disillusionment and shattered perception of American society. Marlowe becomes the American soldier on a quest for heroism in a battle against an unknown enemy, a man sent to an unfamiliar place and who returns with the vain hope of finding recognition and gratitude from those who had sent him there. Yet he finds neither. With each new case he only finds more reason to feel disillusioned with a new and unfamiliar society, and unsurprisingly his initial idealism is hastily displaced as he becomes resigned to his life of mounting cynicism and frustration.

By reexamining the accounts of Chandler's war popularized by MacShane and Hiney and replacing the biographers' assumptions with a case supported by documented evidence, it has been possible to construct a far more accurate and sophisticated picture of Chandler's time in northern France. Additionally, the exercise of placing Chandler within a psychological framework to assess the traumatizing effect of such experiences has exposed the likely origins of the devastating scar that the war left upon the author's mind. It is likely that the incredible brutality of the First World War left Chandler with such turbulent emotions that Marlowe would undoubtedly be endowed with the same eccentricities and psychological profile as his creator. The war binds

Chandler and his detective together, for while Marlowe's character provides a unique window into Chandler's psychological circumstances, Chandler's war experience is likewise the key to decoding Marlowe's behavior and character traits. Philip Marlowe is, by consequence, a character inflicted from his very inception with the symptoms of a severe posttraumatic illness.

3

CHANDLER AND THE AMERICAN WAR WRITERS

There is nothing worse than war.

—FREDERIC HENRY, IN HEMINGWAY, *A FAREWELL TO ARMS*

Widely acknowledged as one of the foremost originators of the hard-boiled school of crime writing, Raymond Chandler's style would not have existed without the birth of an entirely new type of modernist language that developed after the First World War. It was a style that represented, as Chandler remarked, the "terrible honesty" (qtd. in MacShane, *Letters* 453) of American modernism, and significantly, this was "the first literary generation in America to include a significant number of veterans" (Douglas 194). Ann Douglas observes, "Most of the writers who participated in the Great War quickly formed and publicly expressed the view of it that increasingly prevailed in its aftermath in intellectual and artistic circles everywhere: that its corrupt beginnings in imperialist power struggles were matched in ugliness and senselessness only by the unprecedented brutality of combat conditions and the indifference of those in charge to the welfare of the soldiers who were the war's real victims . . ." (195). They were the generation, as Harry Crosby noted in 1925, that "have known war and must never forget war" (qtd. in Douglas 195).

At the vanguard of this modernist mode of writing were the American Lost Generation, a group of writers that had experienced the horrors of war and had returned disillusioned by the decadence and self-indulgence that was to pervade 1920s American society. Ernest Hemingway in particular "integrated the experience of war into the style, the form, the narrative consciousness of what he wrote" (Douglas 196).

Although Douglas, in her book *Terrible Honesty: Mongrel Manhattan in the 1920s* (1996), refers to Chandler in a modernist, post–First World War context—the title of her book, in fact, comes from Chandler's quote above—she by no means firmly identifies Chandler as a member of the Lost Generation. Instead, while acknowledging Chandler's position amongst the group of writers who participated in the war she simultaneously suggests that the Lost Generation was a generation of writers only active in the 1920s. Douglas argues that because Chandler "came to his craft late; he did his apprenticeship in the 1920s, studying the prose of Hemingway and Dashiell Hammett," it is, "this generation, the urban writers of the 1920s, that he is in fact describing" (33). Since Chandler did not publish his first short story until 1933,[1] Douglas, by implication, excludes Chandler from the generation of writers renowned for their "terrible honesty." And yet Chandler's style, although flourishing later than the Lost Generation, provides new modes of understanding and representing the impact of war.

Part of this study, therefore, is to consider the social divide that has traditionally cleaved popular culture and so-called high culture. While this book recognizes Paul Fussell's argument that "life feeds materials to literature" (i), it also seeks to further this view by acknowledging Fredric Jameson's observation that "history . . . as an absent cause . . . is inaccessible to us *except* in textual form [so] that our approach to it and to the Real necessarily passes through its prior textualization, its narrativization in the political unconscious" (35. Emphasis added). As such, literature becomes a "socially symbolic act" (Jameson 12). The First World War not only "gave America's budding literary Modernism its frightfully exhilarating baptism of fire," but it also, as Karsten Piep has noted, provided "its defining gestures of angry protest and disenchantment" (14). In order to locate war noir among other literary work of America's First World War participation we must therefore take Piep's advice and "reconstruct the historical subtexts that surround and underlie individual literary texts" (7).

▼▼▼

Personalizing the hard-boiled crime genre by the application of a first-person narrative, Chandler propelled crime fiction further than his predecessor Dashiell Hammett by relating his work to the inner turmoil so vividly depicted by the Lost Generation writers. Although the critical establishment of the time deemed that the work of Chandler and Ernest Hemingway, for example, was beyond comparison and that their work would never intersect,

Chandler's writing certainly shares a remarkable commonality with that of the influential Lost Generation.

Though enjoying public popularity, Chandler's novels were never received with the literary recognition and critical acclaim of many of his contemporaries. This elusive widespread recognition is all the more surprising when we take into account the fact that many of Chandler's novels were compared positively with those of Hemingway, one of America's most celebrated authors. While the literary and stylistic similarities between the work of Chandler and Hemingway were noted, the importance of this connection was never seriously examined nor its implications fully explored. As Piep observed, relatively little attention has been given to the ways in which post–First World War texts have the ability to "buttress, subvert, or rework cultural assumptions" (4). For example, it was not until the decade after Chandler's death that critics such as Wilson Pollock in his 1962 article "Man with a Toy Gun" for *The New Republic*, began to appreciate the striking similarities between the so-called "low" cultural work of Chandler and the "high" literature of the Lost Generation. Pollock argued that the major difference between Chandler and Hemingway was an artificial demarcation based entirely on the distinction of genre. While Hemingway's reputation and popularity were grounded in novels that had managed to capture the zeitgeist, Chandler's detective novels, written in a genre not normally associated with enduring creative writing, were never able to attain the same literary status. Yet, by putting aside the prejudices associated with genre, it becomes a simple task of recognizing the unmistakably strong resemblance that exists between the styles of their works. This revealing conclusion is grounded in Hemingway's attempt at the hard-boiled style: "The Killers" argues Pollock, "could almost be a 'Black Mask' story except that the ending would probably have cost the author a rejection slip[, . . . and] *To Have and Have Not* is not very much better than *Farewell, My Lovely*" (22). The only significant difference between the two authors, Pollock concluded, was that while Hemingway was able to crown his literary achievements with one of the twentieth century's most revered novels, Chandler was never quite able to achieve this distinction. The single literary achievement that distinguished Hemingway and Chandler's reputations was "that Hemingway [. . .] wrote *A Farewell to Arms*" (22). Pollock's commentary initiates an intriguing discussion that draws direct parallels between the styles of the two authors and suggests that it was Hemingway's war novel that decisively set the two writers apart, thus establishing his place in the American literary canon.

Canonical writers personify the literary spirit of the era, and for Hemingway and other Lost Generation writers this literary force was a reaction against the disillusionment and dislocation they perceived during the postwar era. Harold Bloom noted that the canon reflects "strangeness, a mode of originality that either cannot be assimilated, or that so assimilates us that we cease to see it as strange" (3). Yet this "strangeness, a mode of originality," is also everpresent in the work of many other writers of the era who are *not* considered canonical. This "tang of originality" (6) by which Bloom marks out the canonical is certainly present in Chandler's work, as with Hemingway's. The process of canon formation and evolution is greatly influenced by cultural and historical change, which requires an acknowledgment of all literary forms and genres. Yet these works are habitually confined to certain styles and rely upon the influence of past literary accomplishment. It is the influence of past writers that often drives the canon forward, and it is this impetus that connects the writers of the American Lost Generation with the nation's hard-boiled fiction. The component that ties together Ernest Hemingway, F. Scott Fitzgerald, and William Faulkner, three of the most notable writers of the early to mid-twentieth century, is that "all of them emerge," Bloom argues, "from Joseph Conrad's influence" (11). However, the influence of Conrad's *Heart of Darkness* (1902) upon Chandler's work is also well documented, and the combination of the novel's themes with the hard-boiled influence of Dashiell Hammett, a contemporary of Chandler, certainly supports a case for Chandler's inclusion among the iconic writers who represent the canonical American literary landscape.

Similarities between the work of Chandler and Hemingway were casually noted as early as the late 1940s. Literary critics first became aware of the widespread public anticipation that preceded the publication of a new Chandler novel, which they discovered, to their surprise, was very similar to the reaction which accompanied the publication of a new Hemingway novel. In October 1949, for instance, *Newsweek* announced that "the publication of Chandler's 'The Little Sister' has about the same réclame as would, for *another* literary set, Ernest Hemingway's long-expected novel" (*Newsweek* 69–70. Emphasis added). But while both writers enjoyed a sizeable popular following, Chandler's novels were never able to transcend their generic pulp status and propel him into an elite standing similar to that enjoyed by Hemingway. Chandler's novels were written for *another* literary set and sought after by a *different* type of reader interested in fiction written in a fundamentally different style. Because the detective genre was not considered capable of making a major contribution to American literature, critics exercised their prejudice and effectively denied Chandler the opportunity of achieving a prominent literary status similar to that held by Hemingway.

By the turn of the 1950s, comparisons between Chandler and Hemingway had been taken even further. Critics began to assert that the allure of Chandler's style was not simply equal to that of Hemingway; it was for some a representation of Hemingway's voice relocated in the crime genre. In 1951 H. A. L. Craig wrote in the British journal *The Listener* that Chandler's style of writing was of "Hemingway and Dashiell Hammett born" (513) and suggested that Chandler's work had become a facsimile of Hemingway's writing in a genre that had hitherto never been associated with the Lost Generation. Although Craig believed that Chandler learned his stylistic lessons and methodology from Hemingway and Hammett, it is undeniable that Chandler utilized the modernist style of both writers, which he then advanced into something new, imposing his own unique and contemporary stamp on the genre through his use of punchy language, staccato sentences, and colorful adjectives.

Like Chandler's Philip Marlowe, Hammett's heroes—the Continental Op, Sam Spade, Ned Beaumont—were all violent, but, arguably, that violence was not necessarily sensationalist. Instead, as Philip Durham suggests, "It was rather a kind of meaningful violence, sometimes an explicit description and implicit criticism of a corrupt society" (Qtd. in Nolan xiv). Hammett did not glorify toughness. Instead he portrayed it "honestly," as William F. Nolan argues, "firmly separating his work from the bizarre Spillane school of rampant sex and sadism which followed" (7). Durham asserts that by the 1920s, many Americans had lost faith in their society, and "Hammett's heroes tried both to expose the corruptness and to speak for men who, questioning the values of society, needed to be assured that somewhere—if only on the pages of a pulp magazine—there were heroes who cared" (qtd. in Nolan xiv–xv). Like Hemingway, who was experimenting with writing techniques around the same time, "Hammett was [also] trying to make events truer than life" (qtd. in Nolan xv). Even in his earliest stories, Hammett worked his plots to avoid them becoming too stereotyped. Like Chandler, his protagonist was a common man whom the audience could believe. And using rugged individualism to right social wrongs, he focused on the objective, hard-boiled writing style in an attempt to make his work as thrilling as possible.

Despite Craig's claim that Chandler's writing was of "Hemingway and Dashiell Hammett born," very little has been done to examine the relationship between Hemingway and Hammett, which is vital if we are to understand Chandler's style. Although it is suggested that Hammett was the Hemingway of crime fiction, this idea, as Nolan explains, has not always been utilized in a complementary sense: "Several critics have dismissed Hammett as simply an extension of Hemingway, declaring that he openly imitated that author's terse, understated style and dialogue" (3). However, we must remember that Hammett published his first short story, "From the Memoirs of a Private Detective," in *The Smart Set*, two years before Hemingway published his first book in the United States, *In Our Time* (1925). As Nolan reflects:

> It is fascinating to consider that as a near-starving Hemingway labored in a Paris loft during 1922–23, carving out a muscular, objective prose style which was to become the major influence on mainstream writing, so labored a near-starving Hammett in a San Francisco hotel room, carving out precisely the same prose style, which was to alter completely the fabric of America's popular crime fiction . . . Both men, working independently, became masters of objective realism. (Ibid.)

Similarly although Hammett and Hemmingway entered the same profession during the war, that of ambulance driver, Hammett never actually experienced World War I firsthand, serving instead as an ambulance driver at Camp Mead, Maryland. While Hemingway had been exposed to the traumatic front line of battle in Italy, Hammett had endured the ordeal of transporting severely wounded men who had been returned to the United States for medical attention. Consequently, he contracted Spanish influenza, a condition which would later cause bronchopneumonia and, soon afterwards, untreatable tuberculosis. As Richard Layman notes, "Though he had not seen battle—in fact he had never been more than twenty miles from home as a soldier—Hammett was a war casualty, a disabled veteran" (15). Both Hemingway and Hammett resorted to bouts of heavy drinking in an effort to accept the confusion of postwar readjustment as disabled war veterans. Both writers also chose to reengage with war later in their careers, as reporters: Hemingway during the Spanish Civil War and Hammett during World War II. Walter Blair suggests, therefore, that Hemingway and Hammett are linked by common emotional circumstances: "Wounded by the war and unhappy in the postwar world [respectively] . . . contemptuous of many pre–World War I standards . . . both were battered by disillusionment and cynicism, and both created worlds and characters justifying their attitude" (qtd. in Gohodes 300). And it is certainly possible that the two writers exerted a mutual influence upon each other: "The Killers" (1927) may have influenced Hammett, while *Red Harvest* (1929) may have influenced Hemingway. And despite allegations by Philip Young, Hemingway's biographer, that Chandler was "the only member of [the hard-boiled school that] Hemingway . . . could read," Hammett's was obviously held in esteem, as demonstrated by his inclusion of *The Dain Curse* in Hemingway's *Death in the Afternoon* (1932). Demonstrating an obvious knowledge of Hammett's breadth of work, a character remarks that the novel is "[his] bloodiest [book] to date" (228).

The association of Hammett and Chandler's work with Hemingway and the Lost Generation is therefore a significant achievement for writers of detective fiction. As Douglas noted, Chandler in particular "set himself to learn the new hard-boiled style from Hemingway and Hammett because he believed it to be the most exciting version of the English language to take shape since Shakespeare and the Elizabethans had 'roughed the language around' at the turn of the seventeenth century" (357). Chandler also explained his intentions in a letter from January 1945: "All I wanted to do when I began writing was to play with a fascinating new language, to see what it would do as a means of expression which might remain on the level of unintellectual thinking and yet acquire the power to say things which are usually only said with a literary air" (qtd. in Gardiner and Walker 214).

This new modernist language certainly influenced the styles of many authors. Like many amongst the Lost Generation who rejected traditional forms of literary expression, Hemingway emerged at the forefront of those who chose to express themselves in this innovative manner. In his short stories and novels Hemingway "had vividly illustrated the special power of this 'new language'" (Meador 150), and the power of this new vernacular enabled the writers of the Lost Generation to be far more subtle with their style of writing. Hemingway, in particular, became renowned for what he called the "iceberg style," a method of writing which enabled the author to use language that was far less embellished but still retained the overall message and tone in his work. He believed that if readers had a certain level of understanding there would be no need for the writer to divulge too many details; the overall meaning would be understood. In *Death in the Afternoon*, Hemingway wrote: "If a writer of prose knows enough about what he is writing about he may omit things that he knows and the reader, if the writer is writing truly enough, will have a feeling of those things as strongly as though the writer had stated them" (169). It was, in essence, a style that did not require an elaborate explanation to make the writer's meaning known; it could simply be implied. Hemingway likened this style of writing to an iceberg not only due to its "dignity of movement" but also "due to only one-eighth of it being above water" (*Death in the Afternoon* 183).

Despite Chandler's occasional criticism of the writer, given the similarity in their styles it is hardly surprising that Chandler held Hemingway in such high regard. In 1942 Chandler realized that his admiration for Hemingway was mainly due to Hemingway's own use of "terrible honesty" and realism. "Hemingway sees it all," Chandler said, "not just the flies on the garbage" (qtd. in MacShane, *Letters* 23). He admired Hemingway's writing style, saying, "I wrote melodrama because when I looked around me it was the only kind of writing I saw that was relatively honest and yet was not trying to put over somebody's party line" (qtd. in Gardiner and Walker 214).

Although Pollock believes it was regrettable that Chandler and Hemingway never met, he nonetheless noted that any discussion of Chandler's work would be incomplete if it failed to consider the influence of Hemingway's accomplishments. In any discussion of Chandler's work, he argued that it was "only natural that Hemingway's name should come up" (22) despite the fact that they were normally exponents of different literary genres.

Considering such a contention, it becomes possible to reconfigure the accepted view of Chandler's protagonist Philip Marlowe as much more than simply the battered and disillusioned private eye he is often portrayed to be. By considering the consequences of Chandler's experiences during the First World War in much the same way as critics have deliberated over Hemingway's, and by examining the idiosyncrasies and unconventional behavior that are so essential in understanding Chandler's character, it can be demonstrated that these individualistic qualities were projected or encoded onto Marlowe. The implications upon the crime genre, then, are significant: whatever Chandler's intentions may have really been, Marlowe was not created as a simple detective but instead as a complex character in the mold of Hemingway's Frederick Henry; as someone who was a veteran of the Great War and whose experiences and psychological trauma helped to shape his distinctive behavior and personality. Marlowe may therefore be understood as an entirely different entity than the conventional "chivalric" persona portrayed by commentators such as Jerry Spier and Lee Horsley. The widely accepted perception of Marlowe as a chivalric knight, usually regarded as the foundation for his noble motivations, must be reevaluated because it masks the influence of Chandler's own experiences. Transplanting Marlowe from a medieval mythological perspective to the milieu of postwar America reveals the detective not as a knight but as a soldier, a veteran returned from battle isolated and endeavoring to make sense of the confusion and bewilderment of postwar society. As Marlowe clings to his code of outdated values, he struggles to come to terms with the modern America in which he now finds himself.

Hauntingly reminiscent of the Lost Generation themes of disillusionment and unbridled decadence of the so-called Roaring Twenties, Chandler may be placed alongside this elite group of writers who experienced the First World War. However, this evokes a further dilemma for studies of the Lost Generation since identifying writers of this literary set by genre subsequently becomes nonsensical and meaningless. By the 1920s the concept of genre had become increasingly blurred and imprecise, an impulse directly attributable to the consequences of the war and its aftermath.

Writing about the soldiers returning from the First World War, Gertrude Stein first coined the expression "lost generation." She wrote that "all of [the] young people who served in the war" returned to America a "lost generation" (qtd. in Lynn 333). This group of troubled individuals was identified by F. Scott Fitzgerald's character Amory Blaine in *This Side of Paradise* (1920) as those who spoke for American youth: "Here was a new generation [. . .] grown up to find all Gods dead, all wars fought, all faiths in man shaken" (270). Michael Parish claimed that these returning soldiers were men who "struggled to define the relationship between their craft, their lives, and their place in society in the aftermath of the Great War." He further explained: "They were disillusioned by the savagery of the war and the failure of peacemaking; they rebelled against the moral provincialism and boorishness of their own middle-class upbringing; they distrusted the institutions of mature capitalism and the nation's dominant commercial culture" (184). Malcolm Cowley, however, tells us that the term "Lost Generation" is too narrow and restrictive and argues that a more accurate description of those writing in the interwar period is "the World War One generation" (vii). He explains that it was "the First World War that made . . . a generation, by changing their world and by giving them shares, as it were, in a rich fund of common emotions" (3). The war, he says, "gave them the feeling of having lived in two eras, almost on two different planets. The second era seemed tawdrier in many ways, when they judged it by standards retained from an earlier time" (vii). By articulating themes common to the Lost Generation, and in belonging to, as Cowley notes, the "World War One generation," Chandler can be considered alongside this group of distinguished writers. The traumatizing convergence of emotions that defined the writers of the Lost Generation and the shared experiences that so shaped their lives exemplified an understanding that "those authors were speaking for all for us" (Cowley viii). Chandler can justifiably be discussed alongside canonical writers such as Hemingway, Fitzgerald, Faulkner, and Dos Passos simply because a generation, in historical terms, is a matter of dates and ideology. Arguing that the concept of the Lost Generation arose out of very specific circumstances, Cowley observes that the aspirations and discontent of any given generation are what ultimately define it. He says, "A new generation [. . .] appears when writers of the same age join in a common revolt [. . . , and] in the process of adopting a new lifestyle, they find their own models and spokesmen" (238). Writing of their physical or psychological experiences of war, authors in this era voiced their subsequent disenchantment with postwar American society. They became a generation "lost" to the war, with little acceptance or recognition of their sacrifices.

Cowley argued that the writers of this renowned cohort are generally categorized as those who were born between 1894 and 1900, yet he concedes that older and younger writers (such as Archibald MacLeish or Nathanael West) have been included on certain occasions.[2] Although older than most of the writers of the Lost Generation, Chandler's experience as a soldier during the war and his subsequent psychological trauma are relevant because the postwar torment he suffered was just as debilitating and intense as that of many other writers of the time. His trauma, and what amounted to a thoroughly ignoble reception upon his return to America, would have given him a unique insight into the effect of warfare on society. He would have possessed "shares" as Cowley noted, "in a rich fund of common emotions" (3) that bound the generation together.

Significant to this argument are Fitzgerald and Faulkner, who are included among the Lost Generation even though neither writer actually experienced combat; Fitzgerald "marched on board a transport with full equipment, helmet banging at his side, and was then marched off because the Germans had begged for an armistice" (Cowley 10). But undeterred, the writer drew upon his "lively imagination" and the social discontentment among returning soldiers to portray himself as someone who had suffered "the wounds of an infantry officer in combat" (ibid.). Likewise, Faulkner, who served out his military experience as a Royal Canadian Air Force cadet and who never actually experienced combat, was even "more imaginative," writing "vivid and persuasive stories that ended with dogfights over the German lines" (ibid.). This apparent blurring of eligibility shows that those who did not experience combat or write about their war experiences were nevertheless included among the Lost Generation, simply because they were able to express the "spirit of the times."

Although a lack of wartime experience has not impeded writers from being included amongst the Lost Generation, writing in what was seen as a less important genre appears to have afforded ample grounds for exclusion.

Yet, it appears illogical to maintain an unwavering discrimination against those writers who, while expressing the feelings of the era, were arbitrarily shut out on grounds of style. Given the similarity of experiences, Chandler's choice of literary genre emerges as the single reason for his exclusion from this distinguished group of writers. D. C. Russell noted that Chandler's writing has a "beauty which shows that [he . . .] cannot be pigeonholed, merely as an expert in tough language" (123) and that the undertones of psychological distress that features throughout his writing demonstrate the manifestation of themes far more complex than has been previously recognized.

The grounds for Chandler's inclusion in the Lost Generation become self-evident when measured against Cowley's belief that the literary Lost Generation can be more accurately considered and studied as part of the larger First World War generation. Irrespective of genre, this gifted but disconnected cohort of writers symbolized the disillusionment and isolation felt by many in post–First World War American society. Yet Stein's phrase, which, we must remember described an *entire* generation "lost" to the war, would become the foundation by which to consider a select few writers that best represented the postwar era.

In the aftermath of the First World War, the division that had traditionally separated crime fiction from other styles of fiction, and ensured that the genre remained labeled as a lowbrow yet popular style, began to wane. The style began emulating more "highbrow" styles of writing by acknowledging the impact that war had had upon the nation's servicemen and also upon society itself. In the same way that the Lost Generation had depicted the disillusionment, psychological injury, and readjustment arising from the war, so the crime genre began to portray protagonists as individuals troubled by traumatic events beyond their control and grappling to make sense of their world. Peter Aichinger is at pains to emphasize that after the war, "novels reflected the horror and chagrin of people who had tasted combat for the first time" (x), and Lee Horsley describes how many crime fiction writers, including Hammett and Chandler, set in motion a new phase of detective fiction emphasizing the trauma that haunted society (82). Coping with personal trauma therefore became an integral part of the postwar crime genre.

As the emphasis in literature altered, the conventional description of war literature as anecdotes of soldiers and battles quickly became inadequate because it failed to recognize the psychological effect of war. This development influenced many American authors, including those whose work is not normally recognized as war literature in the traditional sense. Although war is a broad literary theme, the narrow categorization of "war literature" implies a separateness which "sounds too prescriptive, as though war literature exists in a vacuum as a genre hived-off from other forms of writing" (Walsh 1). Even Chandler himself argued that the American "instinct for classification is too strong" (qtd. in Gardiner and Walker 62) and insisted that "it doesn't matter a damn what a novel is about[; . . .] the only fiction of any moment in any age is that which does magic with words, and that the subject matter is merely the springboard for the writer's imagination" (qtd. in Hiney and MacShane 59–60). In terms of writing style, many commentators have come to accept that the meaning of the war *novel* allows "a degree of flexibility" (Aichinger xi). "I would describe the term 'war novel,'" as Aichinger notes, "as any long work of prose fiction in which the lives and actions of the characters are principally affected by warfare or the military establishment [. . . and where] war is the primordial fact dominating the lives of [. . .] the characters" (x). With combat-related PTSD now recognized as a legitimate war injury, Aichinger's assertion that a war *novel* is comprised of written work in which the "lives and actions" of the protagonist are "principally affected by warfare or the military," suggests that a continuation of the theme of war may legitimately include events that not only occur away from the regular theater of war, but also long after combat has ceased. War is not, therefore, confined to battlefields or foreign countries; it remains indelibly imprinted in the minds and behavior of individuals confronted by its horrors. Consequently, it is unrealistic to assume that the psychological trauma experienced by writers *not* normally associated with the war genre should fail to find expression somewhere in their work.

The First World War produced "a collective trauma such as the world had never known" (Cooperman 7), and Jeffrey Walsh notes that "the apprehension of war constitutes a distinctive and central element in the modern American literary consciousness" (1). As the world came to terms with a new reality, American fiction altered with it and became polarized into two opposing camps. Much of the fiction produced by writers who held patriotic inclinations and who, in the main, had no experience of war, were decidedly prowar in tone and mood. Their stories were a celebration of American patriotism, focusing on protagonists who saw it as a noble duty to fight, and when necessary, sacrifice themselves for their country. Willa Cather's *One of Ours* (1922), Edith Wharton's *A Son at the Front* (1923), and Alan Seeger's "I Have a Rendezvous with Death" (1919) are examples of this inclination that propagated the idea that it was a soldier's duty to die for his country in a war that would allegedly fulfill the idealistic objective of making a world safe for democracy. The death of Cather's soldier Claude Wheeler spared him from experiencing the disillusionment of postwar life: "He died believing his country better than it is, and France better than any country can ever be" (485). Similarly, the father of Wharton's character George Campton accepts the death of his son as a divine and meaningful sacrifice. He believes that great things always come from self-sacrifice and finds solace in his belief that "the efficacy of the sacrifice was always in proportion to the worth of the victim" (166). Both Cather and Wharton accentuate the "crusading element" in the American war effort as "America's youth is sent forth not merely to fight a war but to fulfill a sacred trust of heroic magnitude" (Aichinger 5). In a similar manner, Seeger's poem, as in many of his personal writings, demonstrates his desire for a glorious death in battle:

I have a rendezvous with Death,
At some disputed barricade,
When Spring comes back with rustling shade
And apple-blossoms fill the air—
I have a rendezvous with Death
When Spring brings back blue days and fair. (*Poems* 144)

The aggressively desolate usage of wartime imagery throughout the poem is jarringly contrasted with the passively playful imagery of nature but is a sign of Seeger's lighthearted view of death as a meaningful sacrifice. Likewise, in his 1916 poem "Ode in Memory of the American Volunteers Fallen for France," Seeger extols the virtuousness of the fallen American soldiers who had fought and sacrificed themselves for the noble cause engaging the Allies, America having not entered the war by this point. Stressing the glory of having died in Europe, the poem ends:

Hail, brothers, and farewell; you are twice blest, brave hearts.
Double your glory is who perished thus,
For you have died for France and vindicated us. (Qtd. in Stevenson, 664)

At the other extreme were those whose own experiences of war had fundamentally devastated any conviction that battle could ever be a noble enterprise. These writers repudiated the idealistic notion that there was anything romantic to be found in battle, which they knew to be a dehumanizing and meaningless carnage, and completely rejected the idea that death in combat was a worthwhile sacrifice. While vehemently protesting the futility of war, some writers believed that the experience of coming face-to-face with death had rewarded them with a greater appreciation of life and, consequently, had made them better writers. Dos Passos for instance, although a pacifist, firmly believed that "a young man hoping to be a writer [. . .] must experience the war in some fashion" (viii), and likewise, Ernest Hemingway believed that "you have to hurt like hell before you can write seriously" (qtd. in Meyers, *Hemingway* 36). Those who wrote of their experiences—Hemingway, Dos Passos, Faulkner, and others—articulated graphically realistic accounts that smoldered with the terrible reality of death, warfare, and its consequences. For those who had volunteered in search of a romantic adventure and heroism the reality of combat quickly became a shocking experience, and their view of war became one of "accidental, meaningless, [and] purely gratuitous death" (Aichinger 10), an encounter that they would never fully recover from. Aichinger poignantly reminds us: "The sensation of being trapped by a huge and ruthless machine [. . . became] particularly horrifying to a generation that went to war as they might have gone to a picnic" (10).

To these authors war became "the most pointless and destructive of all human activities," frequently "inculcat[ing] in the front-line writer a feeling of existential loss and disorientation, a dawning awareness that the exemplary sacrifice of troops is meaningless and utterly futile" (Walsh 3). The accepted convention of pre-twentieth-century warfare and the related rhetoric acquired new meaning during the war. The existence of a "bleak and nihilistic recognition [. . .] confirms the deep sense harbored by the intellectual of his own alienation" (ibid.) and a profound sense of futility in many of the era's war novels and poetry. Stanley Cooperman declares, "A combination of horror, dehumanization, numbness, and absurdity is the heritage that World War I novelists brought back from their broken world of combat and military glory" (97). Combined with this was the belief that the "total violence, machine civilization, futile terror, and mass death could not be simply accepted. The impact of World War I was unparalleled; it shattered a cultural universe and in the United States shaped the literature of a generation" (Cooperman vii). It was, then, as Cooperman argues, this "Great Crusade which gave to American literature an art not simply 'influenced' by war, but in a vital sense created by it" (vii). The experience shattered the romanticism of war for both the soldiers at the front and civilians at home, a sentiment captured by Faulkner's protagonist Joe Gilligan in *Soldier's Pay* when he declares that "the romance of battle" is "bunk" (40). Hemingway also summed up the futility and absurdity of war in *A Farewell to Arms* during a scene where Captain Rinaldi questions Frederic Henry on the circumstances of his wounding:

> "They say if you can prove you did any heroic act you can get the silver [medal]. Otherwise it will be the bronze. Tell me exactly what happened. Did you do any heroic act?"
>
> "No" I said. "I was blown up while we were eating cheese." (59)

Hemingway's ironic commentary on the absurdity of war is broadened by Aichinger's contention that "the conflict introduced perhaps the most demoralizing aspect of modern war: the dehumanization of combat" (11). Soldiers began to believe they were "degraded slave[s], a number, mere cannonfodder" (qtd. in Dos Passos, *Three Soldiers* xvii). As the protagonist, John Andrews, notes in *Three Soldiers*, "[we] were all so alike, [we] seemed at moments to be one organism" (21). The level of individual dehumanization increasingly troubles Andrews, and as he watches a young boy fishing, he says, "And that boy, too, would be a soldier; the lithe body would be thrown into a mould to be made the same as other bodies, the quick movements would be standardised into the manual arms, the inquisitive, petulant mind would be battered into servility. The stockade was built; not one of the sheep would escape" (*Three Soldiers* 349). Bitterness and detachment are themes that recur throughout *Three Soldiers*, emphasized when Andrews remarks, "[H]ow strange it was that he was not thinking of anything. In the last few days his mind seemed to have become a hard meaningless core" (16).

The work of more traditional war writers exposes not just the physical wounds but also the psychological effects of war, emphasized by the debilitating injuries suffered by Frederic Henry, John Andrews, and Faulkner's Donald Mahon. As the character of Margaret Powers says of Mahon in *Soldier's Pay*, "The man that was wounded is dead, and this is another person, a grown child. It's his apathy, his detachment, that's terrible. He doesn't seem to care where he is or what he does" (114). Similar psychological scarring is conspicuous in *Three Soldiers* where Andrews

> stretched his legs out across the floor in front of him; strange, stiff, tremulous legs they were, but it was not the wounds that gave them their leaden weight. It was the stagnation of the life about him that he felt sinking into every crevasse of his spirit, so that he could never shake it off, the stagnation of dusty ruined automatons that had lost all life of their own, whose limbs had practised the drill manual so long

that they had no movement of their own left, who sank limply, sunk in boredom, waiting for orders. (180)

The most complete and poignant metaphor for the tragedy of the First World War appears, arguably, in Hemingway's collection of short stories, *In Our Time.* Here, as Aichinger notes, "[t]he limitless violence of the war counterpoints the routine violence of the peacetime world; the mules drowning with their legs broken reproduce the agony of the grasshopper impaled on a fishhook; the fisherman's thoughtless cruelty is only a microcosm of the larger barbarity of mankind" (20). *In Our Time* paints a distressing image of the senseless carnage of war where death is raised to the ultimate act of heroism, and survivors are permanently altered to pronounce themselves as "Not patriots" (63). In the short story "Soldier's Home," for example, as war's romanticism turns to hopelessness and terror Officer Krebs is overcome with a sense of "nausea in regard to his [war] experience" (*In Our Time* 70), which is also reflected earlier in the collection by an anonymous soldier's plea: "Dear jesus please get me out. Christ please please please christ. If you'll only keep me from getting killed I'll do anything you say. I believe in you and I'll tell every one in the world that you are the only one that matters. Please please dear jesus" (63). Noticeably in this passage, the lack of capital letters for "jesus" and "christ" suggests the soldier's (and Hemingway's) loss of faith and belief in religion. Herman points out: "In situations of terror, people spontaneously seek their first source of comfort and protection. Wounded soldiers . . . cry for their mothers, or for God. When this cry is not answered, the sense of basic trust is shattered" (51–52).

Reviewing the literature arising from the First World War, Edmund Wilson observed, "The most remarkable effects of this fiction [is that] . . . we are made to feel, behind the appetite for the physical world, the tragedy or the falsity of the moral relation" (101). Not only do soldiers in battle experience a sense of betrayal, but also when returning from war they become aware of society's disaffection and encounter an inexplicable feeling of insensitivity and estrangement from within their own community. Returning soldiers do not seek gratification but instead anticipate acceptance and respect in order to reestablish their self-esteem and rebuild their shattered lives. But a homecoming fit for heroes is often short-lived and quickly becomes a nightmare where they are seen as carriers of a deathly contagion. In William March's novel *Company K*, for example, the reaction of Private Webster's fiancée, Effie, to his wounds is cold and callous. Greeting him upon his return from the war, she says, "If you touch me [. . .] I'll vomit" (156). Moreover, returning soldiers can become a source of embarrassment and chagrin. Aichinger candidly points out that the war "provided an adequate symbol of the selfishness of society" (18). Hemingway's short story "Soldier's Home" portrays this as Krebs, who returns to his hometown in 1919, a year after the war has ended, realizes: "By the time [. . . he] returned to his home town in Oklahoma the greeting of heroes was over. He came back too late. The men from the town who had been drafted had all been welcomed elaborately on their return. There had been a great deal of hysteria. Now the reaction had set in. People seemed to think it was rather ridiculous for Krebs to be getting back so late, years after the war was over" (*In Our Time* 69). This sense of isolation is prevalent among the Lost Generation, who saw the war as "a soul-shattering absurdity beyond the comprehension or control of the human intellect" (Aichinger 14). It was a negation of everything they had once believed and produced what Cooperman calls "a psychic emasculation inherent in the combat environment itself, a sense of violation which had [. . .] vitally important results" (64). This postwar fiction painfully displays a society that is "totally unaware of how soldiers have been re-created spiritually by the war and how they are consequently marked off from society's materialistic concerns" (Walsh 89). They are "like classroom examples of lost generation attitudes" (Walsh 88). It is this postwar disillusionment and insensitivity that provide the link between the combat-related trauma of the war genre and the crime fiction genre as both portray "lost" individuals in a society that cannot acknowledge the horrific consequences of warfare and the enormity of individual sacrifice. After war, many returning veterans, frustrated by society's reaction to them, referred bitterly to the First World War as "The Great Unmentionable" (Herman 70). In such a society, Raymond Chandler's Philip Marlowe feels lost and confused as he tries to come to terms with the feeling that he has somehow been left behind. With the exception of the fellow veterans he meets in the novels, society has little sympathy for his experiences and is instead self-centered and more interested in its own material self-indulgence.

In the postwar era the strong literary bond that had previously linked American intellectuals and their counterparts in the Old World, symbolized by their common values and aspirations, began to loosen and became increasingly untenable. The war had irreversibly changed America, and similarly, American crime writers began to question the traditional rules of their genre which had been established by British writers at the turn of the century. As the British clung to the familiarity of the form, the American crime fiction writers of the postwar era mounted a challenge that resulted in a decisive split from the traditional style, which no longer adequately reflected an increasingly turbulent American society. D. C. Russell noted that Chandler's work uses "characteristic American speech and [. . .] characteristic American humor. In doing this he comes closer to literature than other writers who disdain the native brand of thoughts and language" (123).

Many of those writers now considered as comprising the Lost Generation reacted in a similar manner, no longer content to slavishly reiterate the traditional literary style of the time. Like the evolving crime genre, Cowley notes that members of the Lost Generation "wanted to redeem the language by getting rid of what they often called 'the big words'" (16). In order to clarify what writers meant by this phrase, Cowley explains that many military disasters were disguised by lofty language calculated to mislead both the soldiers and those at home (16). In *A Farewell to Arms* Hemingway sums up his recoil response from this "loftiness" when Frederic Henry, after listening to the haughty remarks of his Italian comrade Gino, muses:

> I was always embarrassed by the words sacred, glorious, and sacrifice and the expression in vain [. . .] I had seen nothing sacred, and the things that were glorious had no glory and the sacrifices were like the stockyards at Chicago if nothing was done with the meat except to bury it. There were many words that you could not stand to hear and finally only the names of places had dignity. Abstract words such as glory, honor, courage, or hallow were obscene beside the concrete names of villages, the numbers of roads, the names of ricers, the number of regiments and the dates. (165)

Haughty sentiments, epitomized by Henry's concerns, are depicted, for instance, in the work of Seeger, whose poetry collection was published in 1917 after his death fighting for the French Foreign Legion the previous year. Seeger's poetry was unsuccessful in capturing the public imagination mainly because it was infused with proud idealism and written in haughty language, which, as Henry notes in *A Farewell to Arms*, was regarded as uncomfortably pompous for many during the early decades of the twentieth century. However, the backlash against lofty language and sweeping sentimentality was much more profound than the subject of poems and prose. Cowley notes:

> It also helped to shape the prose style of a generation [. . .] Outraged by the fake sentiments expressed in wartime [. . .] the generation was trying to learn what it really felt, no matter how simple or shameful,

> and then, in Hemingway's words, "to put down what really happened in action [. . .] the sequence of motion and fact which made the emotion." That search for concrete words to express "what really happened in action" became a distinguished feature of the new literary age. (18)

This alteration in language is a significant factor that links all literary works in the postwar era; the themes and language being employed by the Lost Generation were similarly being utilized in the crime genre. Complimenting Dashiell Hammett on the changing style and tone of the genre, Chandler noted that the types of work being produced by Hammett were similar in tone and texture to those of Hemingway: "Hammett was an ace performer [. . .] [F]or all I know, Hemingway, might have learned something from Hammett [. . .] A rather revolutionary debunking of both the language and the material of fiction had been going on for some time" (*The Simple Art of Murder* 14).

In the postwar era, it was not simply the language of the crime genre that underwent a transformation, the emphasis on plot, puzzles, and clues also became less important than characterization and the emerging protagonists were far more credible and lifelike individuals. Stories became depictions of bad things happening to good people, or good people doing bad things. Like the Lost Generation, the infusion of realism prompted hard-boiled writers to abandon the traditionally British third-person narrative for the more distinct first-person narrative as stories became authentic and more molded to suit an American audience. Stories incorporated accent and regional dialect and integrated colloquial speech by dropping the "g" at the end of certain words, such as "doin'" or "goin'." Private eyes became more internalized, becoming more "I" than "eye" to reflect the changing dynamic of the detective. As a consequence, private and often concealed individual traumas became visible to the reader, observed from within through the probing use of language and a first-person narrative. As stories became more about the "self," Stephen Knight notes,

> It is through this sense of isolation that the private-eye story is in fact more innovative, bespeaking a sense that social values, communal mores, have no real value [. . .] The world-weary feeling of the Hammett-Chandler detective seems related to a growing dismay with modern mercantile society [. . .] but also the post-war period, with its sense of lost dreams and the dangers of over-sophistication [. . .] the between-wars private-eye has a much more personal quest and a much more individualistic set of values. (112–13)

The transformation in the fictional detective that had started as a reaction to the British style of writing quickly developed into a response against the cynicism and materialistic order that dominated postwar America. This environment prompted writers from every genre to create a new generation of fictional characters traumatized by the war who thought and behaved differently from their predecessors by exhibiting a diminished sense of identity and masculinity. Like real veterans, these characters struggled to reintegrate themselves into an amoral nation that was indifferent, insensitive, and ignorant of their suffering and trauma, and where they were shunned and forgotten. Jeffrey Walsh has argued that traditionally, "writers [. . .] have envisioned the soldier as an image of man in society" (ix). Yet the values for which soldiers had supposedly fought and suffered in war to protect were conspicuously absent in the postwar world, debasing their sacrifices as superfluous and immaterial while cynically ignoring the veteran and regarding him as a social embarrassment. In the postwar era, as Aichinger points out, "bravery did not matter, professional competence did not matter, devotion and self-sacrifice did not matter" (11).

It is hardly surprising then, that writers of the era created a new generation of fictional characters unable to reintegrate and suffering profound disillusionment. These were characters who felt compelled to pursue a type of justice which although not shared by the wider society, gave expression to their personalized moral code and individual values. In the era of prohibition, with gangsters prowling the streets and the authorities portrayed as inept, private agencies and detectives "filled the void created by the widespread corruption found in local police and their geographical jurisdiction limitations" (Fagin 191).

It was in these unruly social conditions that Raymond Chandler created his fictional detective Philip Marlowe. Marlowe's personal sense of justice and code of honor appear to resonate with mythic and romantic qualities. Yet they also suggest a warrior mentality, a common theme in the years following the First World War when novels "equate[d] the possibility of romantic love with heroism on the battlefield—of modern-day knight errantry" (Aichinger 19). This notion does not, however, rest easily with Chandler's detective. Marlowe's persona, evoking chivalric knight errantry, comes, in fact, from a much darker place, and his inner conflict and sense of estrangement are suggestive of a far more complex cause. The recurring themes in Chandler's novels are, by contrast, significant indicators of Chandler's affinity with the Lost Generation and the troubling encounters of those who experienced the war firsthand. Chandler's own experiences in the war appear to be every bit as injurious as the recognizable work of those who wrote of war such as Hemingway, Dos Passos, and Faulkner. The influence of war upon Chandler's work is equally revealing, involving numerous examples of both physical and psychological trauma. Yet rather than recount his wartime experiences in a manner similar to those of the Lost Generation, Chandler chose to express himself through a protagonist who had, like his creator, encountered numerous obstacles while trying to reintegrate into a corrupt and heartless world. Marlowe became Chandler's cathartic self-response to the selfishness and unyielding finality of urban America, where it appeared that virtue and honor had unequivocally lost their importance.

Aichinger tells us that "the American writer who had been in action adopted an attitude [. . .] in accordance with a national mythos" (xxiii). The experience of the First World War "shatter[ed . . .] the American attitude towards warfare[,] and the mood of the literature that came out of the war" effectively became a literature of protest (xxv). The undercurrent of protest encouraged many writers in the interwar period to go "beyond realism [and] take the war as a metaphor for the ills besetting their era" (15). Drawing upon his experience of war, Marlowe attempts to reintroduce a sense of justice into an urban landscape that he feels has been blighted by cynicism and moral decay. He is still a soldier, but his theater of war has been transformed from the battlefield to a hostile inner city.

Ralph Willett argues that detective fiction can be used to "display the fragmentation and complexity of modern life and to undermine the tendency of narrative to achieve control and closure" (8). In a similar style to John Dos Passos's *Manhattan Transfer* (1925) and T. S. Eliot's "The Wasteland" (1922), Chandler's novels represent an urban environment as a source of alienation and decay; the city of Los Angeles has been reduced to a hollowed-out void without a soul, a colorless place whose inhabitants have been stripped of identity and compassion. Feelings of "melancholy, regret and emptiness" (Willett 8) are common in the early postwar form of the American hard-boiled genre. Fragmentation, complexity, and diversity, which are unique to early American crime fiction, are characterized by violent tensions and occasional irreconcilable contradictions. In this turbulent urban landscape, Chandler created a war veteran detective who has been robbed of any recognition of "self" in exactly the same way as he had been robbed of his individuality while a cog in the nation's war machine. In the same way that the bootlegger Congo Jake in *Manhattan Transfer* adopts a similar path to wealth and fortune as Jay Gatz in F. Scott Fitzgerald's *The Great Gatsby*, so too can we observe the parallels between the lives of both Joe O'Keefe and Dutch Robinson in

Manhattan Transfer with Chandler's Philip Marlowe. Dos Passos's characters, both of whom are veterans of the First World War, witness the corruption and frivolity of the wealthy and, in Dutch's case, resort to criminal activity as a means of survival. As a veteran of this "fallen world" Marlowe too is struggling to keep his head above water. He cannot accept that his sacrifices and hardships have been for nothing and must find a worthy cause that will redeem him and restore a sense of purpose and meaning to his life.

Chandler's fictional detective is thus an attempt to bridge the gap between the noble ideals for which war was fought and the degrading actuality of contemporary society. Marlowe strives to work to ameliorate society's ills against seemingly overwhelming corruption because if he does not, he believes his sacrifices will have been in vain. Chandler's own traumatic war experience becomes significant when considering Marlowe's characterization, and by recognizing how Chandler's own posttraumatic symptoms were transferred onto his detective it offers a fresh new insight into his writing and more pertinently presents an original understanding of Marlowe's motivations. Chandler's own war trauma suggests that his detective fiction should be interpreted as a literature of traumatic experience located in a crime-fiction setting. Philip Marlowe is not a hard-boiled hero, but a genuine war veteran of a "lost" generation struggling for recognition and unable to accept the disorder of postwar American society.

Although Marlowe is a heroic man driven by a noble code, his compulsions and motivations are driven by his need to make sense of his past experiences. Marlowe, like Chandler, is a veteran of the First World War thrust into a changed and expanded postwar Los Angeles and forced to accept the changing social dynamic while yearning for the supportive company of men like those he relied on so heavily during wartime. Chandler's devastating experience during the war defines the essence of Marlowe's disillusioned and tormented identity.

"A COUPLE OF WRITERS"

Outside the parameters of the hard-boiled style, however, one of Chandler's short stories is particularly revealing and suggestive of how the writer felt about his own experiences. Written in 1951, the story "A Couple of Writers" depicts the psychological effect that war has on a veteran and the difficulty that loved ones have in understanding how their war experience has changed them. Like those among the Lost Generation who witnessed warfare firsthand, Chandler's encounters with the horrors of combat were certainly real, and his experiences had such an emotional impact that they subsequently revealed themselves in his work. The distress that Chandler suffered suggests that the traumatic symptoms caused by his war experience would have surfaced in whatever genre or style he chose to write in.

Written in much the same vein as his 1945 screenplay *The Blue Dahlia*, which focuses upon the interaction between a tight-knit family-like unit of three wartime veterans, "A Couple of Writers" had a personal significance to Chandler not only because of his affinity with the protagonist, but also because of his compulsion to portray the symptoms that he himself suffered. The anxiety he felt while attempting to comprehend his story's rejection by numerous American publishers is apparent in a letter to the English critic and editor of the *Sunday Times*, Leonard Russell. In December 1952, Chandler wrote that although he was not "anxious" or "disheartened" at not hearing from Russell, he impatiently questioned why a response was taking so long. He said,

> Remember me? Chandler? We met once briefly in London [. . . and] it led me to send you a story called A COUPLE OF WRITERS, which was dispatched by airmail on October 29, 1952. And the rest is silence . . . I told you the worst about the story. And after all, you asked me to send it to you. I think some brief acknowledgement might be in order, if the story ever reached you. (Bodleian 58:46)

Despite appearances to the contrary Chandler was indeed anxious to discover the fate of his story, and his agitated tone is suggestive of not just the emotional intensity that he had banking on its successful publication, but also his apprehension over the uncertainty of whether a story featuring an obviously troubled war veteran would ever be seen in print.

"A Couple of Writers" is a candid depiction of married writers Hank and Marion Bruton who torment each other over their personal and literary failures. Similar to the unsympathetic family dynamic depicted in Hemingway's "Soldier's Home," Chandler's story is the study of a couple struggling to come to terms with their crumbling marriage but is set against a complex psychological background. Hank, a war veteran, desperately looks to his wife for compassion, love, and stability, but instead he receives her indifference and desertion. Marion makes no attempt to understand or adjust to her husband's physical and psychological troubles, and she is disgusted by his alcohol dependency. Hank's ailments appear to be the psychological legacy of his war experience, with symptoms that include severe twitching in his legs and thighs, "grinding his teeth," and a constant "nervous feeling in his stomach" (qtd. in Gardiner and Walker 99–100). He also walks "around the house in his bare feet" (qtd. in Gardiner and Walker 99), a mannerism suggestive of the lasting effects of trench foot, an ailment that is also experienced by Philip Marlowe in *Farewell, My Lovely.*

Failing to understand Hank's psychological need for alcohol, the story begins with Marion once again deciding to leave him. When Hank offers to give up drinking whiskey, Marion's response is brutal. She replies: "Oh sure. And then what? You're not a man. You're just a physically perfect specimen of an alcoholic eunuch. You're a zombie in top condition. You're a dead man with an absolutely normal blood pressure" (qtd. in Gardiner and Walker 105). Marion's outburst is shocking because it is two-pronged in nature. First, she cruelly casts aspersions on Hank's masculinity by calling him a "eunuch" (ibid.), effectively emasculating the already psychologically broken veteran. It is an insult that strongly resonates with Ernest Hemingway's novel *The Sun Also Rises* (1926), in which the character Jake Barnes receives a catastrophic wartime wound that physically and symbolically castrates him and denies him the ability to demonstrate his sexual masculinity. Both Hemingway's Barnes and Chandler's Bruton suffer debilitating injuries that, although affecting them in different ways, deprive them both of their sense of masculinity. This connection between Bruton and Barnes not only links Chandler to Hemingway once again, but also opens Chandler's work to many different resonances since both characters originate from similar psychological perspectives and are directed toward questions of masculinity.

Marion's second line of verbal assault upon her husband is to label him a "zombie" and a "dead man" (ibid.), providing the reader with an image of Hank's mental condition and his detached state of mind. He suffers from lethargy, a common behavioral feature among traumatized veterans. Sufferers of this debilitating condition often liken themselves to, as Robert Jay Lifton has noted, the "living dead" (106). They feel disconnected and estranged from those around them, who find it difficult to understand or relate to their experiences. To the veteran, civilians are frustratingly disassociated from the brutal reality of warfare. Lifton observes that on their return from combat the feature that distinguishes veterans from the general public is the physical and psychological burden of comprehending what war is really like. He says, what society "merely sense[s] and resist[s] knowing" contrasts profoundly with the "suffering on the basis of [. . . wartime] knowledge and experience" (67). Veterans often feel that the public, including family and friends, are profoundly insensitive to their circumstances, and this widespread inability to understand a veteran's psychological condition is symbolized by the cruel uncaring actions of Hank's wife, Marion. Instead of trying to understand his suffering by talking to Hank, Marion claims that his alcohol dependency is a consequence of his flawed character and resorts to cruel personal attacks.

Various psychological studies have observed that exposing veterans to responses such as Marion's can have an incredibly detrimental effect. Chandler's protagonist is callously denied the very thing he needs the most, a supportive relationship and community to assist in the psychological reintegration.[3] This is essential because, as Herman states, "a secure sense of connection with caring people is the foundation of personality development. When this connection is shattered, the traumatized person loses [. . . his or her] basic sense of self" (52). Lifton notes that veterans "feel they have come to difficult truths that adult American society refuses to face. Indeed, in their eyes most of America lives in an illusion [. . . Veterans] see themselves sometimes as a victimized group unrecognized and rejected by existing society" (69).

Although "A Couple of Writers" is clearly not a crime story, Hank manifests behavioral traits that are uncomfortably similar to those displayed by Philip Marlowe. This work taken together with Chandler's other writing, including his screenplays, demonstrates that the author was familiar with, and indeed was haunted by, the emotional frailties that are typical of war veterans. As a veteran himself, Chandler penned stories that were based on war, such as "Trench Raid" and his World War Two–based espionage story "No Crime in the Mountains" (1941). He also developed characters deliberately depicted as veterans, such as Hank Bruton, General Sternwood, Bill Chess, Terry Lennox, and Roger Wade, in addition to Johnny Morrison and Buzz Wanchek in *The Blue Dahlia*. Chandler's own experiences were channeled through his characters, making them not only more personal and *psycho*-biographical, but also more realistic, and many of Chandler's characters are tainted with a sense of discontentment and disillusionment that typifies the state of mind of many veterans. Natasha Spender, a friend of the writer in his later years, declared that Chandler almost certainly gave himself a cameo role in most of his novels by creating characters that represented his own mirror image. She believes that in *The Long Goodbye*, in particular, the three main characters—Marlowe, Lennox and Wade—represent discrete facets of Chandler's character that are in constant conflict with each other (Hiney 248–49).

It is probable that Philip Marlowe is an emotionally repressed version of Hank, which is hardly surprising since the two characters originate from the same trauma and disillusionment. When Hank refers to his unhappy life, he evokes emotions hauntingly reminiscing of Marlowe: "[We're] all lonely, all empty, all poor, all gritted with small mean worries that have no dignity. All trying like men caught in a bog to get some firm ground under our feet and knowing all the time it doesn't make a damn bit of difference whether we do or not" (qtd. in MacShane, *Chandler before Marlowe* 59–60). The notion of being unable to gain a "firm footing" in life is a clear articulation of insecurity, and Chandler could almost be referring to Marlowe's own diffidence. His words reveal the faltering manner that Chandler, Hank, and Marlowe share; each appears resigned to the view that life has somehow lost its meaning and reveal a belief that however hard they try they will inevitably fail to achieve the goal that each has set out to accomplish. In the end they have in common the sensation of hopelessness, since their laudable efforts have altered nothing, and their labors have in the end been cruelly frustrated.

An insensitive society combined with the lack of individual self-confidence drives both Hank and Marlowe to find solace in the whiskey bottle. In their own way each feels invisible in a world that has failed to notice their contributions. Their recognition of the terrible and gratuitous loss of life nurtures a sense of resignation toward their own mortality and that of the people they know or have known. When Hank whistles some music from a "symphonic movement [. . . } he tried to remember which it was and when he remembered he thought about the composer, the kind of life he had had, the struggles, the misery, and now he was dead and rotten, like so many men [he] had known in the army" (qtd. in Gardiner and Walker 102). Although Marlowe's ailments are not presented as explicitly as Hank's, the story certainly indicates Chandler's readiness to confront his demons and write about veteran characters. It is quite possible that "A Couple of Writers" prompted Chandler to further develop his veteran characterization when writing *The Long Goodbye*.

While it is tempting to argue otherwise, there is no evidence to substantiate the theory that Marion was intended to be a depiction of Chandler's wife, Cissy. Instead, an examination of Marion's reactions to her husband and the ailments Chandler confers upon his protagonist in the story are more reminiscent of the dismissive reception metered-out to soldiers by society and common public opinion. Marion is the symbolic representation of the indifferent attitude with which society treats its returning war veterans. This depiction underlines the notion of Chandler's own empathetic recognition of the difficulties facing veterans not only upon their return, but also later in life as their experiences begin to affect them psychologically. "A Couple of Writers" can legitimately be considered as an in-depth psychological exploration of Chandler's male protagonists. The story is almost a cipher through which we can the achieve a better understanding of Chandler's work because it not only unlocks Marlowe's character, it provides an insight into the inner thoughts of the author himself, providing a comprehensive understanding of the depth of Chandler's suffering and his intimate identification with veterans.

Chandler created a character that, like himself, suffered the posttraumatic effects of his experiences during the war. Marlowe stands alone in the world not out of choice but because the society he lives in has disregarded him. He is a character from a generation lost to war, a veteran returned from battle and set down in a community that does not wish to acknowledge his sacrifices. Transposing his own symptoms onto his creation, Marlowe became an archetypal Lost Generation character filled with the disillusionment and emotional trauma that plagued his creator.

The argument for Chandler's consideration alongside the Lost Generation therefore brings the discussion back to generic categorization. Despite the genre in which Chandler chose to write, his works unquestionably resonate with Lost Generation themes. If Chandler's style interconnects with that of the Lost Generation, it should not be excluded from consideration simply because it is a form of popular writing. Chandler incorporated similar themes to Hemingway, Dos Passos, and many other writers of the era, yet is considered in a very distinct and separate literary category. As Chandler himself wrote in "The Simple Art of Murder," "There are no vital and significant forms of art [. . .] there is only art" (2). The crime novel evolved by incorporating the realism that addressed the social themes of the era and by modifying its style to become a far more accessible and relevant representation of society. It may therefore be suggested that Chandler tactfully brought Lost Generation themes to the mass population via an appealing and popular genre.

Arguing for the important contribution that Chandler made to American literature, Sean McCann reasons: "The achievement of the hard-boiled crime story . . . proved that "important writing" could be done in popular genres. All that prevented our full realization of the fact was the hidebound prejudice of the cultural elite, on the one hand, and the banal commercial production of mass media on the other" (152). As the line that separates fiction from reality began to blur, the line that separates genres did likewise, allowing for a far wider range of works to be encompassed by the broad heading of crime fiction. These included themes that came directly from witnessed reality, such as the experience of war, which in turn prompted hard-boiled fiction writers to modify the generic expectation of detective fiction. As Paul Cobley points out, it is simply not possible to maintain a pure genre because genres and styles "are decidedly prone to overlaps" (4). Stephen Knight concurs, claiming that "mysteries, detectives and crimes interweave" (xii) in varying ways that move the style forward. As with all other forms of fictional writing, the crime genre is not a static representation, and its conformity and distinctiveness can easily alter as it evolves to reflect new social influences. This blurring of styles is a particular feature of Chandler's work. The author incorporated various facets of the war genre, not only through the characterization and psychology of his protagonist but also through secondary means such as the physical injuries suffered by secondary characters like Bill Chess in *The Lady in the Lake* and Terry Lennox in *The Long Goodbye*. The inclusion of combat-related trauma in a crime novel is, in itself, a transformation into a style of trauma-related and socially disillusioned fiction. Studying genre as an autonomous entity therefore "represents a narrowing of focus which does not fairly reflect the breadth of the generic corpus of texts" (Cobley 4).

The existence of a style of writing that deliberately defies categorization and blurs generic classifications by converging themes and issues from different genres is a positive and rejuvenating development since it consciously creates new work that goes against type or expectation. The subversion of established expectation in a form of writing is important as it reinforces and furthers the verisimilitude of fictional works. Chandler may have adopted this technique along with Hemingway's "iceberg" style to introduce and discuss issues that were considered embarrassing reminders of society's inability to acknowledge them. By molding Philip Marlowe into veteran of war Chandler altered the general mode of crime writing and characterization. In setting aside restrictive generic confinements, what remains in Chandler's work are distinctive Lost Generation themes. The detective can thus be viewed as a broken and disillusioned man on a quest to find justice and decency in an increasingly corrupt and selfish society. Marlowe is reconfigured as a Lost Generation character in a hard-boiled crime fiction setting.

4

CHARACTERIZATION: THE DETECTIVE AS VETERAN

[A] novelist lives through his characters.

—MACDONALD, *THE MOVING TARGET*

For much of the twentieth century the traditional character of the detective in crime fiction has been widely perceived as an iconic and a predominantly mythic individual, an "American image of heroic manhood," and a "cowboy adapted to life on the city streets" (Horsley 74). He was assumed to be "tough [and] modern but also traditional" (Knight 111). Some believed that the detective needed to be a coarse and brutal figure, with an instinct for danger. Julian Symons, for example, argued that the detective's language was raw and unrefined, "as pungent as cigar smoke," while his use of physical violence was "as natural as drinking" (*Bloody Murder* 154). Often operating at the very edge of the law, the detective was considered to be well connected, hard-headed, and unorthodox. Although Andrew Pepper states that the character was "usually violent [. . . and] operates out of selfish as well as selfless motives" (6) this notion often oversimplifies the inner motivations that come together to permeate the detective.

When this generalization is applied to Raymond Chandler, and the series of motives that lie behind the character of Philip Marlowe in particular, the unfaithfulness of this oversimplification becomes immediately apparent. Pepper's notion of the conflict between "selfish" and "selfless" motives is unworkable when trying to comprehend Chandler's detective because Marlowe rarely—if at all—acts selfishly (furthermore, by acting selfishly it would contradict the traditional notion that Marlowe adheres to knightly values, the very values which prohibit him from acting in any way but selflessly). This "selfish versus selfless" argument raises important questions regarding the actual disposition of Marlowe's character. If the detective were acting for himself it would suggest that his sense of "self" has been somehow modified to the extent that his psychological state has moved away from the chivalric traditions we associate with his character.

On the surface, Marlowe is driven by his honorable quest to uncover the truth and attain justice for his clients. As Philip Durham noted, "Marlowe rescued ladies who did not deserve it," he protected the frail and innocent, and he saw to it that "some of the criminal element received its due" (32). Yet, the detective is not superhuman and regularly admits to being scared, thereby attesting to the reality of his character and establishing a sympathetic connection with the reader. Durham argues that Marlowe has the appearance of an ordinary man simplistically trying to restore what he perceives as the balance between "good" and "evil," often ending with him "trying to mete out simple justice" (91). This interpretation is not, however, a strictly accurate image of Marlowe. Throughout the novels Chandler rarely grants Marlowe the satisfaction of a sense of closure, and contrary to Durham's remarks the detective seldom dispenses his own form of justice. In fact, he is often accountable for doing precisely the opposite. Although giving the appearance of endeavoring to redress the balance between right and wrong, Marlowe rarely brings a felon to justice. Instead he allows many of those guilty of crimes to escape or avoid punishment. These include Carmen Sternwood in *The Big Sleep*; Velma Valento in *Farewell, My Lovely*; Elizabeth and Leslie Murdock in *The High Window*; Al Dergamo in *The Lady in the Lake;* and Eileen Wade in *The Long Goodbye*. He also assists in Terry Lennox's escape to Mexico when Lennox is implicated in the murder of his wife in *The Long Goodbye*.

Such commentators as Philip Durham, Russell Davies, and Jerry Speir have offered various theories detailing Chandler's characterization of Marlowe; their theories place the detective in various critical contexts in order to accentuate certain facets of his character and which have become accepted as the primary contexts for studying the writer's works. Richard Slotkin has noted that when considering the foundation of many of America's most celebrated characters, they often originate with "stories drawn from a society's history that have acquired through persistent usage the power of symbolizing that society's ideology and of dramatizing its moral consciousness" (5). While Slotkin's observation relates to the relevance of the gunfighter in American history, his assessment nevertheless accurately depicts the character of the detective, who is often perceived as a modern urban cowboy. The often exaggerated representations of both the gunfighter and the detective are vitally important, symbolizing the essence of the mythic American hero. Horsley contends that "the private eye, as has often been observed, is [. . .] an updated, cynical version of the frontier scout or lawman, patrolling the border between civilization and savagery" (74). It can also therefore be argued that under a macho façade, there is an aspect of an exaggerated characterization that gives the detective "a core of romantic yearning for a lost ideal" (ibid.). This notion is an important component that represents a key theme in Chandler criticism, providing by far the most instructive context to understand Philip Marlowe and subsequently the importance of Marlowe as a prototype for the character of the war veteran—and war traumatized—detective.

Two further theories that have attempted to provide an explanation of Marlowe's character are principally drawn from "the [crime] genre's frontier heritage" and are, as Horsley argues, "related to what are often seen as marked anti-feminist and homoerotic tendencies" (ibid.).

First, as Horsley notes, this tendency may often be observed in many of Marlowe's social anxieties concerning gender, and he is repeatedly categorized as both a misogynist and a homosexual for the simple reason that he routinely seeks out male company. Critics have sought to provide an explanation for Marlowe's affinity for masculine company and have inevitably arrived at the easiest conclusion. Jerry Speir, for example, states that many critics in the field of American literature have "taken great pleasure in declaring Marlowe homosexual" (110). In his article "Marlowe, Men and Women" Michael Mason observed Marlowe's "mixture of tenderness and boyish admiration" (qtd. in Speir 110) for Moose Malloy in *Farewell, My Lovely*, while also noting that "*The Long Goodbye* . . . [is] overtly, a novel of homosexual feeling" (qtd. in Gross 92). He refers to Marlowe's behavior as "morally obtuse" (qtd. in Gross 95) and draws attention to Marlowe's description of the men in the novels; from the "nice easy smile" and "thoughtful grey eyes" (70) of Eddie Mars in *The Big Sleep*, to the "handsome face" (143) of Alex Morny in *The High Window* and the gentleness and civility of Steelgrave in *The Little Sister*. Mason suggests that the only conclusion for a man describing another in this manner is that Marlowe finds these men attractive. Even Marlowe's house-proud nature comes in for homosexual interpretation as a display of the detective's "femininity" (qtd. in Gross 98).

Gershon Legman has made the strongest charge regarding Marlowe's sexuality, believing that in *Farewell, My Lovely*,

> No matter how "strangely" Chandler's detective, Marlowe, moons over these big men, they are always beating him up . . . The true explanation

> of Marlowe's temperamental disinterest in women is not "honour," but his interest in men . . . Chandler's Marlowe is clearly homosexual—a butterfly, as the Chinese say, dreaming that he is a man. (70)

Much of Legman's argument for Marlowe's homosexuality, therefore, rests on "Marlowe's temperamental disinterest in women." This attitude ultimately stems from the belief, as Mason concurred, that Chandler produced novels "full of homicidal females . . . [and] devoid of bad males" (qtd. in Gross 95). Yet this assumption is flawed. Although females are the criminal culprits in four of the seven novels, there are certainly more than a few "bad males" in the mix. Al Dergamo in *The Lady in the Lake*; Terry Lennox in *The Long Goodbye*; and the various corrupt police officers, gangsters, and thugs that appear throughout the series of novels provide frequent foils to Chandler's femme fatales. The one consistency is that Marlowe trusts no one, male or female; from Anne Riordan and Merle Davies to Red Noorgard and Roger Wade, trust is something that must be earned no matter what the sex.

And there are certainly numerous flaws to Legman's argument above. First, the perception of what constitutes "mooning" is entirely subjective; second, Marlowe is never beaten up by any of the "big men" he allegedly "moons" over (Legman is referring here to Red and Moose). The implied suggestion that the physical beatings equate to sexual gratification is simply not part of the novel's plot (nor indeed the series of novels). Instead, as Speir argues, both Legman and Mason overlook key aspects of plot and context in order to read much more into Marlowe's character:

> Red is, like Marlowe, a former policeman . . . [and] his assistance is instrumental in Marlowe's resolution of the case . . . the two therefore, have adequate basis for a relationship without the implications of sexual attraction. Similarly, Marlowe's fascination with Moose, despite his rather uncontrollable violence, stems from the bizarre manner in which they first meet and from his conviction that Moose is only a pawn in some larger game. (111)

Chandler vehemently rejected the theories of Legman and others, responding by noting that such critics "belong to that rather numerous class of American neurotics which cannot conceive of a close relationship between a couple of men as other than homosexual" (ibid.).

While it cannot be denied that Marlowe does idealize certain men, Jerry Speir contends that "to construe that admiration as homosexual lust is to misconstrue an essential facet of Marlowe's character" (ibid.). Marlowe's characterization makes him prone to an exaggerated idealization of *most* things, a feature that becomes particularly noticeable in his relationship with women. However, as will be demonstrated, a more plausible theory—considering the context of his characterization—is that Marlowe's affinity for specific men resonates from military experience and symbolizes the understanding that occurs between soldiers during times of combat, a bonding of men upon whose actions your very life might depend. Herman has noted that "the situation of constant danger [leads] soldiers to develop extreme emotional dependency upon their peer group and leaders" (Herman 25). These wartime bonds, which are further examined in chapter 5, are borne of mutual dependency and shared adversity and are often far more intense than anything experienced in normal civilian life. This represents a far more rational and authentic explanation for Marlowe's affinity for veterans in the novels, given Chandler's own comments upon the subject.

Second, in conjunction with the suggestion that Marlowe is a homosexual, critics such as Geoffrey Hartmann have accused Chandler of "conventional woman hating" (220). Michael Mason further notes that the "moral scheme" of Chandler's novels "is in truth pathologically harsh on women, and pathologically lenient towards men" (qtd. in Gross 95). This argument is both unfounded and flawed since, again, it overlooks Marlowe's characterization in the novels, which in turn flows from inconsistent assumptions regarding both Chandler and Marlowe.

Conflictingly, in addition to suggesting that Marlowe is a homosexual, many critics have maintained that Marlowe is homophobic and a racist. This undoubtedly stems from Chandler's personal attitudes toward homosexuals and African Americans.

However, Chandler's life needs to be placed in context: he was born in the same decade as "Jim Crow" segregation began, and the disfranchisement of African Americans began in the 1890s. Although Chandler was living in England by 1910, segregation became firmly established across the southern United States. When Chandler returned to the States in 1912 the "separate but equal" ruling established in *Plessy v. Ferguson* (1896) had taken root in American society, delegating African Americans as second-class citizens. Even during Chandler's experience of war, combat elements of the US Army were kept completely segregated, and the Ku Klux Klan was flourishing nationwide by the 1920s.

Care must be taken, therefore, to avoid judging the actions of those in the past by contemporary standards. Instead, they should be judged in the context of the society in which they lived. Failure to do this would lead us to consider Ernest Hemingway as racist for using discriminatory language in *The Sun Also Rises* (1926) and also to admonish the implied racism of Dashiell Hammett's *The Dain Curse* (1929).[1]

If, for example, we were to compare the homophobia of Chandler/Marlowe with, say, Dashiell Hammett, there is, equally, very little tolerance toward homosexuality. In *The Maltese Falcon* the openly gay character Joel Cairo is repeatedly singled out for slaps and kicks by the detective Sam Spade, and Cairo's homosexual partner, Wilmer, is called a "gunsel" by Spade. While many readers took this to mean a gun-wielding thug, it actually meant a younger man kept by an older one. Demonstrating the widespread historical context of words such as "pansy" or "sissy," even Joseph Breen, Will Hays's second in command and "chief" of the Production Code Administration, noted in a 1941 letter to Jack Warner: "We cannot approve the characterization of Cairo as a *pansy* as indicated by the lavender perfume, high-pitched voice, and other accoutrements." Similarly, in a 1944 letter to William Gordon of RKO Pictures, he stated with regards to the adaptation of Chandler's *Murder, My Sweet*: "There must, of course, be nothing of the 'pansy' characterization about [Lindsey] Marriott." (Kiszely 98). As Philip Kiszely notes, homosexuality was "frowned upon as the antithesis of Marlowe and Spade's rugged masculinity" (231).

Likewise, Marlowe is neither "harsh" nor unreasonable toward women. In fact he is far more sympathetic than almost any other detective, allowing female criminals, in almost every instance, to evade justice and apprehension by the police. By contrast, the novels of Dashiell Hammett and Mickey Spillane show detectives ruthlessly pursuing the criminals and bringing swift and deliberate punishment, without emotion and especially regardless of gender. Marlowe is far more empathetic, allowing his levelheadedness to guide his moral direction. The transgressors in Chandler's novels are almost always women—Carmen Sternwood, Velma Valento, Elizabeth Murdock, Mildred Haviland, Orfamay Quest, and Eileen Wade—and all avoid punishment for their various crimes, deceptions, and misdemeanors. But this open-mindedness toward female characters is also balanced by the fact that some of Marlowe's closest personal acquaintances in the novels are women, such as Anne Riordan and Linda Loring.

While the propositions espoused by Hartmann and Mason may be regarded as an oversimplification, there is, nevertheless, an undeniable awkwardness to Marlowe when in female company. Horsley believes that Marlowe's "tortured self perceives women as threatening his identity and [he] fears losing control" (82). But it can be argued that this fear has less to do with the women in his life than the fact that he simply identifies more closely with male characters. Like many veterans, Marlowe finds it difficult to form close attachments, especially with those who are unable to understand the callousness of warfare. The detective is instinctively able to recognize those who have undergone experiences similar to his own and as such considers men to be more psychologically accessible. It is no coincidence that Bill Chess, Terry Lennox, and Roger Wade are all men characterized as war veterans, and each is willing to confide in Marlowe and discuss his war experiences, reflecting upon his residual emotional conditions.

The proposition that Marlowe is a misogynist can be questioned still further because the detective's crudeness in the company of women often has its basis in the events of the novel as opposed to being an enduring facet of Marlowe's character. It is therefore imprudent to draw any definitive conclusions without first considering the particular circumstance in which Marlowe finds himself, since there is often a perfectly legitimate reason for his behavior. Jerry Speir, for example, perceptively argues, "Considered in isolation, as they often are, [Marlowe's] remarks do suggest a man with a revulsion for the opposite sex," but, he says, "such an interpretation neglects the circumstances surrounding the scene."[2] It is understandable to view Marlowe as a woman hater if the passages that have achieved such notoriety are read without any consideration of their context. And the legitimacy of Speir's observation is validated when we consider Marlowe's attitude across the broader range of novels. The scene in which Marlowe "tore the bed to pieces savagely" (115) after finding trickster Carmen Sternwood naked there in *The Big Sleep* is in stark contrast to his tenderness at the end of *The Long Goodbye*, where, after spending the night with Linda Loring, Marlowe says:

> We said good-bye. I watched the cab out of sight. I went back up the steps and into the bedroom and pulled the bed to pieces and remade it. There was a long dark hair on one of the pillows. There was a lump of lead at the pit of my stomach.
>
> The French have a phrase for it . . . To say good-bye is to die a little. (308–9)

This scene demonstrates that Marlowe is perfectly capable of displaying compassion and genuine affection for women, a feature that is evident in his friendships with Merle Davies and Anne Riordan and his marriage to Linda Loring in *Poodle Springs* (1989).[3] Marlowe feels protective toward these women and is completely at ease in their company because they do not have an ulterior sexual motive. Unlike the Sternwood sisters, Orfamay Quest, and Eileen Wade, Linda, Merle, and Anne make no effort to use their sexuality to further their own agendas. Despite being occasionally portrayed as prudish characters, Merle and Anne retain a sense of virtue and decorum in the detective's mind. In Anne's case, she actually becomes a strong, admirable female in the male-dominated mean streets of Los Angeles. Likewise, Linda possesses a level of intelligence and mystique that attracts Marlowe. His admiration of caring, resilient, laudable women corresponds with the chivalric notion of Marlowe as a knight. But while he may place women on a pedestal as things to be protected, he nevertheless recognizes, unlike "traditional" hard-boiled detectives, their democratic human value and social parity; a distinct departure from either the highly sexualized femme fatale (for example, Cora in James M. Cain's *The Postman Always Rings Twice)* or, by contrast, nurturing female characters (such as Effie Perrine in Hammett's Sam Spade novels). Marlowe demonstrates this when responding to Terry Lennox's complaint about "goddamn women . . . waving their hands and screwing up their faces and tinkling their goddam bracelets and making with the packaged charm." Marlowe simply replies by saying, "Take it easy [. . .] So they're human [. . .] What did you expect—golden butterflies hovering in a rosy mist?" (21–22). By having Marlowe make such a comment, Chandler effectively dismisses any notion of chivalric or courtly romance that critics have used to categorize the detective. Instead, Anne and Linda are portrayed as competent women that straddle this problematic divide in characterization: they are, as Marlowe states, merely "human." While the femme fatale threatens the stability of the detective's world, and the homemaker exemplifies it, Anne and Linda—both slightly tomboyish yet nevertheless attractive—signify Chandler's (and Marlowe's) willingness to see women not simply as sexual objects or housewives; their characters are far more nuanced and complete (for example, Anne is the daughter of a police officer and possesses valiant qualities that mark her as different). These characterizations represent a significant middle ground in the dialectical argument of female representations in crime fiction.

Two of the most widely accepted explanations for Chandler's motivations for Marlowe's characterization have courtly love as their focus. The first of these is based on the theory of an "anachronistic Marlowe" put forward by Horsley and Speir, which asserts that Marlowe is a man of chivalric values abiding by the rigid code of the knight in his quest for justice. Belonging to a bygone age, his strong sense of duty and his chivalric code of honor possess a mythic and romantic quality. Armed only with his personal integrity and valor that make him resistant to the depraved society around him, Marlowe "assumes a role often compared to that of the questing knight, undergoing tests that involve skill in arms, fearlessness, and integrity" (Horsley 82). Marlowe is, according to Speir, "a character whose values are of another age, dropped down amid the relative valuelessness of the present" (143). Durham also places Marlowe in the role of a knight, saying that Marlowe "work[s] for good rather than for money" (97), which accounts for his numerous noble and chivalric gestures in his battle against the corrupting forces of society.

In Chandler's 1944 essay "The Simple Art of Murder" Chandler noted that the hero goes down "mean streets" but "is not himself mean [. . . and] is neither tarnished nor afraid." He believed the detective should possess "a sense of character, or he would not know his job. He will take no man's money dishonestly and no man's insolence without a due and dispassionate revenge. He is a lonely man and his pride is that you will treat him as a proud man or be sorry you ever saw him. He talks as a man of his age talks—that is, with rude wit, a lively sense of the grotesque, a disgust for sham, and a contempt for pettiness" (18). In this passage Chandler's choice of words resonates with the romantic ideals of Sir Thomas Malory's fifteenth-century tales of *Le Morte d'Arthur* (1485), a text that Chandler may well have studied while at Dulwich College. In this work, King Arthur tells his knights that they should never commit outrageous deeds or murder and always flee from treason. They should by no means be cruel, but give mercy to those that ask for it and always provide assistance to ladies, damsels, gentlewomen, and widows, and treat them with respect and never force them, upon pain of death. The work also urged that no man should fight in a wrongful quarrel for love, nor for worldly goods. By giving the detective this idealized code to serve as a moral compass guiding him through his investigations, MacShane argues that Marlowe's qualities "would appear to be a sentimental position, because it puts Marlowe on a higher plane than any of the other characters." Chandler acknowledged this weakness, but responded to the charge by saying, "I don't mind Marlowe being a sentimentalist because he always has been. His toughness has always been more or less a surface bluff" (qtd. in Frank MacShane, *Life* 206). Reinforcing this, Chandler argued that in order to understand Marlowe the reader had to realize that

> the detective exists complete and entire and unchanged by anything that happens, that he is, as detective, outside the story and above it, and always will be. That is why he never gets the girl, never marries, never

> really has any private life, except insofar as he must eat and sleep and have a place to keep his clothes. His moral and intellectual force is that he gets nothing but his fee, for which he will if he can protect the innocent, guard the helpless and destroy the wicked, and the fact that he must do this while earning a meager living in a corrupt world is what makes him stand out. (Qtd. in Hiney and MacShane 115)

While it is undeniable that Marlowe appears to stand alone in the world, it is not for the reasons commonly accepted.

In contrast to the image of the detective as a chivalric champion, the second major characterization of Marlowe asserts that the detective lives by a *modern* code of values. According to this view Marlowe is not an anachronism but a contemporary man racing to catch up with modernity and suffering its effects upon identity. Woody Haut believes that Chandler "single handedly reinvent[ed] the genre" by "successfully decoding the culture," revealing the sordid reality of a society "saturated with crime and corruption" (*Pulp Culture* 68–69). Arguing in praise of Marlowe's success in deciphering the era, Haut believes the detective's discovery of "crimes within crimes and investigations within investigations" (*Pulp Culture* 75) is indicative of the growing sense of paranoia that prevailed during the early Cold War era. This interpretation is, however, contrary to Chandler's own view that the detective was egocentric: "P. Marlowe has as much social conscience as a horse. He has a personal conscience, which is an entirely different matter" (qtd. in Gardiner and Walker 214). It is probably more accurate, therefore, to claim that Marlowe's discontent and disillusionment provide clues as to the broad social reaction from the 1930s onward. By this time America had become a land of contradiction where men had gone to war expecting adventure and bravery, but had instead returned broken and traumatized by their experiences only to then be cast into the cynicism of rampant consumerism and the inevitably of economic depression. Veterans returned home to be confronted by a "land of plenty" that was driven by consumer greed, and a "land of the free" where, despite the fine sounding principle, many were contemptuously left to suffer from segregation and social discrimination.

Roy Meador argues, "In the 1930s, failure and fear suddenly became avenues of life in America for people who had never met such strange enemies before. Raymond Chandler sent Marlowe to battle them" (152). In an expression of his own war experiences and subsequent disillusionment and cynicism, Chandler reflects that "long before the atom bomb, civilization had created the machinery for its own destruction, and was learning to use it with all the moronic delight of a gangster trying out his first machine gun. The law was something to be manipulated for profit and power. The streets were dark with something more than night" (*The Smell of Fear* 9). Many of Chandler's novels bring together a wide selection of downtrodden civilians from across Los Angeles, highlighting the plight of the era's most demoralized and dejected people. The essential novel for recognizing this social displacement is *Farewell, My Lovely*, in which Philip Marlowe "draws the disparate features of Los Angeles into something that looks like a new deal coalition" (McCann 159). In this particular novel, as Sean McCann notes, "[h]is travels take him from a hotel clerk in Watts; to Jesse Florian, an impoverished and alcoholic widow; to Anne Riordan, the spunky daughter of an honest cop; to Red Norgaard, the operator of a boat taxi—a collection that, along with Moose Malloy, links African Americans, the urban poor, the white ethnics of the working class, and honest middle Americans in a community of sympathy" (ibid.). Chandler creates an image of Los Angeles as "an idealized version of the welfare state," with Marlowe "feel[ing] the pain of working stiffs and those who have been neglected by an unjust society, thus tying the fragmented landscape of Los Angeles into a more or less coherent narrative of victimization" (ibid.). There may be some truth in McCann's interpretation since Chandler clearly had a social conscience (even if Marlowe did not), once remarking that "there are people who think I dwell on the ugly side of life. God help them! If they had any idea how little I have told them about it!" (qtd. in Gardiner and Walker 214).

But Marlowe cannot survive without the city and its sordid deprivation, and his attempts to escape the urban squalor and rationalize the events that have shaped America are repeatedly thwarted as he is habitually drawn back into the quagmire. He manages only brief respite from the city in two novels: *The Lady in the Lake*, during which Marlowe's case takes him to Puma Lake where he is greeted by a laid back environment of the lake-side town; and *Playback*, where he follows Betty Mayfield to Esmerelda, a town which purportedly represents Chandler's own shore-side La Jolla. On all other occasions, however, he is drawn to the city like a butterfly to a glowing lamp. This conflict between the pastoral and the urban is a tradition of American literature that has captured the imagination of many American writers. The escape from the frenzied urban landscape to the peaceful pastoral is a literary cry against the waves of dehumanizing modernity washing through the United States in the early decades of the twentieth century by those who believed that the metaphor of "American innocence" had been lost.

Anxiety caused by the contemporary change that smashed any remnants of community and threw up ugly urban sprawls exuding Replace with "deprivation, providing" fertile ground for the widespread corruption of the inner city are themes explored by many Lost Generation writers. They were writers trying to come to terms with the implications of modernity, as exemplified by some of the more problematic Lost Generation works such as Nathanael West's 1933 novel *Miss Lonelyhearts*. That Marlowe suffers similar disillusionment is a notable indicator that Chandler's literature can be interpreted as being comparable with this particular form of protest writing.

Jerry Speir has noted that "the drive to render the struggle for heroism 'reasonable' in the face of certain death in a harsh world can be seen as the central impulse behind both Chandler as author and Marlowe as detective." He notes that the tensions which arise in the conflicting notions of "noble actions vs. a meaningless end" (82) are what finally define both Chandler's and Marlowe's melancholy and resignation. This struggle, whether it is Chandler's or Marlowe's, is to maintain an ethic—a code—which is rapidly becoming anachronistic (Speir 83) and is being rapidly eroded by the new ethic dictating that corporate profit must come before people, community, and compassion. A generation becomes "lost," according to Michael E. Parish, when "it believes itself to be cut off from the past and unconnected to the future" (184). A veteran's disillusionment and sense of dejection stem from the realization that individualism means isolation, where the sacrifices of the past count for nothing in the present; society simply does not care and is impermeable to the veteran's predicament; he is simply left on the wayside to cope as best he can. Speir argues that this is Marlowe's biggest downfall; the detective "is never able to achieve an understanding of himself as operating within a fallen world" (116). While this is a reasonably accurate summation, Marlowe certainly does acknowledge on many occasions that American society has let itself slide into immorality and corruption. In fact, he describes the decline of this "fallen world" in detail, highlighting the sensation of corruption that lingers throughout the city of Los Angeles. The city is a decaying den of iniquity that is described as symbolically having "the rotten sweetness of a prostitute" (*The Big Sleep* 15). As Ralph Willet says of Chandler's first novel: "General Sternwood's forest of orchids with their fleshy leaves and pungent odour [. . .] is an index of depravity" (22), and "the insidious taint of urban crime and malice [. . .] confronts the protagonist at every turn" (23). The areas outside Los Angeles, however, are described as being almost "Edenic." In contrast to the degenerating urban setting, the location for *The Lady in the Lake*, the fictional Little Fawn Lake, is likened to "a drop of dew caught in a curled leaf" (34).

In hindsight it is somewhat puzzling that Chandler, with all of his social awareness, failed to see the essential correlation between the plight of veterans and the expansion of rampant consumerism in the 1920s. In society, everything, including human labor power has been reduced to a commodity for sale on the market, with consumerism providing the ethos that encourages the consumer to satisfy a need or to gain an instant gratification, to then consume and then to discard. For the culture of continuous consumption to remain it is essential that consumer demand constantly increase, meaning that more and more goods must contain the features to bring about their own obsolescence. Society quickly adopts a mentality where everything is purchased to be thrown away after use and subsequently replaced. But the willingness to discard things had by the 1920s been extended to include human labor power: where the objectification of things that fuel consumerism is extended to include the objectification of people deemed to be surplus. Under these conditions it therefore appears quite normal that this compassionless approach should be applied to the veteran and to any other individual who is judged as being superfluous to society's immediate needs. In the same way that society does not think twice about discarding an item that is no longer needed, so society did not think twice about discarding the veteran; he had served his purpose and having outlived his usefulness was on hand to be cast aside and disregarded.

Society's fragmentation increasingly disturbed Chandler as it placed the accumulation of wealth and power above all else regardless of the consequences, and to the detriment of moral and ethical values. He used the decaying cityscape as a metaphor for the decline in social accountability, and with it, society's ignorance and renunciation of veterans. Those who have witnessed warfare are, according to Edward Tick, aware of the inferior social status heaped upon them by society and recognize the open stigmatization that "having been to hell and back, they are different." Society "expect[s] them to put war behind them and rejoin the ordinary flow of civilian life. But it is impossible for them to do so" (Tick 98). The negative attitudes that the veteran is compelled to endure exacerbate this feeling of rejection. To many veterans returning after the First World War, the country seemed dominated by unregulated free market capitalism that unleashed industrial mechanization which transformed work into drudgery. Michael Parish explains that this awareness stood in stark contrast to the social decadence that made it appear as though America had abandoned every remnant of morality and common compassion in favor of "a full blown, consumer-oriented economy" (x). He says, "In their first sustained experience with consumer culture, Americans learned the truth of the ancient poet Juvenal's observation that 'luxury is more ruthless than war.' A consumer society that sanctioned perpetual technological change, the generation of new fashions and desires, and the ultimate sovereignty of the market did not respect inherited values or the social status quo" (ibid.).

The decade following the First World War was a time when preexisting "bustling new wealth and dismal poverty" (Parish 30) became greatly accentuated as industrial unrest was largely crushed and capital finally triumphed over labor. With the exception of the extremely wealthy, who managed to salvage their fortunes before the Wall Street Crash, much of society's decadence was washed away by the economic crash of October 1929. As Parish has noted, it represented a "curtain call for flush times" (217). The Great Depression affected the entire country, and Chandler was not excluded from the misery. His dismissal from the Dabney Oil Company in in 1932 as a result of heavy drinking severely shocked him and taught him "not to take anything for granted" (Meador 145). However, rather than joining the millions of Americans who waited in "unemployment and bread lines, knocked on doors, applied for relief, sold apples, joined the Marines, hopped freight trains, hitchhiked toward any rumor of work, became prostitutes, begged, borrowed, or stole," Chandler was fortunate enough to be able to stay at home and write (Meador 144). Living on an extremely tight budget while learning his craft, he said later, "I never slept in the park, but I came damn close to it. I went five days without anything to eat but soup once . . . It didn't kill me, but neither did it increase my love of humanity." (qtd. in Meador 145–46). Rather surprisingly then, Chandler's hardships together with the dreadful destitution he saw about him "did not produce an anti-business bias in his writing, although the hypocrisies of the rich apparently rankled" (Meador 145). Instead Chandler exclusively reserved his bitterness and contempt for society as a whole and those who occupied the upper echelons in society in particular, whom he considered "phoney" (ibid.). As Marlowe says in *The Big Sleep*, "To hell with the rich. They make me sick" (66).

Documenting the city's mood in the aftermath of the Great Depression, Meador argues that "Chandler was not simply a Los Angeles resident. He was a scientist dissecting a native society and recording detailed notes. He classified the facts and resonances of Southern California with the precision of a cultural historian and anthropologist combined." Meador favorably compares the atmosphere of utter disillusionment expressed in *The Big Sleep* for example, to John Steinbeck's equally upsetting tone in *The Grapes of Wrath*. Believing that "[b]oth men are crusaders," Meador observes that "[w]hen Tom Joad says goodbye to Ma, telling her that he will be wherever there's a fight so hungry people can eat, it seems not implausible that Tom Joad, on the run, changes his name to Philip Marlowe and opens an office in Los Angeles" (151). Meador's point is interesting since it connects Chandler's work with some of the greatest works of the period. Not only does he observe the disillusioned affinity between Steinbeck and Chandler's novels, but Meador also places them alongside Nathanael West's *The Day of the Locust*; all of which were published in 1939. However, of these novels, Meador argues that *The Big Sleep* is by far the most popular because as a character, "Marlowe [. . .] encompass[es] the others and reach[es] out to new dimensions" (ibid.). As a result, *The Big Sleep* has, in his opinion, "established as permanent a toehold in American culture as Bogart's twitch" (ibid.).

Chandler's social attitude toward the accumulation of wealth, together with his profound distaste for opulence and rampant consumerism, remained with him for the rest of his life. He captured the essence of this increasingly divided society and the hypocrisy that lay behind it when he said critically in 1954:

> The country through its enormous talent for manufacture has worked itself into an economy of overproduction, which is probably a permanent economy. Half the world is starving, or at any rate badly underfed, yet we have to have a new refrigerator and a new automobile every year or so. If we don't, we feel inferior because we are made to feel inferior. The kind of economy we have can only continue to exist if there is an enormous artificial wastage of manufactured products. We get that kind of waste in war. In time of peace you have to try to create it artificially by advertising. (Qtd. in Gardiner and Walker 171)

This increasing depravity and the subsequent decline in standards of every description is a feature of capitalism that Marlowe vehemently resists, and he is resentful toward the effect of modernity and money upon the city's civic governance and its inhabitants. In *The Little Sister*, a novel that deals more freely with Marlowe's social hostility toward the effects of modernity than any of Chandler's other novels, and specifically Hollywood, he says, "California, the department-store state [. . .] More movie stars. More pink and blue bath-tubs. More tufted beds. More Chanel No. 5. More Lincoln Continentals and Cadillacs. More wind-blown hair and sunglasses and attitudes and pseudo-refined voices and waterfront morals" (79–80). Similarly, contrasting the pre- and postwar city Marlowe laments,

> I used to like this town [. . .] A long time ago. There were trees along Wilshire Boulevard. Beverly Hills was a country town. Westwood was bare hills and lots offering at eleven hundred dollars and no takers. Hollywood was a bunch of frame houses on the inter-urban line. Los Angeles was just a big dry sunny place with ugly homes and no style, but good hearted and peaceful [. . .] Now we've got the big money, the sharp shooters, the percentage workers, the fast dollar boys, the hoodlums out of New York and Chicago and Detroit—and Cleveland. We've got the flash restaurants and night clubs they run, and the hotels and apartment houses they own, and the grifters and con men and female bandits that live in them . . . the riff-raff of a big hard-boiled city with no more personality than a paper cup. Out in the fancy suburbs dear old Dad is reading the sports page in front of a picture window, with his shoes off, thinking he is high class because he has a three-car garage. Mom is in front of her princess dresser trying to paint the suitcases out from under her eyes. And junior is clamped on to the telephone calling up a succession of high-school girls that talk pidgin English and carry contraceptives in their make-up kit. (*The Little Sister* 181–82)

Marlowe is clearly able to distinguish the contrasting identities of pre- and postwar Los Angeles, suggesting that he has been away from the city for a long enough period to immediately feel an enmity toward an LA that he no longer knows. The war became a pivotal event for Marlowe because it heralded the advent of a *new* Los Angeles. He notes the contrast between prewar LA, in a time when he felt comfortable with the city, and the postwar environment of the 1940s. This passage from *The Little Sister* not only clearly shows that those differences bother the detective, but also that by this time the war had started to influence Chandler's writing as he began to imprint this aversion clearly onto his character.

With this point in mind, Ross Macdonald's assertion that writers portray aspects of themselves through their characters (*The Moving Target* 28) becomes extremely pertinent. It validates the contention that Philip Marlowe can be understood as a semipsychobiographical rendering of his creator and that Chandler consciously or otherwise imbued his detective with individual characteristics similar to his own.

TRACING MARLOWE'S LINEAGE

When tracing Marlowe's lineage it is interesting to note that although the detectives in Chandler's short stories project some of his own posttraumatic symptoms, his characters are not only connected to war by their behavior or psychology. The connection to war is far more explicit and can be traced through the development of the detectives themselves. As well as being recognized by their symptoms, it is also feasible to link the names Chandler gave certain detectives and correlate these names with Chandler's own experiences and influences. His various detectives—Mallory, Malvern, and Marlowe—each has specific connections to Chandler's background, to war, and to the notion of chivalry.

Philip Marlowe's character is the synthesis of a chivalric lineage that began with Chandler's first detective, Mallory. In Chandler's first two stories he gave his detective this name probably in veneration of Sir Thomas Malory and honoring his tales of *Le Morte d'Arthur*. His detective is epitomized by his romantic attitudes and chivalric codes that seem to flow directly from the tales of King Arthur and his gallant Knights of the Round Table. The knights' virtues are a fair summation of the moral code that Chandler gave to his fictional detectives. Chandler had studied Shakespeare, Addison, and Milton at Dulwich, and had a deep appreciation of English literature, which MacShane argues, "helped mold his own character" (*Life* 9) and which he would later bestow on his detective creations. Chandler cherished the education he had received at Dulwich, particularly in the classics, and this helps explain why his detective has been perceived as a modern-day knight. The knight's code is one of fearlessness and honor through self-sacrifice, and it would have been natural that in a number of the stories and novels Chandler's detectives would be powerfully drawn to the knightly symbols they encounter during their investigations. These scenes conjure up the pageantry of medieval quests of courage and heroism, which are regularly included in Chandler's short stories and later transposed directly into his novels. In the short story "The Curtain," for example, detective Carmady notices "several suits of time-darkened armour on pedestals of dark wood. High over the huge marble fireplace hung two bullet-torn—or moth eaten—cavalry pennants crossed in a glass case, and below them the painted likeness of a thin, spry-looking man with a black beard and moustachios and full regimentals of about the time of the Mexican War" (qtd. in *Killer in the Rain* 110). In another example, from *The Big Sleep,* while calling at General Sternwood's mansion Marlowe notices "a broad stained-glass panel showing a knight in dark armour rescuing a lady who was tied to a tree and didn't have any clothes on but some very long and convenient hair" (9). In keeping with the chivalric side of his character, Marlowe exclaims: "The knight had pushed the visor of his helmet back to be sociable, and he was fiddling with the knots on the ropes that tied the lady to the tree and not getting anywhere. I stood there and thought that if I lived in the house, I would sooner or later have to climb up there and help him. He didn't seem to be really trying" (ibid.). This chivalric motif can also be seen in many of the surnames of Chandler's characters surnames, such as Orrin and Orfamay *Quest* in *The Little Sister*, and Mr. and Mrs. Lewin Lockridge *Grayle* in *Farewell, My Lovely*. The fact that Mrs. Grayle turns out to be the missing woman Marlowe has been searching for conjures vivid resonances with the mythic search for the Holy Grail.

At school Chandler would have undoubtedly been influenced by the English literature of the time. One possible influence, extremely popular in England at the turn of the century, may have been W. S. Symonds's *Malvern Chase*. Originally published in 1881, it is a romantic novel set in Herefordshire during the War of the Roses. The characters and surroundings were described vividly and evocatively with the intention of stimulating interest in the area's history and traditions which had become all but extinct. The idealism depicted in this type of classic English literature would have appealed greatly to Chandler, and it is quite conceivable that his character Ted Malvern was named in reverence to Symonds's novel. Like Chandler's novels, this passage from *Malvern Chase* almost has a duality about it: "The companions of his youth are borne to the grave with every passing year, and drop like autumn leaves into their mother earth. But with all this, often [. . .] I have slumbered in a sleeping as I rested under a broad bank by a burnside, and dear old faces have come back, and old familiar voices have been again eloquent, faces which are now dust, and voices which have long been silent" (336). As well as exhibiting a romanticism that would have appealed to Chandler, this work also has overtones of disillusionment that would later become a powerful theme running through Chandler's own work. The references to "dear old faces" and "old familiar voices" that have "long been silent" also resonate with memory and loss.

By taking as his inspiration the popular classical literature of the time, it is likely that Chandler was stirred into naming his most famous detective, the "shop soiled Galahad" (*The High Window* 214), Philip Marlowe. Critics have often attributed the surname to Marlowe House, named for the playwright Christopher Marlowe, at Dulwich College where Chandler was educated

(Hiney 99). However, the House system at Dulwich was introduced only in 1919, fourteen years after Chandler had left the College. As such, it is highly unlikely that the detective was named after Marlowe House.

Despite this, however, there is a direct link between Dulwich College itself and the ill-fated Christopher Marlowe. It is believed that the original seventeenth-century founder of the college, Edward Alleyn, created Dulwich as a direct result of Marlowe's 1590s play, *The Tragical History of Doctor Faustus*. According to Dulwich legend, after hearing that the play's satanic content had apparently driven many of its spectators mad, Alleyn, the lead actor of the drama company the Admiral's Men, who had performed *Doctor Faustus*, devoted his life to charitable enterprises. One of these charitable enterprises was Dulwich College. However, given Chandler's passion for classical literature there are two other possible explanations for naming his protagonist, Philip Marlowe.

A more likely scenario was that Chandler chose the name from an amalgamation of Philip Sidney and Christopher Marlowe—two English Renaissance writers he admired—that together represented the characteristics he wanted for his fictional hero. Sidney struck a characteristically Renaissance pose of studied intelligence, and his style, like Chandler's, was one of someone extremely clever, with a well-developed sense of humor, who wrote fluently and often with a very light touch. Sidney appears to have been considered by the Elizabethan court as the very epitome of chivalry. He was an exemplar of the ideal courtier but also a man of contradictions: learned, astute, and generous but also naturally impulsive and brave. Christopher Marlowe was not only a notable writer, but is also thought to have been a spy for the British government, potentially one removed from a private detective.

It is certainly feasible that Chandler named his detective after two of the best-known Renaissance writers of the sixteenth century. He would have undoubtedly been aware of Sydney's and Marlowe's importance in English literature, and Marlowe's poem "Accurs'd Be He That First Invented War!" (1587) would have taken on a much greater significance after his experiences during the First World War. As the first monologue of part 1, act 2, scene 4 shows:

Accurs'd be he that first invented war!
They knew not, ah, they knew not, simple men,
How those were hit by pelting cannon shot
Stand staggering like a quivering aspen-leaf
Fearing the force of Boreas' boisterous blasts! (Qtd. in Pendry 23)

This supposition is even more plausible when we consider how some characters react to the detective in the novels. For example, in *The Long Goodbye*, when introduced to a woman at a party, Marlowe's name illicits the following response:

> "Ah, Marlowe," she intoned. "Such a sad beautiful name." She put her glass down damn nearly empty and closed her eyes and threw her head back and her arms out, almost hitting me in the eye. Her voice throbbed with emotion, saying:
>
> "*Was this the face that launch'd a thousand ships*
> *And burnt the topless towers of Ilium?*
> *Sweet Helen, make me immortal with a kiss.*" (153)

These words are taken directly from Marlowe's play *Doctor Faustus* and not only show Chandler's appreciation for his classical sense of poetry, but again reinforce the connection between Chandler and Christopher Marlowe.

A second possible explanation is that Chandler was influenced by certain elements in the work of other writers. There is much to suggest that Joseph Conrad especially influenced Chandler in a number of ways, having used both a first-person narrative and also a protagonist called Marlow in his novel *The Heart of Darkness* (1902), which chronicled the effects of European colonialism in Africa. But while Conrad's Marlow lived literally in the jungle, Chandler created his own metaphorical jungle for Philip Marlowe on the streets of Los Angeles. Peter J. Rabinowitz has noted the similarities between the two characters by observing that both Conrad and Chandler "tell of idealists whose adventures seem destined to bring them in contact with some kind of truth, but who in fact find only a hollowness and a horror" (235). On his adventures, Conrad's protagonist does not turn away from exposure to murderous horror; he is instead fascinated by it in much the same way as Chandler's Philip Marlowe is keen to expose the same horror on the "mean streets" of Los Angeles. However, Rabinowitz continues, "both these lovers of truth learn that the only way to deal with the horrors they have exposed is to bury it once again with a lie, a lie that leaves the hero perhaps wiser, but also more bitter; and a lie that leaves the evil fundamentally untouched" (ibid.). These lost causes further add to the sense of frustration that is evident in Chandler's novels. Herman has argued that "[t]he ordinary response to atrocities is to banish them from consciousness [. . .] Certain violations of the social compact are too terrible to utter aloud" (1). Yet by continually burying the horrors they attempt to exorcise through their honorable actions, they are compounding their symptoms further. This is part of the endless cycle associated with the psychological trauma of PTSD. As Gabriel noted, if emotions are continually buried "deep in the soldiers psyche . . . the overt manifestations become symptoms of deeper symptoms of even deeper underlying causes" (qtd. in Grossman 48).

While Chandler joked that he had used a process of "cannibalization"[4] to create the Marlowe novels, this notion is far too simplistic because, as Jerry Speir has noted, the short stories exhibit "considerable experimentation in subject matter, style, point of view, and detective types" (145). Writing in 1950 Chandler stated that, "although he wasn't called Marlowe until *The Big Sleep*, he certainly had his genesis in two or three of the novelettes; and he probably hadn't changed any more relatively between say, *Finger Man* and *The High Window* than he will have changed between *Finger Man* and the next one I turn out" (qtd. in Gardiner and Walker 226). This genesis is reflected in the fact that four of Chandler's short story detectives were renamed Philip Marlowe for later publications. These were Mallory in "Blackmailer's Don't Shoot," the unnamed detective in "Finger Man," Ted Carmady in "Goldfish," and Johnny Dalmas in "Red Wind."

When writing his short stories Chandler adopted a definite style and developed fictional characters whose temperaments he felt comfortable with. His character needed to be someone he could not only relate to but also depend on. In this way Philip Marlowe became burdened with his creator's psychological scarring, emerging as Chandler's embodiment of himself still fighting meaningful battles but assigned to a different location.

Jerry Speir has used Chandler's own words to create a convincing context to examine the reasoning behind the writer's work, and also one by which we can reconsider Chandler's short stories and novels as a literature of traumatic experience. Speir notes that Chandler maintained the conviction that "the best way to comment on the large things is to comment on the small things" (viii), by which he meant character and language. By "concentrating on the motives of individual characters," Speir argued, Chandler "approaches larger themes such as the unpredictability of human emotion under pressure and the manner in which changing times appear to alter one's ethical possibilities" (viii). These themes are crucial to understanding the literature that Chandler produced. Chandler had witnessed firsthand the unpredictability of humans under pressure from his experience during the First World War and incorporated it into his work. Even in his later life this was still something that deeply affected him, and as Hiney has noted, the "gut wrenching" nature of many of Chandler's short stories can be considered gory even by today's standards. An example is the following excerpt from "Bay City Blues," published by *Dime Detective Magazine* (1938):

> Big Chin's face was a mass of blood [. . .] His hands were free and what the kick to his groin had done to him was long ago, on the far side of oceans and pain. He made a croaking noise and turned his left hip suddenly against De Spain and went down on his right knee and lunged for the gun.
>
> De Spain kicked him in the face [. . .] He twisted the foot quickly, with both hands. Big Chin's body seemed to leap in the air and dive sideways, and his shoulder and face smashed into the ground, but De Spain held onto the foot. He kept on turning it [. . . and] gave the foot a sudden hard wrench. Big Chin screamed like a dozen sheets tearing. (Qtd. in *Killer in the Rain* 292)

Here, as elsewhere in his work, Chandler uses powerful imagery that leaves the reader in no doubt of the degree of pain and the extent of the injuries suffered. It is extremely suggestive of his own experiences of war, which implanted a brutal realism into his stories that left little to the imagination.

Because the short stories were the precursors to the novels and had yet to undergo any form of "cannibalization" they provide explicit wartime contexts through subtle character dialogue and plot ideas. In "Pearls Are a Nuisance" (1939), for example, Chandler uses a wartime context as the background for the story. When discussing a missing pearl necklace, the fiancée of amateur detective Walter Gage notes how the heirloom was "made in Bohemia [. . .] and *the way things are going over there now*, [the owner] might never be able to get another set of really good imitations" (qtd. in *The Smell of Fear* 57. Emphasis added). Furthermore, in "No Crime in the Mountains" (1941) the entire plot revolves around a German-Japanese plan to produce and spread counterfeit currency in California to fund the work of the Nazis in Central and South America.

Chandler also introduced characters that were physically affected by war. In "The Lady in the Lake" (1939) Chandler introduces a veteran character with a notable war injury "copped [. . .] in France" (qtd. in *Killer in the Rain* 333). Chandler contrasts this image of the wounded veteran with a sheriff who believes that "veterans give themselves too many privileges in my opinion. Some of 'em did three weeks in a camp and act like they was wounded nine times" (qtd. in *Killer in the Rain* 348). While this remark could be interpreted as an attempt to chastise those among the Lost Generation who had unduly embellished their wartime experience, it is also suggestive of the view Chandler held of his own war experience. It hints at the frustrations of someone who had spent only three months in combat and had been left with the deep-seated emotion that he had been denied a sense of heroic privilege that so many men had sought. The war ended too soon for some, and as Malcolm Cowley noted, many "would never know whether or not they were brave men. Some were ashamed of being unmedaled and unwounded" (12).

The influence of Chandler's experiences during the First World War is therefore evident in the progression and development of Chandler's fictional detective, and its effects were not something easily shaken off. As Kardiner and Spiegel noted, during warfare,

> the whole apparatus for concerted, co-ordinated and purposeful activity is smashed. The perceptions become inaccurate and pervaded with terror, the co-ordinative functions of judgment and discrimination fail [. . .] the sense organs may even cease to function [. . .] The aggressive impulses become disorganized and unrelated to the situation in hand [. . .] The functions of the autonomic nervous system may also become disassociated with the rest of the organism. (186)

Tick believes that combat veterans often remain immersed in the imagery and emotion of war for years afterward and sometimes for their entire lives (1). As detective Carmady confesses in "Goldfish," "The quiet of the house made ghosts in my brain, ghosts of a lot of years ago" (qtd. in *The Smell of Fear* 459). Chandler's detectives clearly understand the imagery and emotion of war through their recognition and acceptance of death and its unpleasantness. Philip Marlowe, in particular, is completely unperturbed by the sight of a corpse and in almost every novel is quick to recognize the unmistakable "harsh, sharp bitter smell" (*The High Window* 73) of death, which he says is "not quite like any other smell" (*The Lady in the Lake* 104). Chandler is very precise with his choice of words to conjure up the imagery of the "horrible, sickening" and "pungent" (*The Lady in the Lake* 53, 104) smell of decomposition. In *The High Window*, upon discovering the body of Louis Vannier, Marlowe notes how, in "the air of the room a rather heavy perfume struggled with the smell of death, and lost" (219). But the smell of decomposition is unmistakable to only those who have spent some time close to a corpse. Life on the front line brought with it the inescapable reality of death and enduring images of a landscape strewn with dead and decomposing bodies. It is likely that these visions and smells remained with Chandler for the rest of his life, and it is details such as these, however small and seemingly insignificant, that reinforce the notion that Chandler transplanted his own experiences into the Marlowe novels.

Chandler's descriptions of fatal injuries are exceptionally graphic, as shown in *Farewell, My Lovely* when Marlowe put into words the grim sight of Lindsay Marriott's beaten body: "He lay smeared to the ground, on his back, at the base of a bush [. . .] His face was a face I had never seen before. His hair was dark with blood [. . .] and some thick greyish ooze, like primeval slime [. . .] I held the light on his face. He had been beaten to a pulp. One of his hands was flung out in a frozen gesture, the fingers curled [. . .] There was a trickle as black as dirty oil at the corner of his mouth" (65). The description of a female corpse in *The Lady in the Lake* is equally disturbing: "The thing rolled over once more and an arm flapped up barely above the skin of the water and the arm ended in a bloated hand that was the hand of a freak. Then the face came. A swollen pulpy grey white mass without features, without eyes, without mouth. A blotch of grey dough, a nightmare with human hair [. . .]" (48).

Chandler had a special ability to perfectly describe the anatomical features of a lifeless corpse, and in every novel Marlowe is drawn instinctively to the unresponsive eyes of a lifeless body. In *The Big Sleep*, when he eventually rediscovers the body of Arthur Geiger he notes, "His eyes were almost closed, but not entirely" (102). Upon locating Chris Lavery after he is shot to death in *The Lady in the Lake*, Marlowe says, "His eyes had a curiously bright and expectant look, as if he smelled the morning coffee and would be coming right out" (104). After Roger Wade's supposed suicide in *The Long Goodbye* Marlowe says, "I bent over him, peering at the edge of the wide-open eye [. . .]" (215). And also in *The Little Sister* the detective says of Orrin Quest, "He had eyes an eighth of an inch deep, pale gray-blue, wide open. They looked at me but didn't see me" (151). Marlowe's description of the varying "appearances" of death—eyes partially closed, the look of surprise upon a face, the unseeing stare—is indicative of the traumatic imprint of witnessing sudden death at close quarters.

Marlowe's fascination with eyes, however, may have an alternate interpretation. His captivation with the eyes of a corpse may be an extension of the interest he has in the eyes of everyone he meets, especially those of male characters. Although his fascination with the eyes of men has been construed as a sign of Marlowe's supposed homosexuality, when the detective comments upon a character's eyes he presents a striking and almost comforting comparison between the emptiness of death and the vivacity of life he sees in those around him. It suggests that while he accepts the finality of death, Marlowe appreciates the enthusiasm and zeal he sees in the eyes of others.

It is evident that Chandler makes these gruesomely real observations from his own experience. Because the eyes and face tend to show the initial signs of death most clearly, it explains why a former soldier would naturally be drawn to these first. In *The Big Sleep,* Marlowe notes how Owen Taylor's "face was bluish white and his eyes were a faint dull gleam under the lowered lids and his mouth had sand in it" (50). The corpse of Muriel Chess/Mildred Haviland is subjected to similar scrutiny in *The Lady in the Lake*: "There were dark bruises on her throat. Her mouth was open and a swollen tongue filled it to overflowing. Her eyes bulged and the whites of them were not white" (191). While these descriptions appear exaggerated, and at times seem to dwell on the grisly detail, they come from a mind that had been etched with images of death and carnage. In *Farewell, My Lovely*, for example, Marlowe says, "I thought of dead eyes looking at a moonless sky, with black blood at the corners of the mouths beneath them" (206). Although Marlowe says this in reference to the death of Lindsay Marriott, his words have a weight of knowledge behind them. Chandler's use of the plural (eye*s*, mouth*s*) is suggestive of something far larger than Marriott's murder; Marlowe's words could almost have come straight from a war poem. Although hard-boiled detective fiction is known for its embellished and brutal descriptions, the vividness of Chandler's scenes delivers authenticity into a form of literature not always known for its realistic and lifelike depictions.

In Chandler's novels his detectives all "exhibit some degree of alienation [. . . and] all are committed to high ideals against great odds" (Speir 94), battling a world of madness and mayhem passing for normalcy. It is well known that Chandler used many of his short stories as the basis for his later novels, and initially this process worked well, with *The Big Sleep* finished in only three months. *The Lady in the Lake*, however, took much longer, and it was almost four years before it was completed, mainly, as Speir notes, due to "disturbances in the world and within Chandler's own life; the war, for example, was a powerful distraction" (86). Speir contends that the motif of "Appearance vs. Reality" (100) becomes an increasingly relevant aspect of Chandler's detective because he created a character that *appears* to be a hero, yet in *reality* is the opposite. It is only in the Marlowe novels that the essentials of Chandler's style achieve their maturity. The difference is due, in the main, to his use of "space to allow for dramatic and character development, . . . to get away from the requisite, lavish devotion to plot [. . . and create] the voice of Marlowe who, though he may appear in the stories as a prototype, is only realised completely in the longer works" (Speir 104). Unlike his short stories, Chandler's novels leave a lasting impression upon the reader because they evoke an understanding for Marlowe's traumatic past. Edward Tick argues that by returning to war in one's own imagination, it is quite possible for the mind to reemerge with a new perception of one's identity, which is generally understood as an attempt to alter the outcome of the original event (198). What makes Chandler's work so engaging is that it appeals on two different levels. On the one hand, it appeals to readers who wish for realism in the often gruesome depictions of crimes in a genre that was known for its tough guys and violence. Yet, on the other hand, it appeals to those who seek a sense of order and justice through an individual psychological framework.

Although Chandler conceded that the character of the private eye was an exaggeration, he also believed that Marlowe was "at least [. . .] an exaggeration of the possible" (qtd. in Gardiner and Walker 60). He believed that the popularity of the murder and crime novel had a psychological foundation that had never been fully considered. In 1943 he argued, "There is a lot more to this subject than most people realize [. . .] [I]t is just possible that the tensions in a novel of murder are the simplest and yet most complete pattern of the tensions in which we live in this generation" (qtd. in Hiney and MacShane 95).

Chandler's writing came to fruition with the creation of Marlowe. Yet, despite this fact, Marlowe's background and character justification have long been shrouded in mystery. Chandler divulges very little about his character's past, providing only hints for the reader to follow. On a basic level the information Chandler provides relates to Marlowe's appearance:

> No visible scars. Hair dark brown, some grey. Eyes brown. Height six feet, one-half inch. Name, Philip Marlowe, Occupation, private detective [. . .] I have some nice inlays and one very high-class porcelain jacket crown. Eighty-seven dollars' worth of porcelain jacket crown . . . up my nose . . . A lot of scar tissue in there for you. Septum operation and was that guy a butcher! [. . .] I got it playing football [. . .] a slight miscalculation in an attempt to block a punt. I blocked the guy's foot instead—after he kicked the ball. (*The Long Goodbye* 46)

Intriguingly Chandler gave Marlowe a physical imperfection similar to his own. While at Dulwich, Chandler's nose "was broken during [. . . a] rugby game" (Hiney 16). Chandler likewise gave Marlowe a broken nose, an injury sustained as a result of a football game, the American equivalent of the traditionally English game of rugby. Hiney suggests that his broken nose gave Chandler a tough look, and it is logical the writer would have wanted Marlowe to have the same distinction. In *Farewell, My Lovely*, for example, Marlowe draws specific attention to his "battle-scarred frown" (84), suggesting a face that is imperfect and tough.

In the same quotation Chandler makes reference to Marlowe's past sporting prowess by suggesting that he had played football. Similar clues regarding Marlowe's past are found in further passages from two other novels. First, in *The Big Sleep*, Marlowe notes: "I'm thirty-three years old, went to college once and can still speak English if there's any demand for it. There isn't much in my trade. I worked for Mr. Wilde, the District Attorney, as an investigator once . . . I'm unmarried because I don't like policemen's wives [. . .] I was fired. For insubordination. I test very high on insubordination" (15). To this, he adds in *The Long Goodbye*,

> I'm a licensed private investigator and have been for quite a while. I'm a lone wolf, unmarried, getting middle-aged, and not rich. I've been in jail more than once and I don't do divorce business. I like liquor and women and chess and a few other things. The cops don't like me too well, but I know a couple I get along with. I'm a native son of Santa Rosa, both parents dead, no brothers or sisters [. . .]. (79)

In April 1951 Chandler revealed further details of Marlowe's education to his English correspondent D. J. Ibberson. In the letter Chandler divulged what he believed his character's background might be, although these details were never disclosed in the novels or confirmed in any other correspondence. Chandler states that Marlowe "has a couple of years of college, either at the University of Oregon at Eugene, or Oregon State University at Corvallis, Oregon" (qtd. in Hiney and MacShane 227). It is known that both after his return from the war and also later in his life Chandler spent time in the Pacific Northwest, and may have taken inspiration for Marlowe's university life from his travels.

While it is impossible to deduce what subjects Marlowe may have studied at college, the information Marlowe himself reveals certainly makes it possible to speculate. It is feasible that he studied subjects that relate either to law or to literature. From his own self-description we know he was an investigator for a district attorney, a job that would have required Marlowe to have previous law enforcement experience. His primary duty would have been to provide prosecutorial support in the form of locating and processing prosecution witnesses and conducting additional pretrial investigations.

Marlowe has detailed knowledge of a number of literary works, which suggests that he is widely read and knowledgeable in the subject. In *The Long Goodbye* for instance, Marlowe shows an understanding of the difficulty in writing good literature when he says to Roger Wade, "[It] depends on who the writer is, maybe [. . .] It didn't come easy to Flaubert, and his stuff is good." To which Wade replies, "Okay [. . .] So you've read Flaubert, and that makes you an intellectual, a critic, a savant of the literary world" (148). Marlowe also makes reference to Hemingway in *Farewell, My Lovely.* After detective Galbraith repeats Marlowe's words, the detective begins calling Galbraith "Hemingway." He says "Listen, Hemingway, don't repeat everything I say" (140). Once he had provoked Galbraith sufficiently for Galbraith to ask, "Who is this Hemingway person at all?" Marlowe replies, "A guy that keeps saying the same thing over and over until you begin to believe it must be good" (143). That Marlowe believes Hemingway's work to be repetitious complements Chandler's own opinion of the writer later in his life. In letters to Blanch Knopf, the wife of his publisher Alfred Knopf, he referred to "Hemingway and his eternal sleeping bag" as "pretty damn tiresome" (qtd. in MacShane, *Letters* 23). Despite his great admiration for the writer, Chandler argued that one of Hemingway's biggest problems was that "[n]inety per cent of it is the goddamnest self-imitation. He never really wrote but one story. All the rest is the same thing in different pants—or without pants. And his eternal preoccupation with what goes on between the sheets becomes rather nauseating in the end" (qtd. in MacShane, *Letters* 72).

As well as Flaubert and Hemingway, there is also reference to T. S. Eliot. In *The Long Goodbye* Marlowe is driven to meet the imposing Harlan Potter, father of the murdered Sylvia Lennox. He says: "I went on out and Amos had the Caddy there waiting. He drove me back to Hollywood. I offered him a buck but he wouldn't take it. I offered to buy him the poems of T. S. Eliot. He said he already had them" (201). Chandler also makes an extremely revealing reference to William Shakespeare in *Farewell, My Lovely*. After being beaten and drugged, Marlowe makes his way to the house of Anne Riordan, one of the few women the detective trusts. Her reaction to the sight of Marlowe is obvious:

> The door opened wide and Miss Anne Riordan stood there in a pale green slack suit looking at me. Her eyes went wide and scared. Her face under the glare of the porchlight was suddenly pale.
>
> "My God," she wailed. "You look like Hamlet's father!" (160).

Chandler's reference to King Hamlet's ghost provides masterful imagery of Anne's horrified reaction to Marlowe's appearance. Her description of the detective not only gives us a startling visual description of the detective's pale and haggard visage, but it is also suggestive of Marlowe's psychological condition at the time. Marlowe's belief throughout the novels is that the society in which he lives is unappreciative and corrupt, and he has been left feeling invisible; he says earlier in the novel: "I was a blank man. I had no face" (*The Little Sister* 177). Marlowe almost sees himself as an apparition, a shadow of his former self who believes his self-sacrifice has been for nothing and has been left feeling like "a grain of sand on the desert of oblivion" (*The Long Goodbye* 201). Like Hamlet, Meador observes that Marlowe "occupies a world badly out of joint and has the nontransferrable duty to set it right" (151). "Chandler," Meador argues, "knew his detective-crusader could not win, at least not permanently [. . .] but he keeps trying to make it happen [. . .]" (152). Chandler's use of a Shakespearean character in such a way supports the sense of literary realization in Marlowe. Moreover, by using such stark symbolism it also points to the psychological torment Marlowe endures through each of his investigations.

Marlowe is therefore not the typical hard-boiled detective. He hides a deeply disguised anguish that cannot simply be attributed to the circumstances he finds himself in or the people he meets. His strict adherence to a rigid ethical code, as well as the possible origins of his name, implies Chandler's deep desire to present the detective as an icon of chivalry who has been severely ravaged by combat and has the distinctive characteristics of a veteran. His imperfect character carries troubling effects of warfare on his personality, and he is plagued with the symptoms of trauma that are the outcome of a harrowing war experience. Although he functions quite normally, he is nonetheless a haunted man plagued by past events that have left his world disordered. His capacity for meaningful relationships has been eroded to include only those who are either similarly broken or persons who understand his psychological condition. His traumatic past forces him to view those outside this small circle with disdain. It is only with other veterans that he feels truly comfortable.

While Marlowe may consider aspects of his investigations as a chivalric quest, his psychological condition and repeated rejection force him to realign himself and drive him to the inevitable disappointing conclusion. Marlowe's complex character encapsulates the dichotomy of the knight and the traumatized war veteran, suggesting that the widely accepted idea of Marlowe's chivalric and knightly persona may not have been Chandler's original intention when he created Philip Marlowe.

5

THE PHILIP MARLOWE NOVELS

There's no tragedy, no real sorrow, just a flat emptiness.
—HANK BRUTON, "A COUPLE OF WRITERS," QTD. IN GARDINER AND WALKER

While critics have postulated numerous theories concerning the key themes and issues that have shaped the character of the hard-boiled detective—race, gender, sexuality, class, politics—few, if any, of these theories acknowledge that there are characters that simply do not fit the traditional mold of the macho detective. Neither do these theories acknowledge the impact of war upon the style and characterization of American private eyes. By reevaluating the significance of Chandler's combat experience it is clear that the First World War had a profound effect upon the author's emotional stability and, consequently, upon all aspects of his life and work. This shift of focus—from a chivalric knight to a traumatized soldier—significantly alters the way in which Chandler and his work can be viewed because it not only exposes the depth of trauma suffered by the author, but also shows how the effects of his experiences are reflected in the characters and works he created. Chandler's emotional state was increasingly erratic and introverted, and he believed that writers "drain their hearts and souls to write at all and therefore become introspective" (qtd. in Gardiner and Walker 10). In a society that, at the time, did not recognize or understand the devastating effect of war upon a person's mind, Chandler's salvation came in the form of writing. The symptoms of PTSD that he suffered intruded into almost every aspect of his work. Philip Marlowe, in effect, acted as Chandler's sounding board and someone he could take strength from. The detective became a catharsis to alleviate Chandler's stress and someone he could pour all his thoughts, emotions, and traumas into. Although there are only seven Marlowe novels to draw upon, Chandler's books are significant not only because they highlight the troubled nature of his detective, but they also provide a context for our understanding of the veteran's reception in society. Through his protagonist Chandler transferred his trauma onto the page in an attempt to relieve his physical and psychological posttraumatic symptoms and in doing so became a witness to history by interpreting the society around him. Consequently, Marlowe came to personify the image of an antihero, and Chandler's trauma became his detective's trauma.

As with chapter 1, which discussed the peculiarities of Chandler's personality and argued that when considered collectively the symptoms of severe emotional stress begin to emerge, so too can the same be realized for Philip Marlowe. When taken in isolation some may argue that many of the character traits described in this chapter could be interpreted simply as the behavior of a downtrodden detective. But when we consider them collectively they begin to display a distinct pattern of behavior, and it becomes apparent that Marlowe's persona displays distinct similarities to that of his creator. Utilizing the Marlowe novels, this chapter highlights a number of personality traits from across the range of texts to focus on the distinct idiosyncrasies of a war-traumatized veteran.

In order to more precisely capture each of the different aspects of Chandler's work, this chapter has been split into two separate, but interrelated, sections, each exploring a different facet of the Marlowe novels in relation to postcombat trauma and the particular influences that were projected by Chandler onto his protagonist. The first section focuses upon the psychological basis of PTSD and the symptoms that are witnessed in Chandler's protagonist Philip Marlowe. Drawing upon the Marlowe novels specifically, this section uncovers the symptoms that plagued Chandler and were subsequently encoded onto his detective. The second section explores how Chandler moved his theater of war from the trenches of northern France to the urban environment of Los Angeles, considering how he substitutes the carnage of physical combat for the metaphor of the chessboard and the "knightly" quest for justice.

THE PHILIP MARLOWE NOVELS

Raymond Chandler's war experience encoded his protagonists with the distinctive behavioral traits and emotional distress which are unmistakable markers of combat-related PTSD. The behavioral characteristics of the war veteran Hank Bruton in Chandler's 1951 short story "A Couple of Writers" and his detective Philip Marlowe are alike because they both suffer from, and have their origins in, the trauma of military combat. In order to formulate such authentic depictions Chandler would have certainly suffered from those same troubling posttraumatic symptoms. Only by suffering the effects of warfare would he have been able to imbue his characters with the intimate mannerisms of a traumatized veteran.

As noted previously, Bruton and Marlowe's most noticeable trait, and that of veterans in general, is their disillusionment with society. In much the same way as Judith Freeman describes Marlowe as having "the spirit of the man who wins and yet never really wins, because the forces he opposes never really go away" (71), so the same can equally apply to Bruton. However, the estrangement experienced by Chandler's characters manifests itself not only in their attitudes towards others, but is also evident in their attitude toward mortality and death. Bruton's preoccupation with death for instance, is very similar to Philip Marlowe's disillusionment and gloom at the end of *The Big Sleep.* In the final pages of the novel even nature has lost its vitality and appears sinister and corrupt. As Marlowe says, "Outside the bright gardens had a haunted look, as though small wide eyes were watching me from behind the bushes, as though the sunshine itself had a mysterious something in its light" (220). At the end of *The Big Sleep* Peter Rabinowitz has noted that Marlowe "contemplates the meaning of death and decides that this world is so ugly that death can only be seen as a liberation" (240). It is an outlook that is captured in much of Chandler's early romantic prewar poetry and a perspective that often haunts the detective throughout the novels. Marlowe's experiences have given him an attitude toward death that was similar to Chandler's: he accepts its inevitability and accepts the knowledge that one day he too will cease to exist. He even jokes with Mona Mars about funeral arrangements, stating that once he is dead he won't care for pomp or mourners: "Just a plain pine box . . . Don't bother with bronze or silver handles. And don't scatter my ashes over the blue pacific. I like the worms better" (*The Big Sleep* 184).

The detective's almost nonchalant attitude toward death is most prominently displayed in *The Big Sleep* when he faces the dead body of Harry Jones, poisoned by cyanide and now "beyond fear, beyond change" (174). This demonstrates the most chilling aspect of Marlowe's character. While eavesdropping on a discussion between Lash Canino and Jones, Marlowe overhears the gangster threatening Jones, who once described Canino as "tough like some guys think they are tough [. . .] He'd bump a guy off between drinks" (*The Big Sleep* 162). After discovering the two in Jones's office, Marlowe realizes that the "little man" (*The Big Sleep* 169) will not survive the encounter once Canino has the information he requires. But because Marlowe is also seeking the same information, he remains silent as the hoodlum poisons the unsuspecting Jones with cyanide. Marlowe's lack of intervention in Jones's death is calculating and indifferent because it suits his own motivations, and he effectively allows Jones to be sacrificed.

Jones himself also realizes that the situation he is in is extremely precarious and knowing Canino's character, surely comprehends that he is in grave danger. But rather than capitulate to the gangster's threats, he remains tragically defiant, an act that, despite his good intentions, results in his death. Acting in a noble manner reminiscent of Marlowe, Jones refuses to divulge information regarding his client even under duress. He is willing to put his own life at risk to protect the whereabouts of Agnes Lozelle, a vital witness in the case of Rusty Regan's disappearance. By giving Canino false information he commits an act of heroism that saves his client but ultimately proves fatal. After Marlowe discovers Jones's body, the detective shows no remorse for his nonintervention, but instead exhibits the utmost respect for Jones's deception of Canino and the protection of his client. He says, "Well, you fooled him Harry [. . .] You lied to him and you drank your cyanide like a gentleman. You died like a poisoned rat, Harry, but you're no rat to me" (*The Big Sleep* 173).

At the end of *The Big Sleep*, Marlowe's unemotional view of death deepens as he considers, "What did it matter where you lay once you were dead?" His conclusion is that whether it is "[i]n a dirty sump or in a marble tower on top of a high hill . . . You were dead, you were sleeping the big sleep, you were not bothered by things like that. Oil and water were the same as wind and air to you. You just slept the big sleep, not caring about the nastiness of how you died or where you fell" (220). It is no coincidence that Bruton and Marlowe share a similar attitude toward death. Yet, their view appears to differ from Chandler's personal beliefs regarding his own mortality. While Marlowe does not appear religious and consequently has a straightforward attitude toward death, Chandler's attitudes are suggestive of someone who was caught in a religious dilemma. Although he considered death to be a permanent termination of life and did not believe in any form of afterlife, Chandler certainly believed in God and the notion of salvation. Admitting that he had an "antipathy to dogmas," he showed the stark contrast in his personal faith when he wrote in 1957, "I am one of those who do not believe in personal immortality, since I see no need for it [. . .] God probably finds something to preserve, but what I don't know" (qtd. in MacShane, *Letters* 420).

Believing in God but not in Heaven or Hell, Chandler instead appears to have craved a sense of comfort from the notion of faith. Having little belief in Heaven or Hell is a consequence of war that many soldiers tend to suffer from. Once soldiers have experienced battle they can become extremely disillusioned by the idea of religion. Failing to comprehend what they have witnessed, their experiences "undermine the belief systems that give meaning to human experience" (Herman 51). War violates any sense of faith in a natural or divine order and can cast the victim into a state of existential crisis (ibid.). Chandler believed that a person's earthly qualities and sense of spirit were the attributes God considered worth preserving and reasoned that because of the way a person's experiences shape his or her life and attitude, whether good or bad, they diluted a person's sense of purity. He said: "[God] might find even in me, a sensual, sardonic, cynical man, some essence worth preserving, but I don't think it is anything I could recognize. So much of us is external, environmental, caused by our experiences here on earth, so little of us is pure and undiluted" (qtd. in MacShane, *Letters* 420). Revealingly, Chandler implies that the qualities God would salvage are attributes that he once possessed, a small "essence" from a distant past, which has now become unrecognizable due to certain "environmental" experiences. He believes that "external" influences combined with "experiences here on earth" shape our lives, and as a result most people lose all sense of innocence. Chandler's earthly experiences made him feel that he had forever lost a part of himself, leaving him with a sense of detachment.

Only two years before his death Chandler was able to equate his acceptance of mortality with his war experience, which he believed had given him a more practical view of death. It is conceivable, then, that Chandler's apparent indifference toward death can be construed as a symptom of survivor guilt, an emotional affliction that haunts war veterans. Lifton has argued that this guilt can manifest itself as a "sense of having defeated death and been rendered vulnerable from it—of having crossed over and returned." However, he warns that "[t]his feeling of invulnerability [. . . is] fragile, and mask[s] a more powerful sense of heightened vulnerability underneath" (106). As we have seen, Chandler appears to have indeed been a fragile character in his later years, and his erratic emotions are certainly suggestive of the survivor guilt that began after the war.

From his earliest short story, Chandler's works incorporated a number of recurring tropes that are suggestive of a psychologically wounded veteran and which quickly became a distinctive feature of his work. The solitary experience of pain is a theme that regularly recurs in his work, reinforcing the recurring "pain" suffered by the author during the war. J. W. Appel and G. W. Bebbe have emphasized that in warfare "psychiatric casualties are as inevitable as gunshot and shrapnel wounds" (1470). The First World War saw a new and awful type of warfare where "the probability of a soldier becoming a psychiatric casualty was greater than that of his being killed by enemy fire" (Grossman 55). Under these sorts of circumstances very few soldiers escaped completely unscathed and often continued to suffer either physically or psychologically for years afterward. In view of this, Chandler's characters are viewed not as static personalities, but like their creator, as individuals traumatized by their wartime experiences. This immense mental suffering inflicted upon serving troops is the often unseen but devastating consequence of war. And yet the fear of death is not the only or perhaps the major cause of psychiatric injury incurred by soldiers engaged in combat, since, as Grossman notes, "the whole truth is far more complex and horrible . . . resistance to overt aggressive confrontation, in addition to the fear of death and injury, is responsible for much of the trauma and stress on the battlefield." The overpowering sense of fear, Grossman says, "combined with exhaustion, hate, horror, and the irreconcilable task of balancing these with the need to kill, eventually drives the soldier so deeply into a mire of guilt and horror that he tips over the brink into that region that we call insanity" (54). Chandler was certainly qualified to know how the indescribable horror of war could inflict itself on the human psyche no matter how mentally robust and confident the individual appeared, saying as if from personal experience, "Anyone can be broken by suffering" (qtd. in Hiney and MacShane 234). Combat produces unpredictable human emotions and responses under pressure, and aspects of these certainly found their way into Chandler's works.

The cruel irony of war is that it is not just the frontline soldiers who suffer the traumatic contagion arising from combat. Being *indirectly* involved in the carnage is often enough to induce psychological injury. Peter Leese, for example, has said, "Barrage and battle, the hard labour of fighting and surviving, meant a constant physical struggle against exhaustion; feelings of isolation, helplessness and extinction imposed a further psychological strain. None the less, stress and trauma were not only associated with the active phases of the war. Low-level combat shaped trauma just as powerfully" (17). This psychological anguish can cause symptoms that vary from person to person, and, as Leese notes, there are a "variety of emotional and physical symptoms associated with the diagnosis" of PTSD (ibid.). The human mind is therefore "infinitely capable of bringing about any number of combinations of symptoms and then, to make matters worse, burying them deep in the soldier[']s psyche so that even the overt manifestations become symptoms of deeper symptoms of even deeper underlying causes" (Grossman 48). Despite the difficulty that specialists have in diagnosing PTSD, experts have identified three separate and distinct categories into which the main symptoms fall. These are intrusion, hyperarousal, and constriction. While each of these can be individually tormenting to the sufferer in their own right, depending on the severity of posttraumatic symptoms it is possible for victims to suffer elements of all three categories.

Intrusion, generally considered the most disturbing and intruding of the categorizations, occurs when a single traumatic moment creates a permanent imprint on the sufferer's mind, which Kardiner and Spiegel described as a "fixation on the trauma" (1). Symptoms of intrusion occur when long after an event has passed a victim relives the original event as though it were happening in the present with all the emotional force of the original event. This symptom is exposed in Marlowe's own experience at the conclusion of *The Big Sleep* where he suffers what he calls "waves of false memory." When he experiences these waves, he feels that he does the same things "over and over again, go[ing] to the same places, meet[ing] the same people, say[ing] the same words to them, over and over again." Consistent with the symptoms of intrusion, Marlowe describes his "false memory" as having the feeling of being "real, like something actually happening, and for the first time" (*The Big Sleep* 199).

A person suffering symptoms of intrusion experiences what Herman labels an "indelible image" (38), where one particular set of memories crystallizes a traumatizing experience. These visions may continually interrupt the sufferer's life, and "the intense focus on fragmentary sensation, an image without context, gives the traumatic memory a heightened reality" (Herman 38). Trauma tends to be encapsulated by one repetitive recollection and has a tendency to "become encoded in an abnormal form of memory" (Herman 37). Herman states: "The traumatised person may experience intense emotion but without clear memory of the event [. . .] [T]raumatic symptoms have a tendency to become disconnected from their source and to take on a life of their own [. . .] This kind of fragmentation, whereby trauma tears apart a complex system of self-protection that normally functions in an integrated fashion, is central to [. . .] post-traumatic stress disorder" (Herman 34). There is much to suggest that Chandler suffered from intrusion and that this indelible image, which, although not well documented in his daily life, certainly filtered through into his work and into the behavioral traits of Philip Marlowe. Tom Hiney believes: "Chandler could not help but absorb the details he had witnessed in wartime France; from the way a man's eyes look just after death to the viscosity of blood that seeps from a fatal head wound. These observations he would use in his later fiction" (45). However, it was not only the violent detail that Chandler absorbed. There are scenes in Chandler's novels that resemble the actual physical suffering resulting from war. For example, in a scene reminiscent of the wartime condition trench foot, Marlowe states in *Farewell, My Lovely*, "I took off my shoes and walked around in my socks feeling the floor with my toes. They would still get numb again once in a while" (234). Marlowe's comment here implies that his affliction has a specific cause, and more importantly his emphasis on the word "still" suggests that this is an ongoing condition caused by a past event. It is evident that this sentence was incorporated for a reason, because as Hemingway noted, "A writer who omits things because he does not know them only makes hollow places in his writing" (*Death in the Afternoon* 169). As an admirer of Hemingway's work Chandler would have probably been aware of this, and he appears to imply so in a letter to James Sandoe in 1947. He stated that when it came to writing, "[p]hysical clue a. has meaning only when added to psychological clue b" (qtd. in MacShane, *Letters* 100).

Marlowe's uncomfortable condition appears to resonate with the painful condition trench foot, which is caused by prolonged exposure to damp and cold. Thousands of soldiers trapped in the stalemate of trench warfare typified by the First World War had it. When treated correctly, however, complete recovery was normal, though it often left sufferers prone to further bouts during cold or wet conditions. It is no coincidence that in the scene preceding Marlowe's comment about the numbness of his feet, he has been walking around the Bay City waterfront and takes two boat rides to Laird Brunette's gambling ship *Montecito*, moored off the coast. The numbness in Marlowe's feet, triggered by the cold and dampness of the Bay City Harbor, connects him back to Hank Bruton's symptoms in "A Couple of Writers," a man we explicitly know to be a war veteran. Since Marlowe and Bruton suffer similar conditions it might suggest that the condition was something Chandler suffered from and that once again it was transferred to his characters.

Returning to the notion of an indelible image, the regular violent assaults that Marlowe sustains are also symptomatic of Chandler's own mental susceptibility to this condition. We regularly witness Marlowe receiving blows to the head and being rendered unconscious, but despite the claims of MacShane and Hiney there is no factual evidence to support the theory that Chandler himself suffered such an occurrence during the war. Although Herman has stated that those who suffer a traumatic event "often feel impelled to re-create the moment of terror, either in literal or in disguised form" (39), it is evident that this is not the reason for Chandler's inclusion of these scenes. Yet there are enough of these incidents to consider them important. For example, Chandler's detective John Evans describes in the short story "No Crime in the Mountains" (1941), how his "head came off and went half-way across the lake and did a boomerang turn and came back and slammed on top of [his] spine with a sickening jar" (qtd. in *Killer in the Rain* 375).

Instead, a more likely explanation for the repetitious use of such scenes suggests that Chandler intended to convey a far simpler image of a sensory response to his wartime experience. Bessel van der Kolk argues that the senses are extremely fine-tuned to capturing traumatic events. When the central nervous system is under severe stress, memories of a traumatic event can become so overwhelming that they bypass all linguistic encoding, and instead the nervous system reverts to capturing the memory in sensory or symbolic form. While van der Kolk argues that these forms of memory can be difficult to retrieve, "they can be reactivated by affective, auditory, or visual cues" (232). Chandler's experiences on the front line may have been sufficiently traumatic to encode the disturbing events in the form of vivid sensations and images that were later projected into his stories. Noting the terrifying experience of being under attack, and bearing in mind its potential for sensory encoding, one American soldier from the First World War described the experience of war as "scary business [. . .] when the shelling begins, the rockets and flares all along the near horizon lighting up the weird scene [. . .] the everlasting crack and roar of our own artillery all around us and the whine of the innumerable shells passing overhead [. . .]" (qtd. in Freidel 131). Consequently the imagery Chandler uses can be interpreted as a sensory reaction to the experience of an enemy barrage. The combination of deafening gunfire, ground tremors, and fear would have undoubtedly imprinted themselves onto the minds of those who experienced it.

Events documented in the Seventh Battalion's war diaries support the argument that the sensory responses Chandler incorporated into his work reflect the ordeal endured by soldiers. In particular, scenes where Marlowe is knocked unconscious have very definite Lost Generation attributes. Like Chandler's novels, which are also written in a first-person narrative, we experience the exact event through the eyes of Hemingway's protagonist. For example, Frederic Henry notes in *A Farewell to Arms*:

> I heard a cough, then came the chuh-chuh-chuh-chuh—then there was a flash, as when a blast-furnace door is swung open, and a roar that

> started white and went red and on and on in a rushing wind. I tried to breathe but my breath would not come and I felt myself rush bodily out of myself and out and out and out and all the time bodily in the wind [. . . and] then I floated back [. . .]. (50)

Chandler's language is equally descriptive. When Lash Canino knocks Marlowe unconscious in *The Big Sleep*, the detective says,

> I had the stunned moment of shock when the lights danced and the visible world went out of focus but was still there [. . .] There was no sensation in my head. The bright glare got brighter. There was nothing but hard aching white light. Then there was darkness in which something red wiggled like a germ under a microscope. Then there was nothing red or wiggling, just darkness and emptiness and a rushing wind and a falling as of great trees. (183)

In these scenes, although Marlowe has been physically beaten, the imagery appears reminiscent of a sensory response to an exploding shell.

These dramatic descriptions suggest Chandler projected a traumatizing sensory experience onto his detective, and further evidence is implied by the writer's use of warlike imagery to describe Marlowe's blackouts. For example, in Chandler's short story "Bay City Blues," detective Johnny Dalmas says: "A naval gun went off in my ear and my head was a large pink firework exploding into the vault of the sky and scattering and falling slow and pale, and then dark, into the waves. Blackness ate me up" (qtd. in *Killer in the Rain* 275). Similar imagery occurs in Chandler's final novel, *Playback*, where Marlowe says that "at that moment an army mule kicked me square on the back of my brain. I went zooming out over a dark sea and exploded in a sheet of flame" (34). These descriptions have a specific military context. In *Farewell, My Lovely* the detective is beaten unconscious only to awake after "[t]wenty minutes' sleep. Just a nice doze [. . .] In twenty minutes you can sink a battleship, down three or four planes, hold a double execution" (59). Later, Marlowe is again rendered unconscious, held prisoner, and drugged for three days. He wakes to find that the "room was full of smoke [. . .] The smoke hung straight up in the air, in thin lines, straight up and down [. . .] in the middle of the room, all across the room" (*Farewell, My Lovely* 144–45). Although Marlowe is hallucinating, this scene is certainly reminiscent of a hazy battle scene. It appears that when turned inward under the influence of drugs Marlowe's mind relives the event as though he is experiencing the original traumatizing incident. He indicates his unease at this occurrence by saying, "[T]he smoke bothered me" (*Farewell, My Lovely* 145).

As a veteran Marlowe relives his experiences in a different type of war where the trenches of northern France have been transformed into the hard-boiled streets of Los Angeles. Edward Tick noted, "The healing cleansing of veterans can only occur when we relive memories and their accompanying feelings so that they may be expressed and relieved [. . .] Years after combat is over, our souls may still wander in the horror of the war zone" (194). In the postwar period "writers of hard-boiled novels, especially Chandler, Cain and their Hollywood counterparts [. . .] constructed a sinister, malignant image of Los Angeles, exploding the myth of the city as a golden nirvana gracing the California coast [. . .] LA's fragmentation has produced a city of strangers, where the claims of the community are acknowledged less strongly" (Willett 20). For Chandler, the dirty reality of war is given a new urban setting in which Los Angeles suffers "the big money, the sharp shooters, the percentage workers, the fast dollar boys, the hoodlums" (*The Little Sister* 181). It becomes a city associated with loss, displacement, and denial. Chandler's novel *The Lady in the Lake* in particular records the degree of estrangement and the sense of alienation that the Second World War brought to Chandler's work, reflected by the detective's need to escape the "warlike" city for the sanctuary of Little Fawn Lake. As he told his publisher in August 1939: "The effort to keep my mind off the war has reduced me to the mental age of seven," and by the summer of 1943 Hiney notes that Chandler was feeling "mentally finished" (qtd. in Hiney 111, 134). Although Marlowe is physically beaten in the *Lady in the Lake*, the imagery is once again reminiscent of an exploding shell: "The scene exploded into fire and darkness [. . .] Fire and darkness and just before the darkness a sharp flash of nausea" (289). It is no coincidence that Chandler should use such powerful imagery at precisely the time that the carnage of the Second World War in Europe was reaching its height. During times of stress such terrible reminders can "evoke [. . . traumatic] memories, which often return with all the vividness and emotional force of the original event" (Herman 37).

The exposure to drugs also features prominently in *Farewell, My Lovely* and *The Little Sister,* where they are administered to the detective, rendering him unconscious. The imagery in these scenes is less savage, and Marlowe merely "slips" into unconsciousness instead of being forcibly dispatched. In *The Little Sister,* after smoking a drugged cigarette offered by the corrupt Dr. Lagardie, Marlowe states: "I started to get up off the floor [. . . It] looped the loop. After a while it steadied a little [. . .] A face swam towards me out of the darkness. I changed direction and started for the face. But it was too late in the afternoon. The sun was setting. It was getting dark rapidly. There was no face. There was no wall, no desk. Then there was no floor. There was nothing at all [. . .] I wasn't even there" (147–48). By the time *The Little Sister* was published in 1949 drugs had come to feature prominently in Chandler's life. He had been prescribed morphine on numerous occasions for painful skin rashes, and the numbing experience of the drug may have begun to influence his work.

Herman believes that symptoms of intrusion can be interpreted as "spontaneous attempts to integrate the traumatic event" (41) into a sufferers personal life, and the trauma is only resolved when the sufferer develops a new understanding of the event. Yet intrusion also carries with it damaging consequences. Robert Jay Lifton points out that a common form of intrusion is the "death immersion" (323) in which "[t]he long term impact is extensive. Survivors typically suffer nightmares that may recapitulate traumatising incidents" (Tick 138). Marlowe experiences nightmares that are generally related to the case he is working and feature vivid descriptions of death or dying. They are based on characters in the novels and are often combined with graphic imagery. In *Farewell, My Lovely,* Marlowe is almost strangled to death and later recalls: "Sometimes I wake up in the night. I feel [. . . his hands] there and I smell the smell of him. I feel the breath fighting and losing and the greasy fingers digging in. Then I wake up and take a drink and turn the radio on" (136). Even after being drugged once again he regains consciousness and remarks, "I undressed and went to bed. I had nightmares and woke out of them sweating" (*Farewell, My Lovely* 165). Such experiences are not uncommon for those suffering from PTSD, where shocking events occur "both as flashbacks during waking states and as traumatic nightmares during sleep" (Herman 37). Although these events are based in the plot, it indicates that these traumatic occurrences are not forgotten easily and may awaken buried memories themselves. In the graphic nightmare that Marlowe suffers in *The Lady in the Lake* he again combines his experience of discovering a body at Little Fawn Lake with vivid imagery. He says:

> I was far down in the depths of icy green water with a corpse under my arm. The corpse had long blonde hair that kept floating around in front of my face. An enormous fish with bulging eyes and a bloated body and scales shining with putrescence swam around leering like an elderly roué. Just as I was about to burst from lack of the air, the corpse came alive under my arm and got away from me and then I was fight-

> ing with the fish and the corpse was rolling over and over in the water, spinning its long hair. (90)

Although they are flashbacks to a specific plot-oriented event, the nightmares suggest that a certain aspect of Marlowe's investigation triggers an emotional response akin to his original traumatic episode. As van der Kolk suggested earlier, visual or sensory triggers can reactivate traumatic memories that have been stored as images or sounds. This trigger awakens the traumatic memory with the full force of the original event and can once again prove terrifying for the victim.

Trauma sufferers tend to avoid reliving a distressing event because it often increases emotional distress. This in itself is problematic, however, because efforts to prevent reliving the trauma can actually aggravate posttraumatic symptoms despite the self-protective intention of the sufferer. As such, reliving a traumatic event can in some cases prove to be cathartic for the victim, and it can have a cleansing effect in which, Herman notes, survivors "may find a way to integrate reliving experiences into their lives in a contained, even useful manner [. . . and] manage to re-create some aspect of his war experience in civilian life" (40). By reliving an injury through Philip Marlowe, Chandler may have been unconsciously attempting to recreate his battle in Los Angeles, a safer front line. The city therefore becomes a more controlled method of coming to terms with a traumatizing occurrence without reliving the actual horror of the original event. For Chandler, Marlowe was the soldier in the city, but revisiting a traumatic event, although adaptive, may also entail high emotional intensity. As well as creating a sense of stability for himself through his work, Chandler continued a compulsive pattern that, like other veteran writers, would be prominent in his work until the end of his life.

The second major set of PTSD symptoms encompasses anxiety caused by a persistent expectation of danger, a condition referred to as hyperarousal. This can occur after a traumatic event causes the entire system of self-preservation to be overloaded and become permanently alert, making it almost impossible for the sufferer to relax in social situations and in surroundings that would normally be considered safe. It is, Herman states, "as if the danger might return at any moment" (35). The perceived existence of a threat "initially arouses the sympathetic nervous system, causing the person in danger to feel an adrenaline rush and go into a state of permanent alert. Threat also concentrates a person's attention on the immediate situation [. . . It] evokes intense feelings of fear and anger. These changes in arousal, attention, perception, and emotion are normal, adaptive reactions. They mobilize the threatened person for strenuous action, either in battle or in flight" (Herman 34). Herman argues that this chronic psychological arousal often means "the traumatised person startles easily, reacts irritably to small provocations, and sleeps poorly" (35). It may also cause fatigue and bouts of irrational anxiety, symptoms that Chandler himself suffered from for most of his adult life. Herman notes, "People with post-traumatic stress disorder take longer to fall asleep, are more sensitive to noise, and awaken more frequently during the night than ordinary people" (36). Grossman concurs, saying that anxiety is common among PTSD sufferers and is characterized by "feelings of total weariness and tenseness that cannot be relieved by rest or sleep, which degenerate into an inability to concentrate" (47). Chandler spoke of similar feelings in a letter to Jamie Hamilton while writing *The Little Sister* in 1948. He said, "I have a very, very tired mind [. . .] Lately I have been trying to simplify my life [. . .] But I am not happy. I need a rest badly [. . .]" (qtd. in MacShane, *Letters* 124–25).

In combat situations soldiers often unconsciously activate a survival instinct that causes the "mobilisation of mind and body for danger, the vigilant sharpening of the senses, the tense readiness to kill an attacker" (Shay, *Odysseus* 39). In extreme cases this instinctive behavior may trip over into hyperarousal, with symptoms that stimulate a permanent sense of danger when the machinery for intensive, coordinated, and focused action is shattered by the traumatic experience. When faced with such an event as war, "profound and lasting changes in psychological arousal, emotion, cognition, and memory" (Herman 34) can occur. The threat of danger may cause the nervous system to go onto high alert and may continue unabated, even when the sufferer is removed from the threatening situation.

In warfare, a soldier must rely upon basic instinct and alertness to stay alive, and in Chandler's mind the same is true for the detective. Symptoms of hyperarousal are reflected prominently in Chandler's work by Marlowe's instinctive reaction to danger and to the unknown. In "The Lady in the Lake" detective Johnny Dalmas says, "I swung around hard, as if somebody were trying to sneak up on me with a blackjack, but nobody was. The silence held. The room was full of it, brimming over with it. A bird chirped outdoors in a tree, but that only made the silence thicker. You could have cut slices of it and buttered them" (qtd. in *Killer in the Rain* 326). The detective often appears abnormally alert and unnaturally aware of his surroundings, using highly descriptive imagery to heighten the tension and encourage the reader to identify with his apprehensive state of mind. In *The Big Sleep* Marlowe notes, "Something was wrong. Something on the air, a scent. The shades were down at the windows and the street light leaking in at the sides made a dim light in the room. I stood and listened" (150). Marlowe's exaggerated alertness surfaces throughout Chandler's novels, and in *The High Window*, the detective is even unnerved by the sound of the telephone: "The ringing bell had a sinister sound, *for no reason of itself, but because of the ears to which it rang.* I stood there braced and tense, lips tightly drawn back in a half grin. Beyond the closed window the neon lights glowed. The dead air didn't move. Outside the corridor was still. The bell rang in the darkness, steady and strong" (99. Emphasis added). Later in the same novel, after discovering the body of Elisha Morningstar, Marlowe is unnerved by "Silence. Not even the sound of breathing. The hair moved on the back of my neck" (110). Marlowe experiences similar anxiety in *The Little Sister* where, confronting Dr. Lagardie, a disgraced doctor selling narcotics, a nervous Marlowe says, "I'm just talking . . . Waiting for something to happen. Something's going to happen in this house. It's leering at me from corners" (139).

Hyperarousal can also extend to feelings of anxiety triggered by the immediate environment, where a person lives or works. As Lifton has mentioned, social restlessness combined with varying levels of bitterness, distrust, and suspicion are all symptoms of PTSD (35). In Chandler's novels, as well as in his own life, these symptoms are very pronounced. Just as Chandler would change location when he became restless, Marlowe does exactly the same, moving four times in seven novels. The detective begins *The Big Sleep* residing at the Hobart Arms, a place he describes as "barren" (114). He changes his residence in *Farewell, My Lovely* where, although not mentioning it by name, he makes it clear that it is not the same apartment house as in the previous novel. Unlike the Hobart Arms, where the "door was put on lock at ten" (ibid.), in his new apartment, "[t]hey lock the lobby door at eleven" (*Farewell, My Lovely* 165). By the time we reach *The High Window*, Marlowe achieves a degree of stability, giving his address as the "Bristol Apartments, 1624 North Bristol Avenue, Hollywood" (107), where he stays until *The Long Goodbye*. In this novel, however, he states: "I was living that year in a house on Yucca Avenue in the Laurel Canyon district. It was a small hillside house on a dead-end street with a long flight of redwood steps to the front door and a grove of eucalyptus trees across the way" (*The Long Goodbye* 7). Marlowe remains at this address throughout *Playback*. It is noticeable from such details that there is far more of Chandler in Marlowe than has been previously acknowledged. Judith Freeman believes that Chandler's relocation around Los Angeles added a vital element to his work. It "reflects one of the [most important] things Chandler did for the mystery novel," she says, which was "to imbue it with extraordinary detail and create an atmosphere so thick and rich that the landscape really comes alive" (32).

The final category of posttraumatic symptoms is constriction, an alteration in a victim's consciousness initiating a numbed response to surrender and withdrawal into seclusion, where, as Herman notes, "[t]he helpless person escapes from [a] situation not by action in the real world but rather by altering [his or her] state of consciousness" (42). Situations of danger may provoke unexpected emotions accompanied by terror and rage, or conversely, detached calm. Herman notes that "it is as though these events have been disconnected from their ordinary meanings" (ibid.). Alterations in perception can combine with feelings of indifference, detachment, and passivity and are viewed as a barrier against the "pain" of trauma. While the "heightened perceptions occurring during traumatic events resemble the phenomena of hypnotic absorption, the numbing symptoms resemble the complementary phenomena of hypnotic dissociation" (ibid.). Therefore, while intrusion and hyperarousal require the absorption of traumatic stimuli, constriction is the dissociation from those stimuli, which encourages a sustained emotional detachment and the fluctuation of emotions commonly associated with PTSD.

Although the biological reason for this altered hypnotic condition is unknown, Ernest Hilgard believes the brain "may be acting in a manner parallel to morphine" (246). The constructive process helps to keep intrusive memories out of the normal range of consciousness, allowing only minor details of the original memory to emerge. Jonathan Shay argues that when the senses are "stuck in the on position and [this] persists into civilian life, the veteran may embark on a frenzied search for calm" (*Odysseus* 39). The symptoms associated with intrusion and hyperarousal may actually lead to constriction, and as a result veteran trauma sufferers may attempt to achieve a similar calming state of consciousness with the aid of intoxicants such as alcohol or narcotics. When facing combat, soldiers' use of alcohol appears to be "an attempt to obliterate their growing sense of helplessness and terror" (Herman 44). It is a dependency that typically continues when soldiers return home as the means of combating their heightened symptoms of intrusion and hyperarousal, which often include insomnia, nightmares, irritability, and rage. Once back in civilian life a soldier is unable to simply switch off and will continue to rely upon—even becoming dependent upon—these agents for relief. Shay believes: "Both hyperarousal and numbing may persist into civilian life, paradoxically coexisting as constantly inflamed anger, but numbing of everything else. Or they may alternate with one another, giving the veteran a history of 'cycling' between over-excitement and numb withdrawal" (*Odysseus* 40). These symptoms can often result in increased levels of violence and eventually prison sentences.[1] The combination of hyperarousal and constriction can therefore have devastating effects on both the individual and the social perception of veterans.

Although there is no evidence that Chandler ever experienced fits of violent behavior, he did suffer from fluctuating emotions and bouts of alcoholism, both recognizable symptoms of constriction. It is reasonable to assume that if Chandler suffered such symptoms they would have transferred into his work and into the distinctive behavioral idiosyncrasies of Philip Marlowe. Like Chandler, Marlowe's emotions were often erratic, swinging between a need for company and complete isolation. In *Farewell, My Lovely* he says to Anne Riordan, "I don't want any help. I've got to think. I want to be by myself for a while" (69). While later, in *The Little Sister* he craves any form of human contact: "Let the telephone ring, please. Let there be somebody to call up and plug me into the human race again [. . .] Nobody has to like me. I just want to get off this frozen star" (177).

Since veterans often have a need for numbing agents it is not unrealistic to see Marlowe's weakness for alcohol as an indicator of his PTSD. Even after being knocked unconscious, having been hit on the head with a bottle of gin, Marlowe wakes covered in the spirit and craving alcohol. He says, "I got my knees under me and stayed on all fours for a while, sniffing like a dog who can't finish his dinner, but hates to leave it" (*The Lady in the Lake* 190). Although clearly not an alcoholic, Marlowe does display signs of alcohol dependency. In stressful situations, he is not averse to drinking in his office, admitting, "I'm a fellow that will take a snort myself, if I'm tired and nervous and overworked" (*The Long Goodbye* 52). In particularly tense situations he becomes almost desperate, saying, "I needed a drink badly and the bars were closed." Later, with a glass in his hand, he says, "[T]he drink made me feel a lot better" (*Farewell, My Lovely* 76, 82). Marlowe appears to know what he is doing to himself, and although he acknowledges, "I like to drink" (*The Lady in the Lake* 38), he prefers to let his "self-respect ride its own race" (*The Big Sleep* 126).

Like most veterans Marlowe uses alcohol as a relaxant to numb his memory and senses. He admits he will regularly "bang myself to sleep with a bottle," while drinking coffee the following morning to make himself feel more "human" (*Farewell, My Lovely* 80, 168). He believes that alcohol makes him feel "just right, and the first swallow is like a peak into a cleaner, sunnier, brighter world" (*The High Window* 117). In one of the most noteworthy examples of this symptom of constriction in Chandler's work, Marlowe is unable to resist the temptation to drink after solving the case in *The High Window*:

> I drove back to Hollywood, bought a pint of good liquor, checked in at the Plaza, and sat on the side of the bed staring at my feet and lapping the whisky out of the bottle.
>
> Just like any common bedroom drunk.
>
> When I had had enough of it to make my brain fuzzy enough to stop thinking, I undressed and got into bed, and after a while, but not soon enough, I went to sleep. (160–61)

Chandler's use of military symbolism appears in most of his novels and in many instances is combined with Marlowe's craving for alcohol. An example of this is found in *Farewell, My Lovely* when Marlowe refers to empty liquor bottles as "dead soldiers" (28). This connection, however, also appears with other characters. In *The Lady in the Lake* for example, Bill Chess is not only named after the warlike board game but is additionally depicted as a disabled war veteran heavily dependent upon alcohol. Marlowe describes him as being "heavily built and not very tall and he limped as he walked, giving his right leg a little kick out with each step and swinging the foot in a shallow arc [. . .] In spite of his weathered appearance he looked like a drinker" (34). Instinctively understanding exactly how Chess's mind works, Marlowe encourages him to talk about his marital problems. Producing a bottle of whisky, Marlowe asks: "Anything a drink would help?" (36). Recognizing the severity of Chess's battle with alcohol addiction, Marlowe says, "He leaned to pick the bottle off the rock and stare at it. He seemed to fight with it in his mind. The whisky won the fight, as it always did" (39). For those like Marlowe and Chess, the temptation of alcohol is often too hard to resist.

A further symptom of constriction is the veteran's disheartened response to what is perceived as a frivolous and superficial life he returns to after war. Even though Marlowe is quick to defend those he recognizes as helpless, he is nevertheless usually disappointed by the outcome of his own well-intentioned heroics, and we often find him "disillusioned [. . .] and unable to assimilate the meaning of his case or of his own role in it [. . . He is] unable to comprehend how the world could have sunk—so unexpectedly—to such depths of dishonesty" (Speir 109–10). Chandler depicts Marlowe as someone who also seems to simply wash his hands of life. In *The High Window* Marlowe ponders his situation and says, "I filled and lit my pipe and sat there smoking. Nobody came in, nobody called, nothing happened, nobody cared whether I died or went to El Paso" (201). Marlowe's feeling of detachment from others is part of the reason for his nonchalant attitude toward death. In spite of his good intentions and courageous endeavors, he considers himself to be worthless. He summarizes his life as degraded and having little meaning, "as if I had spent my life knocking at doors in cheap hotels that nobody bothered to open" (*The Little Sister* 48). Marlowe is reconciled to the fact that his work will never be fully appreciated and is inconsequential in a culture that does not care for him. In his own words, he has become "a grain of sand on the desert of oblivion" (*The Long Goodbye* 116). This tension even transfers to his physical appearance: "I had a strained look. I'd been living too fast . . . I looked as if I had made my mind up to drive off a cliff" (*The Little Sister* 135).

Marlowe's indifference and disillusionment are suggestive symptoms of survivor guilt. As Grossman notes: "The dead soldier takes his misery with him, but the man who killed him must forever live and die with him. The lesson becomes increasingly clear: killing is what war is all about, and killing in combat, by its very nature, causes deep wounds of pain and guilt" (Grossman 93). This is the sentiment that Marlowe expresses in *The Big Sleep*. In his disillusioned tirade at the end of the novel he includes the revealing line, "You just slept the big sleep, not caring about the nastiness of how you died or where you fell. Me, I was part of that nastiness now" (220). Although seeming resigned to his fate, Marlowe alludes to the burden of pain and guilt he must endure, in contrast to the dead who take their suffering with them. It is his guilt and listlessness that lead Marlowe to believe that he has become "as empty of life as a scarecrow's pockets" (*The Big Sleep* 156).

Disillusionment and passivity became increasingly prominent in Chandler's later work where Marlowe has been fully developed as the shattered veteran of war. Tom Hiney believes that in *The Lady in the Lake*, "Marlowe certainly does not feel like a hero any more" (130). Looking in a mirror, Marlowe says, "I brushed my hair and looked at the grey in it. It was getting to be plenty of grey in it. The face under the hair had a sick look. I didn't like the face at all" (*The Lady in the Lake* 140). Marlowe repeatedly says that he feels "jaded and old" (*The Little Sister* 48), yet his disillusionment is mainly reserved for the corruption he sees around him. He says, "The white moonlight was cold and clear, like the justice we dream of but never find" (*The High Window* 244).

Like many other emotionally detached veterans, Marlowe feels his sacrifices in war have been inconsequential and forgotten by a cynical world. Although recognition and acceptance are essential in aiding the healing process, the veterans who look to their community for support and approval rarely find them. Grossman notes that for society, "it is simply too painful [. . .] to address what it does when it sends its young men off to kill other young men in distant lands [. . .] And what is too painful to remember, we simply choose to forget" (Grossman 95). The veteran feels "isolated [. . .] by the images of the horror that he has witnessed [. . . and] imagines that no civilian [. . .] can comprehend." All too often civilians share the view of the veteran as a man apart from the rest of society. However, the "[r]estoration of the breach between the traumatised person and the community depends [. . .] upon public acknowledgement of the traumatic event" (Herman 66, 70).

The last chapter of *Playback* is a poignant reminder of Chandler's own circumstances, concluding with Marlowe returning to a home similar to the lonely La Jolla apartment in which his creator was now living. He says: "I opened a couple of windows and mixed a drink in the kitchen. I sat down on the couch and stared at the wall. Wherever I went, whatever I did, this was what I would come back to. A blank wall in a meaningless room in a meaningless house [. . .] I put the drink down on the side table without touching it. Alcohol was no cure for this. Nothing was any cure for this but the hard inner heart that asked for nothing from no one" (156). Yet however dismally Marlowe describes his living space, his home is his sanctuary. This is where he feels safe surrounded by his possessions that have special sentimental value. When Carmen Sternwood calls him a "filthy name" in *The Big Sleep*, he promptly throws her out, saying: "I didn't mind what she called me, what anybody called me. But this was the room I had to live in. It was all I had in the way of a home. In it was everything that was mine, that had any association for me, any past, anything that took the place of a family. Not much; a few books, pictures, radio, chessmen, old letters, stuff like that. Nothing. Such as they were they had all my memories" (154). Carmen's language debases Marlowe's sanctuary. The hissing noise she makes when Marlowe asks her to leave only serves to aggravate the sensation that Carmen has compromised and tainted the serenity of the retreat that he has carefully created, and he vents his anger after she leaves by viciously attacking the bed covers, tearing them apart.

As part of the larger symptom of constriction Grossman observes that a trauma sufferer can experience what he calls "conversion hysteria," a condition which can occur either during combat or years later as a feature of PTSD (Grossman 45). This manifestation causes a trauma victim to suffer selective amnesia, which expunges the traumatic event caused by "a "constriction of the field of consciousness" which keeps painful memories split off from ordinary awareness" (Herman 45). This could explain why Chandler never attempted to provide a biography for Marlowe, and may indicate that Chandler, and through him Marlowe, did not want to dwell on his past and has instead chosen to concentrate on the present. Although Chandler may have allowed Marlowe to forget certain aspects of his past, Chandler could not. As Merle Davies states in *The High Window*, "People are always telling you to forget unpleasant things. But you never do" (233). By denying Marlowe a past, Chandler may have been granting the detective a freedom that he himself did not have, a life free from emotional or familial ties. In *The Lady in the Lake*, after being knocked unconscious, Marlowe says, "Someday it will all come back to you. And you won't like it" (191). By withholding Marlowe's past, Chandler may be signaling his own desire to forget his war experiences by allowing Marlowe a clean slate from which to restart his life. As well as Marlowe, many of Chandler's other characters forget past events. In *The Big Sleep*, for example, Carmen Sternwood, without recollection, kills her brother-in-law, Rusty Regan, during an epileptic seizure. Similarly, in *The Long Goodbye* Eileen Wade accuses her traumatized war veteran husband of Sylvia Lennox's murder, blaming blackouts caused by heavy drinking.

As well as amnesia, Grossman argues that a susceptibility to states of confusion is another prominent symptom of PTSD which often leads to sufferers becoming dissociated from reality. The most notable example of this condition is Ganzer syndrome, where a sufferer tries "to ward off the horror with humour" (Grossman 45), a defensive mechanism that Marlowe displays with disturbing regularity. The most consistent evidence of this condition is the way Marlowe uses sarcasm and wit. MacShane argues that Marlowe's sarcastic dialogue is "not just for the sake of the jokes and wisecracks. [It is] his chief weapon. Chandler has Marlowe choose his words in such a way as to throw his opponents off base" (*Life* 113). While this style of banter is common in Chandler's novels, the detective's behavior when confronted with more frightening situations becomes increasingly erratic and develops into heightened agitation that includes unnerving outbursts. When placed under pressure the detective's emotional state becomes chaotic and unstable. In circumstances where Marlowe's nervous response to danger takes control, his display of humor is displaced by a state of mind akin to delirium. He also has an aversion to killing which is unusual for detectives of the period. The only killing he commits throughout the entire series of novels is Lash Canino in *The Big Sleep*. Even here, despite committing the act in self-defense, Marlowe allows his uneasiness to show, saying, "I began to laugh like a loon" (194), following Canino's shooting. Earlier in the same novel, Marlowe is accosted by one of Eddie Mars's gangsters and says, "I grinned at my own foolishness" (114), and even after Carmen Sternwood tries to shoot Joe Brody he says, "I began to laugh. I laughed like an idiot, without control" (88). In *The Lady in the Lake*, we find a similar reaction when, after discovering that Chris Lavery has been shot to death, Marlowe recounts: "I laughed. It was rather a ghoulish laugh" (105). These incidents reveal just how unstable and irrational Marlowe becomes when confronted by emotionally stressful situations.

Yet, paradoxically, in other stressful situations when in the company of men, Marlowe is at relative ease. As with soldiers who have no alternative but to endure the enormous emotional and physical intensity of combat it is not unusual that men should group together for reassurance and mutual support. Because "war affects our physical, emotional, and spiritual dimensions" (Tick 222), this instinctive banding together may explain why the detective is drawn to certain men and why, as a result of a common bond, some critics have interpreted this instinctive reaction in such a way as to raise questions about Marlowe's sexual orientation. This interpretation, however, does seem to be an excessive explanation for the natural bond and interdependence forged by combat, one which creates a sense of brotherhood that is akin to what Grossman describes as a "love relationship" (Grossman 90). For example, Vietnam veteran John Early explains that "the man next to you—you're depending on him for the most important thing you have, your life, and if he lets you down you're either maimed or killed. If you make a mistake the same thing happens to him, so the bond of trust has to be extremely close, and I'd say this bond is stronger than almost anything [. . .] It's a hell of a lot stronger than man and wife" (qtd. in Grossman 90). In *Farewell, My Lovely*, "Moose" Malloy and "Red" Norgaard are both characters that Marlowe is drawn to. He says of Red, "His voice was soft, dreamy, so delicate for a young man that it was startling. It made me think of another soft-voiced big man I had strangely liked" (213). Marlowe says this about Red but is in fact referring to Malloy, showing his respect and feeling for both characters. Later in the novel he admits: "I told [Red] a great deal more than I intended to. It must have been his eyes" (218). The language here is unusually sensitive, and some have argued that it is an indication of Marlowe's homosexuality. Gershon Legman believes that in *The Long Goodbye* Marlowe appears to "moon" over Terry Lennox and after receiving news of Lennox's supposed death, sentimentally pours him a cup of coffee and lights him a cigarette, a scene that will be discussed further in chapter 6.

With regard to the hypothesis that Marlowe is homosexual, Freeman notes, "There was always the possibility that if Chandler, and by extension

Marlowe, did harbour any homosexual inclinations they might have been so deeply repressed as to never have been acknowledged, leaking out instead, via the unconscious, in certain passages of prose" (164). Yet this argument falters if we consider that Marlowe's actions toward certain male characters are a consequence not of sexual attraction but of his loneliness and recognition of others who are also part of the brotherhood produced under combat conditions. As the next chapter will consider, Marlowe's attraction to Lennox and Wade is far more complex than simply theorizing upon the detective's sexuality; at the heart of Marlowe's actions and emotions lies a bond with the two veterans that runs incredibly deep.

PHILIP MARLOWE, WAR, AND CHESS

While critics such as Philip Durham and Jerry Speir have located Philip Marlowe in a chivalric context and interpreted the detective as a modern-day knight, such an interpretation has become increasingly inadequate. Although initially Marlowe appears to have the features that emanate from a chivalric lineage with the customary traits of a questing knight, these traits are incidental. Rather than being a knight himself, Marlowe, as Judith Freeman alludes, is instead merely "associated with the *idea* of the knight" (141. Emphasis added). As a result it may be argued that Chandler did not actually intend for his detective to be molded into a chivalric knight, but instead the reference refers to Marlowe as a knight in a game of chess evaluating his progress and playing out his moves across the game board of Los Angeles. Marlowe is surrounded by mayhem and the turbulence of the society in which he lives, and in order to find stability he increasing finds solace and certainty in the game of chess as the sole means of regaining a sense of order in his life. It is comforting for the detective because he is able to place himself within a meaningful and structured context, where the rules are fixed and progress is certain. As this section will demonstrate, Marlowe possesses the actual qualities of a knightly chess piece while his character resonates only momentarily with the attributes of the chivalric knight.

With only fleeting references to Marlowe's personal history his character manifests itself through his favorite pastime, chess, and offers significant insights into the detective's troubled mindset and noble ambitions. The complexities of chess quite often enable Marlowe to "work out problems" (*The High Window* 115) by using its intricate strategy to piece together his next best move.

When Chandler arrived in California in 1912 he very quickly became firm friends with Warren Lloyd and his family, and through Lloyd, the Pascals. MacShane notes, "On Sundays, Warren Lloyd would play a ritualistic game of chess with this contemporary Julian Pascal, and the whole house would be silenced so as not to disturb them." This social set and their group activities "were to be very important in [Chandler's] life" (MacShane, *Life* 27, 24). To Chandler, chess increasingly became much more than just a mere game; it became the symbol of his social standing as well as mental stability.

Yet chess also has a far more fundamental significance to everyday existence. David Shenk argues that chess can alleviate daily stresses and strains and represents a satisfying method of achieving a sense of structure and organization in most aspects of life. When human beings are faced with disorganization and dislocation, they seek a method of managing their feelings. They seek a disciplined yet therapeutic coping mechanism that assists in regaining control of their emotions and alleviating the anxiety and contradictions of everyday life within a constantly changing social framework. Shenk believes that the ancient game of chess is one of the more beneficial ways that enable people to achieve this aspiration. "On the board [the player] could see the whole action," he says, "On the board he could neatly make sense of significant past events and carefully plan his future. On the board he still might win" (3). Given this thoughtful insight, it is reasonable to suppose that Chandler saw the benefits of chess and went so far as to bequeath to Marlowe his own interest in the game to utilize as a coping mechanism. The game itself differs from almost any other pastime because the outcome does not in any way rely on the element of chance. Without involving the luck of the draw and with no dice, winning rests on the unfolding of a strategy solely motivated by rational action on the board. To those who first played the game it was a revelation; human beings were able to make conscious decisions and forge their own destinies, albeit on a board, but without any reliance upon chance or fate. Chess then, "stood for the new empowerment, the idea of making one's way in the world based on one's own effort and ability" (Shenk 53). The effects of chess on humans are well noted because "it offered a unique insight into the human endeavour" (Shenk 3). In medieval England for example, chess was not only a popular game, but also a method of conveying abstract ideas and a mirror for individuals to examine their role in society. Chess also allowed Europeans to understand their identities at a time when new codes of social morality developed. "So ensconced [was chess] in the culture of medieval chivalry," says Shenk, "that it was listed as one of the seven essential skills for every knight" (50).

The aggressive nature of chess is well understood, for as former world champion Bobby Fischer once noted: "Chess is war over the board" (qtd. in Shenk 5). When played seriously, chess encourages a "forbidding atmosphere of unforgiving rules, insider jargon, and the general aggressiveness and unpleasantness that seem[s] to accompany even reasonably casual play" (Shenk 5). Former chess master Alfred Kreymborg claims that chess is not just confined to the board but can spill over into life. Chess, he notes, "is warfare in the most mysterious jungles of the human character" (qtd. in Shenk 6). Even keen chess player Benjamin Franklin stated in 1786, "Life is a kind of Chess, in which we have often points to gain, and competitors or adversaries to contend with" (qtd. in Shenk 88). In other words, when played to a certain standard chess can influence our decisions when engaging with the realities of life. The close relationship between war and chess is one that goes back to the origins of the game in which the very nature of the pieces dictates that the game should have the appearance of armies in battle. Samuel Rosenthal, a former chess master, encouraged this comparison in late nineteenth-century Paris. He believed,

> Both soldiers and players, regardless of their talent, must know a certain theory and certain principles. Indeed, [the soldier's] theory resembles ours. Isn't it true that it teaches him to conduct his troops on a battlefield according to established rules, to reassemble at the opportune moment, to have them converge at a determined point, in the briefest span of time? Shouldn't he try to make the others attack him there where he is the strongest, to charge fronts when the opponent attacks him at his vulnerable point, to manage his soldiers' lives for the ultimate moment? (Qtd. in Shenk 114–15)

He went on to say: "I could make an infinite number of comparisons, for the two are sisters: the path one follows, the method one uses to succeed in chess, are absolutely identical to those that the greatest commanders recommend" (ibid.). By arguing that war and chess are so closely connected Rosenthal not only echoes Franklin, but also many other observers over the years, including the twelfth-century Jewish scholar Abraham ibn Ezra, who wrote of chess:

> *All slaughter each other*
> *Wasting with great wrath each other*
> *[. . .] with yet no bloodshed.* (Qtd. in Shenk 116)

Shenk argues, "Enabling people to see themselves on the board would turn out to be [. . .] the great metaphorical contribution of chess over the centuries." This use of symbolic metaphor is important because it can "help us navigate complexity by reducing it to simpler, more manageable concepts. Chess is a powerful reducing agent. It can reduce a whole battlefield or city or planet down to sixty-four squares. And yet, within that simplistic frame, chess retains its active quality; like a snow globe, it shrinks things down but retains its dynamic essence" (Shenk 55–56). As a proponent of the game it is quite possible that Chandler used chess as a metaphor for the world in which the detective finds himself. He plays a game of order in a world devoid of order, where the rules of chess serve as a beacon of stability in a society too decadent and corrupt to abide by the laws that he struggles to defend. Chess, it would seem, is Marlowe's catharsis in a world turned on its head by world war, moral degeneration, and economic collapse.

Although Chandler noted that Marlowe's chess is not of tournament standard (qtd. in MacShane and Hiney 159), the detective is nevertheless an enthusiastic player. In the novels Marlowe acknowledges the mid-nineteenth-century Austrian chess master Wilhelm Steinitz and the Cuban world chess champion Jose Raul Capablanca, and considers both to be worthy opponents. Marlowe's recognition of the latter is especially important because Capablanca reached his peak at an important time in Chandler's life, becoming the world chess champion at the same time as Chandler was settling back into postwar life. Consequently, Chandler's references to these chess masters suggest that not only did he have a keen interest in the game but, more importantly, that they were real people who were transposed into his work to be admired by the fictional Marlowe. Since, as MacShane has noted, "Marlowe evolves from Chandler's own character" (69), it seems logical to assume that Chandler imprinted this aspect of chess reality into his work, and consequently it is not unreasonable to suppose that he also imprinted his own persona, including personality and methodology, onto his detective.

In Chandler's novels the world appears to turn inside out as Marlowe adopts the rules of the game in his quest to beat his real-life opponent. Assuming for a moment that the detective is a chess piece, and Los Angeles is the chessboard, Marlowe's unbending honesty and questing nature make him a perfect character in a real life game of chess played out across the city. Marlowe is the only character in the novels that, like the Knight, makes leaps of logic throughout the stories. The rules of chess also explain why Marlowe continues from case to case without ever appearing to win. A stalemate in a game of chess means that the game is concluded without either a winner or a loser, and the players have no alternative but to continue to the next game. This viewpoint explains Marlowe's continued perseverance; he is determined to win his cases despite his constant stalemates and is thus prompted to take on new cases. As Mardi Horowitz has noted, "Action is the prototypic terminator of stress states because action changes events. The knight who slays an attacking dragon terminates the threat. He [can] also discharge (or change) the state of his own rage and rage-action plans as activated by the [. . .] dragon's attack" (117). This discharge of emotions is short-lived for the detective, however; the end of a case brings no respite and provides an explanation for Marlowe's mounting disillusionment that gathers momentum throughout the series of novels.

Although Marlowe may possess knightly tendencies, he often unwittingly becomes a pawn in someone else's scheme, a perception competently demonstrated by his unwitting involvement with Lindsay Marriott in *Farewell, My Lovely*. The rigid nature of the rules of chess may therefore explain why Marlowe is more at ease with his board and pieces than with the deceitfulness and counterfeit sincerity that pervade the real world. The game allows him to relax while contemplating his next move; without extraneous influence he is able to plan his subsequent efforts. He practices using the games of the chess masters who become his confidants, people who understand his world. They are fellow crusaders who have sought to uphold the "rules" for which they fight. As Marlowe says in *The Long Goodbye*: "I set out the chessmen and played a French defense against Steinitz. He beat me in forty-four moves, but I had him sweating a couple of times . . . I might have been sore enough to beat the hell out of Steinitz—except that he had been dead for fifty years and the chess game was out of a book" (14–15).

Marlowe's mind works like a chess champion, continually reappraising and then amending strategy, as he does, for example, while attempting to fend off the advances of Carmen Sternwood in *The Big Sleep*. His feelings are unmistakable as he says, "I looked down at the chessboard. The move with the knight was wrong. I put it back where I had moved it from. Knights had no meaning in this game. It wasn't a game for knights" (153). This scene provides a rare insight into Marlowe's state of mind. Even though he is looking at the chessboard and appears to be referring to the game pieces, Marlowe is not actually referring to chess itself. Instead he is reassessing his most recent line of thought in the ongoing case. He senses that his current strategy is mistaken, and he needs to reconsider the move before committing to a better alternative that will eventually enable him to solve the case. It is when the tired detective discovers Carmen Sternwood in his bed that he realizes he has been chasing the wrong piece on the board. Instead of pursuing Carmen after the disappearance of Rusty Regan he has allowed his investigation to focus on Eddie Mars, the gangster whose wife disappeared at the same time. By placing the knight back in its original position Marlowe can now see clearly how the game will eventually play out and the tactics his opponent, Carmen, will pursue. He understands the game Carmen is playing, a game she has played in the past with Rusty Regan, to his downfall. He therefore understands the repercussions of his refusal to play. The detective realizes that Carmen is using her sexuality and sense of coy vulnerability as a strategy against him, and because of this knowledge, he loads her gun not with bullets but with blanks at the end of the novel. His awareness of Carmen's strategy and the caution he employs turn out to be well founded and eventually save his life.

Toward the end of *The Big Sleep* Marlowe appears to identify with the early twentieth-century playwright Samuel Beckett, who proposed that in his ideal game of chess the pieces would "move around for a while in futility, [and] in the end are back in their starting positions" (Shenk 192). By the end of the novel Marlowe senses the futility of his quest and is overwhelmed with disillusionment and disgust, which nullify any feeling of relief with his final "success." This same sense of disgust surfaces again in *The Lady in the Lake*, after the arrival of Derace Kingsley at Marlowe's apartment. Delivering five hundred dollars to Marlowe, the detective notes how "Kingsley tossed the envelope across and it fell on the chess table. I looked inside. It was money all right [. . .] I let it lie on the small polished table with its inlaid squares of brown and pale gold" (173–74). Taking the chessboard as a representation of how Marlowe perceives society, this single scene depicts the corruptive influence of money that serves to negate society's rules, which would otherwise be straightforward and logical. The gesture of leaving the money lying upon the chessboard is a clear representation of contemporary Los Angeles, a city in which everything may be bought. The casual "tossing" of the envelope contrasts with the delicate detail used to carefully describe the chess table and serves to emphasize the hypocrisy of Kingsley's request for Marlowe to find a way to clear his wife of murder, even though all the evidence points toward her guilt.

The chessboard is given further symbolic meaning in *The High Window*, when Merle Davies arrives at Marlowe's apartment deeply distressed, claiming to have killed Louis Vannier. Calming her down, Marlowe seats her in his "easy-chair behind the chess table," in a position "[t]hat put me just on the other side of the chess table from her" (202–3). The placing of Merle across the board from the detective symbolizes that Marlowe must solve the case before he can save Merle from her captor, Mrs. Murdock. In order to rescue the damsel in distress he must use all his skills to work his way across the board to win her freedom. For Chandler, it appears that chess was the simplest form of symbolism to convey the most basic of ideas and motifs.

Although Marlowe puts everything into his investigations, this effort exacts a severe physical and mental penalty. Yet he always comes back to the certainty of chess, which has a stabilizing effect on the detective. So, for example, at the conclusion of *The High Window*, he says: "I went home and put my old house clothes on and set the chess-men out and mixed myself a drink and played over another Capablanca. It went fifty-nine moves. Beautiful, cold, remorseless chess, almost creepy in its silent implacability" (272). To Marlowe, being comfortable means putting on his "house clothes" and setting up the chessboard. The "silent implacability" is exactly the calming atmosphere Marlowe craves to shut out the lawlessness and hypocrisy and soothe away the contempt he holds for society. He continues:

> When it was done I listened at the open window for a while and smelled the night. Then I carried my glass out to the kitchen and rinsed it and filled it with ice water and stood at the sink sipping it and looking at my face in the mirror.
>
> "You and Capablanca," I said. (Ibid.)

Marlowe strives to see beyond the chaos and ambiguity for the order and the rationality that only playing chess against a master, such as Capablanca, can provide. The mirror in this scene symbolizes two distinct things. First, it represents the two games that Marlowe has been playing, the chess game being a reflection of, and diversion from the game he plays at society's behest. Second, it represents the duality between the honest motivations of the detective and the corruption and depravity of society, a contrast represented by the traditionally light (good) and dark (bad) colors of the chess pieces.

Marlowe's fascination with chess is noted in many of the novels, and the detective regularly inspects his pieces as a general might inspect his troops. In *The High Window* Marlowe says, "The chessmen, red and white bone, were lined up ready to go and had that sharp, competent and complicated look they always have at the beginning of the game" (112). In *The Long Goodbye*, before playing a "championship tournament game between Gortchakoff and Meninkin," Marlowe inspects his pieces. He says, "I filled a pipe, paraded the chessmen, and inspected them for French shaves and loose buttons."[2]

Marlowe describes the game as "seventy-two moves to a draw, a prize specimen of the irresistible force meeting the immovable object [. . .] and as elaborate a waste of human intelligence as you could find anywhere outside an advertising agency" (*The Long Goodbye* 159). Speir has suggested that Marlowe's comment in this scene is one of disdain intended to signal that while he still has the desire to play the game he no longer holds it in such high regard (139). However, this is a misinterpretation of Marlowe's rationalization of what the game actually represents. By using chess as a representation of the detective's cynical view of society, Marlowe's contempt is reserved not for the game, but for society itself. Marlowe, in his most ambitious case to date, feels as though he has played "seventy-two moves to a draw," showing how weary the detective has become. He is playing the game to the best of his abilities, but all he can achieve is a stalemate in a social order that thrives on deception. Life itself has become a literal contest of "irresistible force meeting the immovable object." The object of Marlowe's disdain is a way of life that renders everything meaningless and trivial, and to sum it up he refers to it cynically as an "elaborate a waste of human intelligence as you could find anywhere outside an advertising agency." This interpretation also explains why "Mendy" Menendez insists on calling Marlowe "Tarzan on a big red scooter" (*The Long Goodbye* 64) in the same novel. As Speir explains, "Tarzan is a character of the heroic mould, but to have 'Tarzan on a big red scooter' suggests the hero well out of his element, in a new age." Marlowe, like the heroic Tarzan, "is drawn to the grand, heroic act but the modern world has rendered such acts 'plain foolish'" (Speir 77). This thread is also raised in *The Little Sister* when Delores Gonzales says to Marlowe, "You are a ridiculous character, amigo. You really are. I did not know they made such people any more." To which Marlowe replies, "Pre-war stock . . . We're getting scarcer every day" (160–61). Marlowe is, as Speir has argued, a hero out of his time, representing the ideals of a prewar era. He no longer feels he belongs and is left feeling like a "page from yesterday's calendar crumpled at the bottom of the waste basket" (*The Little Sister* 177).

Marlowe's fascination for the warlike game of chess, this "battle without armour, a war without blood" (*The Long Goodbye* 159), is suggestive of his own warrior background. As a veteran, chess would provide the military order and discipline absent in a society that has become so chaotic and where law and order had all but broken down. Unlike society, which often treats its members with disdain, chess is a game where every piece is valued and no piece is abandoned without a fight to protect it. As will be discussed later, according to these rules a sacrifice is never offered unless the benefits are clear. Marlowe's conscious nonintervention in the death of Harry Jones during *The Big Sleep* is clear evidence that this rule has meaning for the detective.

According to Chandler, Marlowe studies his chess games from a "little paper-bound book of tournament games published in Leipzig" which came into the detective's possession from an unknown source (Bodleian 57:172–268, p. 219). It is interesting that he should have a copy of a book published in Germany because it is suggestive of a European connection, yet as far as we can tell the detective does not speak the language and has never been to Europe. However, Chandler himself undertook "instruction in French, German, and Spanish" (MacShane, *Life* 8) at Dulwich, and later, at the age of seventeen, spent a year in Paris and Munich. He indulged his interest in languages later in life and often incorporated them into the dialogue of his stories. As Hiney says, "Unlike many of the middle-class Californians who saw Mexico as a kind of glorious hobby, Chandler spoke Spanish" (286). In *The Long Goodbye* Chandler introduces a Chilean housekeeper who banters with Marlowe in Spanish, and as Hiney notes: "As late as 1956, [Chandler] had his Olivetti typewriter customized to incorporate Spanish accents, so that his Mexican gangsters could insult Marlowe in their native tongue" (ibid.).

It is natural to assume that whatever languages Chandler had mastered, Marlowe could also speak. It is an indicator that while developing Marlowe's character Chandler gave the detective a reason for spending time in Europe and points toward parallels between author and protagonist. While it is certainly possible that Marlowe discovered the book in Los Angeles, it is equally possible that he brought it back as a souvenir from Europe. Although Marlowe does not mention leaving the United States, the chess book ties him quite specifically to Europe. Opportunities for Americans to go to Europe at the time would have been limited, and since Marlowe does not appear to be wealthy enough to have visited Europe on his own, it is conceivable that he left America to perform military service during the First World War. If the book is from Europe, it could have come into Marlowe's possession if he had been involved in the First World War.

Chandler noted that his detective "prefers the continental method of designating the squares on a chess board" (Bodleian 57:172–268, p. 219). This is almost certainly a reference to the descriptive notation used to identify the squares in a game of chess. This method is a technique that had become firmly established in English-, French-, and Spanish-speaking countries during Chandler's lifetime, where "the files of the board [the vertical columns] are named after the pieces which stand in them at the start of the game [...] But the ranks [the horizontal rows] are numbered by each player beginning to count from his own side of the board, with the result that each square has two different names, depending upon whether White or Black describes them" (Lasker 15). For example, if a knight is moved to queen's bishop three, the descriptive method requires that it be noted as Kt–QB3, and so on. The alternative algebraic notation is far simpler, but was not as widely used as the more traditional descriptive method. According to the algebraic method the vertical columns (files) are lettered a to h from left to right, and the horizontal rows (ranks) are numbered 1 to 8 beginning at the bottom left corner of each player's board. Recording movements in this method would, for example, denote pawn to queen's bishop four as c7–c5.

Chandler's novels reveal that Marlowe uses the descriptive method of notation used mainly in Europe. As he says in *The High Window*, "I opened a little paper-bound book [...] picked out a dashing-looking Queen's Gambit, moved the white pawn to Queen's four" (112). This comment points to the fact that Marlowe was familiar with the continental chess notation and at some point had acquired a German chess book. Marlowe was also the proud owner of another European acquisition, a German Luger. These small details hint that Marlowe could be the soldier Chandler describes in his short story "Trench Raid," who, like the later Marlowe, is resigned to endure his fate, whatever it may be. The anonymous soldier "began to concentrate on the shells. If you heard them they never hit you. With a meticulous care he set himself to picking out the ones that would come near enough to be reckoned on as a possible introduction to immortality. To these he listened with a sort of cold exhausted passion" (qtd. in MacShane, *Life* 29–30). Although written in the third person, it is not implausible to assume that not only did Marlowe have his genesis in Chandler's short detective stories, but also in the much earlier war-related story "Trench Raid." As such, the Marlowe novels can be interpreted as Chandler's attempt at portraying a veteran who adapts by becoming a soldier in another theater, and reveals the reactions he receives and difficulties he faced when trying to reintegrate into society.

Chess may also have a larger significance in our understanding of Marlowe. As well as being a retreat from the real world, Shenk has noted that chess can become an obsession that is capable of exacerbating underlying mental illness, and in extremely severe cases may even cause it. This happens because "chess taps into primal forces far beyond our immediate control. Clearly, something profound, thrilling, and even somewhat terrifying takes place on its mental stage. And the game's close association with a particular variety of mental illness suggests that something potentially destructive may lurk beneath the surface for some players" (qtd. in Shenk 149). And Tim Redman questions, "After all, what is a chess tournament? [It] is, by definition, an activity in which you spend many hours each day, using your best intellectual and imaginative abilities to figure out how the other player is out to get you. [It is a] constant exercise of [the] 'paranoid faculty'" (ibid.). Playing against oneself or from a book, as Marlowe does, is allegedly one of the foremost ways of exacerbating this connection. As the Austrian writer Stefan Zweig concluded in one of his short stories,

> The fundamental attraction of chess lies, after all, in the fact its strategy develops . . . in two different brains, that in this mental battle Black, ignorant of White's immediate manoeuvres, seeks constantly to guess and thwart them, while White, for his part, strives to penetrate Black's secret purposes and to discern and parry them. If one person tries to be both Black and White you have the preposterous situation that one and the same brain at once know something and yet does not know it; that, functioning as White's partner, it can instantly obey a command to forget what, a moment earlier as Black's partner, it desired and plotted. (Qtd. in Shenk 149–50)

Ironically, this particular psychological disorder is reflected in a comment Chandler jokingly made to Dale Warren in 1949, when he said, "If I ever wrote a non-fiction book, it would probably turn out to be the autobiography of a split personality" (qtd. in MacShane, *Letters* 176).

Yet Marlowe is clearly aware of the intellectual torment of chess and the psychological effect it can have on those playing it. In *The Long Goodbye*, he says:

> I put the chessboard on the coffee table and set out a problem called The Sphinx [. . . It] is an eleven-mover and it justifies its name. Chess problems seldom run to more than four or five moves. Beyond that the difficulty of solving them rises in almost geometrical progression. An eleven-mover is sheer unadulterated torture.
>
> Once in a long while when I feel mean enough I set it out and look for a new way to solve it. It's a nice quiet way to go crazy. You don't even scream, but you come awfully close. (243)

Although there are no grounds to suggest that Marlowe suffered from schizophrenia, he is certainly a man at war with himself. As a traumatized war veteran, playing too much chess may have aggravated some of Chandler's symptoms, which were subsequently transposed to Marlowe. Zweig identifies something that Chandler may have been subconsciously aware of, that the total absorption in war, whether on a board or in reality, can induce psychological illness. Chess, then, can become on the one hand a refuge but on the other an aggravating factor for mental deterioration.

The typical ending to a Marlowe novel sees the detective disillusioned, having suffered physiological as well as physical injury in his struggle against injustice. Yet still he does not concede. Although troubled, he is sustained by his dogged resolve in much the same way as Chandler described Hemingway: "[W]hen he can no longer throw the high hard one, he throws his heart instead. He throws something. He doesn't just walk off the mound and weep" (qtd. in Hiney 206). Marlowe displays the same determination that embodies the perseverance and courage of a knight during battle on a chessboard. Benjamin Franklin also noted this temperament of single mindedness in 1786. He believed that chess taught three essential lessons to a player, "the habit of not being discouraged by present bad appearances in the state of our affairs, the habit of hoping for a favorable change, and that of persevering in search of resources" (qtd. in Shenk 282). Franklin believed that chess players were resilient types who did not give up and simply walk away in frustration, but instead, like Marlowe, they were unyielding in the face of adversity.

While Marlowe's character appears to stem from knightly origins, the detective's character is considerably more complex. Because of the turbulent society he lives in, Marlowe has come to rely on the game of chess as the only form of regaining a sense of order in his life. It is comforting for the detective because he is finally able to locate himself within a meaningful and structured context. Although Marlowe feels dislocated and disillusioned, qualities that are constantly reinforced throughout the novels, his affinity for the warlike game of chess keeps him focused and gives him a sense of order. The use of an intimate first-person style provides a far deeper insight into Marlowe's innermost thoughts and reveals his private psychological struggles. For all of Marlowe's honorable intentions, he is frustrated by society's ignorance of his sacrifices. The conflicting aspects of Marlowe's character are clear, for while he wants to be a modern-day knight he cannot prevent the overwhelming sense of disillusionment and cynicism toward the world in which he lives. Chandler's own emotional trauma is mirrored in his detective, and although

Marlowe displays definite veteran tendencies on the surface, these do not provide the whole story. It is the detective's dislocated and traumatized mind that provides the key to unlocking his tormented character. Marlowe's private battle to come to terms with his demons and regain control of his emotions is vital for understanding the weary detective's motivations.

6

THE LONG GOODBYE

Nobody understands me . . . I'm enigmatic.

—PHILIP MARLOWE, IN CHANDLER, *THE LONG GOODBYE*

The Long Goodbye, Raymond Chandler's penultimate novel, was to be his most personal and ambitious work. The novel is, at one and the same time, a psychobiographical work and a bold experiment to consciously go beyond the limitations of the traditional detective genre. It is a novel in which John S. Whitely notes that "the conventions are used so flexibly that, without actually transgressing the formula, he incorporated a kind of love story, full of pathos and subtle character definition, within those conventions" (22). Published in 1953 the novel is significant because it demonstrates Chandler's identification with the character of the veteran, revealing evidence of PTSD in all three veteran characters: Philip Marlowe, Terry Lennox, and Roger Wade. The two main characters are both psychologically troubled veterans of the Second World War, haunted by their harrowing experiences. Although Lennox and Wade never meet, Philip Marlowe is drawn into a complicated case that reflects upon traumatic war experience, lost wartime love, and murderous jealousy that has far-reaching consequences.

Yet the significance of *The Long Goodbye* goes still further since it symbolizes the pinnacle of Chandler's traumatic literature, a synthesis of the recurring theme of trauma and the characterization of psychologically flawed individuals of his previous novels brought to skillful fruition in a work generally considered to be Chandler's greatest novel. Published two years after Chandler wrote "A Couple of Writers," *The Long Goodbye* is noteworthy for the supportive attachment that links together the characters of Marlowe, Lennox, and Wade, emblematic of a complex yet loyal bond between three similarly characterized men. Yet, as this chapter will demonstrate, while each character individually represents a distinctive facet of life as a war veteran, their foremost importance lies in the fact that, understood together, they all ultimately personify Chandler himself: the cynicism and disenchantment that emerged from his war experience and additionally his uncertainty about his own place in the American literary landscape. Natasha Spender, Chandler's friend and confidante in his final years, drew attention to the three highly conspicuous self-portraits presented within the novel. She explains that Lennox adopts the persona of an emotionally and physically scarred war hero with an English accent and manners, while Wade is an aging, disillusioned, alcoholic writer of popular fiction whose writing causes him extreme anxiety and extreme self-loathing. Marlowe, by consequence, represses his trauma and acts as the writer's conscience. It was the Marlowe within Chandler "which pushed the Roger Wade within him[,] though not without commendation for achievement[, . . .] and befriended the Terry Lennox within, not without censure" (qtd. in Gross 135).

Ultimately, however, *The Long Goodbye* seeks to expose human sympathies and weaknesses in the counterfeit sincerity that engulfs a hostile American society. It is a wide-ranging condemnation of the shallow sources and corrupted output of American culture in the early 1950s. Along the way Chandler and an increasingly sensitive Marlowe absorb the phony superficiality of American society through the tawdriness of American media; the outrageous betrayal of medical ethics by numerous quack doctors; the insincerity and worthlessness of people who run for public office; the boredom of the rich; and the culture of deceit that inextricably binds successful business to the dishonesty of organized crime.

While Chandler had included fleeting glimpses of veteran characters in previous novels—General Sternwood in *The Big Sleep*, Bill Chess in *The Lady in the Lake*—Terry Lennox is the first fleshed-out character explicitly characterized as a veteran war hero. Lennox is a principal character in *The Long Goodbye* despite the fact that he is absent for the majority of the novel; his background, personality, and war experience act as the fulcrum of the novel. Introduced in the very first sentence, Marlowe befriends the inebriated war veteran when he is abandoned by his selfish wife, Sylvia, who drives away leaving him all but in the gutter. Noticing that Lennox has a "young-looking face," Marlowe also observes that "his hair was bone white" (5). But besides these immediately noticeable features, Marlowe is drawn to the most distressing aspect of Lennox's appearance: "The right side of my new friend's face was frozen and whitish and seamed with thin, fine scars. The skin had a glossy look along the scars" (*The Long Goodbye* 7). We later discover that these unsightly scars are the enduring legacy of an injury incurred during the Second World War. As Lennox's hoodlum acquaintance and fellow veteran "Mendy" Menendez recounts:

> "We were three guys in a foxhole eating," he said. "It was cold as hell, snow all around. We ate out of cans. Cold food. A little shelling, more mortar fire. We are blue with the cold, and I mean blue, Randy Starr and me and this Terry Lennox. A mortar shell plops right in the middle of us and for some reason it don't go off. Those Jerries have a lot of tricks. They got a twisted sense of humour. Sometimes you don't think it's a dud and three seconds later it ain't a dud. Terry grabs it and he's out of the fox hole before Randy and me can even start to get unstuck. But I mean quick, brother. Like a goof ball handler. He throws himself face down and throws the thing away from him and it goes off in the air. Most of it goes over his head but a hunk gets the side of his face. Right then the krauts mount an attack and the next thing we know we ain't there any more." (*The Long Goodbye* 66)

Marlowe warms to Menendez's honesty and says, "Thanks for telling me" (ibid.). He begins to identify with Lennox and appreciates the protectiveness shown by Menendez and Randy Starr toward their fellow veteran. Menendez, moreover, seems to recognize something in Marlowe, and after an uneasy first encounter he feels a kinship for the detective, saying, "You're okay" (ibid.). Menendez continues his story by explaining how the experience dramatically altered Lennox's life and instigated a physical and psychological deterioration as soon as he arrived home: "[W]hat happened to Terry Lennox was enough to screw up any guy's brains [. . .] All Terry gets out of saving our lives is half a new face, white hair, and a bad case of nerves. Back east he hits the bottle, gets picked up here and there, kind of goes to pieces. There's something on his mind but we never know about it" (ibid.). This depiction is soon corroborated by Eileen Wade when she reasons that Lennox "must have been insane" (*The Long Goodbye* 88) when he brutally murdered Sylvia, a murder that we later learn was committed by Eileen herself. Significantly, Marlowe responds: "He must have been. He was badly wounded during the war" (ibid.). This comment is a highly significant moment in the novel, and indeed for Chandler's body of work as a whole, because it is here that the detective (and Chandler) openly accepts that war *can* cause serious psychological problems for veterans. Marlow believes that the trauma received during the war serves to mitigate Lennox's actions.

As Marlowe begins to understand the dynamic that exists between Lennox and the mobsters Menendez and Starr, his concern about the veteran Lennox palpably grows. After their initial meeting Marlowe reveals just how protective he has become toward Lennox, and after a few short hours in each other's company, he admits: "I drove home chewing my lip. I'm supposed to be tough but there was something about the guy that got to me. I didn't know what it was unless it was the white hair and the scarred face and the clear voice and the politeness. Maybe that was enough" (*The Long Goodbye* 9). Significantly, the war experience and polite demeanor are strongly reminiscent of the influences and behavior that shaped Chandler's own life. Marlowe further reveals his fear for his new friend and says to Lennox that he might find himself "in worse trouble than I can get you out of" (*The Long Goodbye* 13). Assuming that it is because of his facial wounds Lennox self-consciously "touched the right side of his face gently with two finger-tips. "Maybe it's this. It does make me look a little sinister, I suppose. But it's an honourable wound—or anyhow the result of one" (*The Long Goodbye* 13). Nothing could be further from Marlowe's mind, and rejecting Lennox's assumption he states: "It's not that. That doesn't bother me at all" (ibid.). Chandler's own compassion for fellow veterans made him eager to not just include veteran characters in his novels but go to great lengths to try to educate his reading public that they deserved accreditation for their adversity, a point consciously reflected in Marlowe's own sympathetic relationship with Lennox.

In many ways Lennox and Marlowe are very similar, yet Marlowe's harsh opinion of Lennox at the end of the novels reveals how deeply betrayed the detective feels by Lennox's actions:

> For a long time I couldn't figure you at all. You had nice ways and nice qualities, but there was something wrong. You had standards and you lived up to them, but they were personal. They had no relation to any kind of ethics or scruples. You were a nice guy because you had a nice nature. But you were just as happy with mugs or hoodlums as with honest men. Provided the hoodlums spoke fairly good English and had fairly acceptable table manners. You're a moral defeatist. I think maybe the war did it and again I think maybe you were born that way. (*The Long Goodbye* 319)

In Marlowe's condemnatory opinion of Lennox the morally ambivalent attitudes of the detective are plain to see. Although Marlowe feels betrayed by

Lennox they ultimately share a very similar moral viewpoint. And in defense of his actions Lennox argues:

> "I don't get it," he said. "I really don't. I'm trying to pay you back and you won't let me. I couldn't have told you any more than I did. You wouldn't have stood for it . . . I got in a bad jam. I happened to know the sort of people who know how to deal with bad jams. They owed me for an incident that happened long ago in the war. Probably the only time in my life I ever did the right thing quick like a mouse. And when I needed them, they delivered. And for free. You're not the only guy in the world that has no price tag, Marlowe." (*The Long Goodbye* 319)

Lennox demonstrates here that he and Marlowe share the same sense of honor as Menendez and Starr, who helped Lennox in his time of need. Despite their former friendship, Lennox is quick to point out that Marlowe is acting haughtily by pointing out that the detective is not the only person with good intentions and a moral code; like Marlowe, Lennox did what he had to do in a difficult situation. Dismayed that Marlowe does not understand, Lennox shows his emotion when we are told: "There was suddenly a glint of tears in his eyes. He put his dark glasses back on quickly" (ibid.).

What becomes plain, however, is that Marlowe's stubborn refusal to come to terms with Lennox's argument exposes two distinct possibilities. On the one hand, it can be argued that Marlowe had long since accepted Lennox's death and is wounded by his sudden return and drastic change of appearance. Appearing to backtrack from his earlier stance following Lennox's admission that his torture by the Nazis "did something to me" (*The Long Goodbye* 320), Marlowe says: "I know all that, Terry. You're a very sweet guy in a lot of ways. I'm not judging you. I never did. It's just that you're not here any more. You're long gone. You've got nice clothes and perfume and you're as elegant as a fifty-dollar whore" (ibid.).

On the other hand, however, this exchange displays Marlowe's real concern about Lennox: he has become the very thing that Marlowe rails against in the novel, a user and manipulator—a "fifty-dollar whore"—and as such, Lennox becomes part of the unstable society that the detective is constantly resisting. Lennox pleads for Marlowe to recognize that his behavior was "just an act" (ibid.), yet he knows that he will not change the detective's mind. Leaving Marlowe to wallow in his own self-pity, Lennox leaves him with these final words: "'In here'—he tapped his chest with the lighter—'there isn't anything. I've had it, Marlowe. I had it long ago'" (ibid.). As he stands listening to Lennox's footsteps echo down the corridor, the degree of Marlowe's regret at seeing Lennox leave is clear, and yet his pride prevents him from pursuing his former friend: "I listened to his steps going away down the imitation marble corridor. After a while they got faint, then they got silent. I kept on listening anyway. What for? Did I want him to stop and suddenly turn and come back and talk me out of the way if felt? Well, he didn't. That was the last I saw of him" (ibid.). The detective's level of disillusionment is palpable, and the novel ends on a distinctly pessimistic and dejected note.

Many of the symptoms that psychiatrists have observed in veterans can be seen quite clearly in the three veteran characters in *The Long Goodbye*. We see the signature signs of "startle[d] reactions, hyperalertness, vigilance for the return of danger, nightmares, and psychosomatic complaints" which "could be understood as resulting from chronic arousal of the autonomic nervous system" (Herman 35). What's more we witness these symptoms throughout the novel; as the following passage illustrates, the level of self-control Marlowe requires in order to function shows that he himself is by no means a stranger to many of these distressing symptoms. He explains: "Why do I go into such detail? Because the charged atmosphere made everything little stand out as a performance, a movement distinct and vastly important. It was one of those hypersensitive moments, when all your automatic movements, however long established, however habitual, became separate acts of will. You are like a man learning to walk after polio. You take nothing for granted" (*The Long Goodbye* 25). But while Marlowe's behavior is self-evident, it is in the characters of Lennox and Wade that we see the most prominent indications of postcombat trauma. Lennox is a "wounded war-hero" (*The Long Goodbye* 56), and Wade "has a war record and a good one" (*The Long Goodbye* 91), making it apparent that both have suffered from the effects of war. Marlowe is especially aware that Lennox has suffered acutely from his time at war. Eileen Wade explains: "In October 1942 [. . .] Hitler issued an order that all Commando prisoners were to be turned over to the Gestapo. I think we all know what that meant. Torture and nameless death in some Gestapo dungeon" (*The Long Goodbye* 256). Although Eileen believed that Lennox was dead, he had actually survived only to suffer his own living death. "The krauts got him. They worked him over, for about a year and a half," Menendez reveals. "They did a good job but they hurt him too much" (*The Long Goodbye* 66). As well as Menendez's revelation, Lennox himself admits: "I got badly hurt and it wasn't any fun with those Nazi doctors" (*The Long Goodbye* 76). His experiences of torture during the war have left him not just physically but also deeply psychologically scarred. He has become an alcoholic and despite his heroic ordeals still considers himself "a weak character, without guts or ambition. I caught the brass ring and it shocked me to find out it wasn't gold. A guy like me has one big moment in his life, one perfect swing on the high trapeze. Then he spends the rest of his time trying not to fall off the sidewalk into the gutter" (*The Long Goodbye* 22). Lennox like Marlowe suffers from extreme disillusionment, yet his belief that he has "caught the brass ring" only "to find out it wasn't gold" is comparable to Hank Bruton's despair and sense of utter dejection in Chandler's short story "A Couple of Writers." It is also reminiscent of Dashiell Hammett's "Flitcraft parable" in *The Maltese Falcon* (1930) in which Sam Spade comments on Charles Flitcraft's observation that "somebody had taken the lid off life and let him look at the works" (61), a parable that resonates strongly with the disillusionment of all three veteran characters in *The Long Goodbye*.

As the story unfolds, Terry Lennox's war experiences come under inspection on a number of occasions, and though the details of Roger Wade's war experiences are never conveyed, we know that he too is a war veteran and an author by profession whose alcohol dependency is so damaging that he no longer has the will to write. Much like Marlowe and other veterans of war, Wade uses alcohol as a means of escaping the memories of the past and drudgery of the present. Marlowe believes that Wade "has a guilty secret and he tries to drown it in alcohol" (*The Long Goodbye* 81). Recognizing the damaging effects of combat Marlowe concludes: "[W]hat's the matter with Roger Wade is something that happened a long time ago [. . . , and] it has caught up with him now, and is hitting him harder than he can take" (*The Long Goodbye* 91). As seen in "A Couple of Writers," the war veteran's use of alcohol as a calming device is viewed by family and friends as an embarrassment, and Wade's wife responds in a similar way to Marion Bruton by ignoring his desperate and pitiful state of mind after

> [S]he was standing in the open doorway with a cigarette in her mouth [. . .] She looked at me calmly. If there was any excitement around there I had brought it with me.
>
> "He fell down [. . .] He cut his head on something. There's a little blood, not much."
>
> "Well, that's fine [. . .] We wouldn't want a whole lot of blood. Where is he now?"
>
> She looked at me solemnly. Then she pointed. "Out there somewhere. By the edge of the road or in the bushes along the fence."

> I leaned forward and peered at her. "Chrissake, didn't you look?" [. . .]
>
> "No, I didn't look," she said quite calmly. "You find him. I've had all of it I can take. I've had more than I can take. You find him."
>
> She turned and walked back into the house, leaving the door open. (*The Long Goodbye* 161–62)

Taken aback by her bluntness, Marlowe contemplates her outburst and thinks, "[I]t didn't quite add up. You'd expect her to look for him and find him and make sure he wasn't hurt [. . .] you wouldn't expect to find her standing in the open doorway smoking a cigarette, not knowing except very vaguely where he was" (*The Long Goodbye* 170). Later in the novel Marlowe confronts Eileen directly by stating: "You don't really want to save him, do you? You just want to look as if you are trying to save him" (185).

By refusing to acknowledge Wade's problems Eileen effectively forces her husband to find refuge with the "barred window boys" (*The Long Goodbye* 106), as Marlowe calls the rogue doctors who live by offering false hope and phony drying-out treatments. Eileen justifies her behavior in belittling her husband's problems by arguing, "You can't treat a grown man like a child with a sore throat" (*The Long Goodbye* 93), to which Marlowe disparagingly responds: "You can if he's drunk. Often you damn well have to" (ibid.). Marlowe is quick to inform her that in severe cases such as Wade's, immediate treatment is essential, and here we get the distinct feeling that he is speaking from his own experience. While it is well known that the detective routinely resorts to alcohol during stressful situations or as a means of escape, it is in this novel that we begin to uncover more about Marlowe's battles with alcohol dependency. In an earlier conversation with Terry Lennox—during which Lennox considers: "Maybe I can quit drinking one of these days. They all say that don't they?"—Marlowe's informed response is intuitive. He simply says, "It takes about three years." While Lennox is shocked that it will take so long, Marlowe's words suggest that the detective speaks from personal experience: "Usually it does. It's a different world. You have to get used to a paler set of colors, a quieter lot of sounds. You have to allow for relapses. All the people you know well will get to be just a little strange. You won't even like most of them, and they won't like you too well" (*The Long Goodbye* 12). Wade also recognizes that Marlowe has battled alcohol addiction and later probes the detective for further information, asking: "Not everybody gets drunk. What are *you* running away from?" a question that Marlowe avoids answering (*The Long Goodbye* 148). Significantly, Wade has had a longstanding problem with alcohol, confessing to the detective: "It's got worse, but I was always a hard man with a bottle. When you're young and in hard condition you can absorb a lot of punishment. When you are pushing forty you don't snap back the same way" (ibid.). It is quite possible that Chandler is telling us here that Wade's excessive drinking has its roots in his youth, potentially as a consequence of his war experience.

Throughout the novel, Wade is consistently characterized as a person who is not only troubled and anxious, but one who has subconsciously blanked from his memory a lingering secret. Wade says to Marlowe during a dinner party held by his wife:

> "There's something I want to know, that I have to know. You don't know what it is and I'm not sure I know myself. All I'm positive of is that there is something, and I have to know it."
>
> "About who? Your wife?"
>
> He moved his lips one over the other. "I think it's about me," he said. (*The Long Goodbye* 150)

Marlowe instantly recognizes the trouble Wade is having and is quick to suggest a course of action to his wife:

> "He needs a psychiatrist, Mrs Wade."
>
> She looked startled. "A psychiatrist? Why?"
>
> "You want an amateur opinion, here it is. He thinks he has a secret buried in his mind and he can't get at it. It may be a guilty secret about himself, it may be about someone else. He thinks that's what makes him drink, because he can't get at this thing. He probably thinks that whatever happened, happened while he was drunk and he ought to find it wherever people go when they're drunk—really bad drunk, the way he gets. That's a job for a psychiatrist." (*The Long Goodbye* 155)

Later it is taken for granted that Wade has committed suicide because, in the words of Marlow, "He's a haunted man. He has a massive guilt complex" (*The Long Goodbye* 200), a verdict that could just as easily be a description of Chandler's own experience and behavior. By putting his own words and feeling into the mouths of each of his characters Chandler is divulging his personal view that in the end, as Marlowe says, "the only salvation for a writer is to write," even if "he has fallen out of love with the kind of stuff he writes" (*The Long Goodbye* 81, 90).

Many of the seemingly obscure notes written by Wade when intoxicated are inscrutably cryptic yet also revealing. In one instance Wade writes a letter in which he refers to F. Scott Fitzgerald. The letter, read by Marlowe, says, "I do not care to be in love with myself and there is no longer any-one else for me to be in love with. Signed: Roger (F Scott Fitzgerald) Wade. P.S. This is why I never finished The Last Tycoon" (*The Long Goodbye* 92). This note yields an insight into Wade's state of mind and intriguingly into Chandler's literary admirations. In clarifying Wade's words, Eileen admits that her husband has "always been a great admirer of Scott Fitzgerald. He says Fitzgerald is the best drunken writer since Coleridge, who took dope" (*The Long Goodbye* 92). The reference here to Samuel Taylor Coleridge, the English poet, literary critic, and philosopher who, with along with William Wordsworth, was a founder of the romantic movement in England, is clearly a reference to Chandler's own classical reading. Yet Chandler's linking of Coleridge and Fitzgerald is fascinating since it uses their common addiction to numbing agents—opium and alcohol respectively—to connect the two legendary writers from different literary movements. Fitzgerald was a writer that Chandler greatly respected; a decade after Fitzgerald's death of a heart attack, brought on by years of heavy drinking, Chandler wrote to Dale Warren, the publicity director of Houghton Mifflin, noting: "I think he just missed being a great writer, and the reason is pretty obvious. If the poor guy was already an alcoholic in his college days, it's a marvel that he did as well as he did. He had one of the rarest qualities in all literature [. . .] the word is charm" (qtd. in MacShane, *Letters* 239). Such was Chandler's reverence for Fitzgerald that it was only a disagreement with the studios that had prevented Chandler from working on a film adaptation of *The Great Gatsby* in the 1940s. It was a novel that Chandler once described as: "not perfect; evasive of the problem often, side-stepping scenes which should have been written, but somehow passing along, crystallized, complete, and, as such things go nowadays, eternal, a little pure art" (qtd. in Hiney and MacShane 235). However, Marlowe in very simple terms believes that "the Scott Fitzgerald allusion [. . .] might be merely an off-beat way of saying good-bye" (*The Long Goodbye* 95). In a novel full of goodbyes, Marlowe's theory is more suggestive of Wade's frustration with his life and with his writing. His goodbye, if that is what his letter really is, might in fact represent an admission of his desire to escape from both his rich but phony life and his writing, by drinking and then disappearing.

Chandler would have been mindful of the attraction of escaping from the self-imposed confinement of his writing as he labored to complete *The Long Goodbye* during one of the most painful periods of his life, a subject that weighed heavily upon his mind: "I guess I don't mind being destroyed very much anymore [. . .] I watched my wife die by half-inches and I wrote my best book in the agony of that knowledge, and yet I wrote it. I don't know how. I used to shut myself in my study and think myself into another world" (qtd. in Hiney and MacShane 228). The ridicule that Wade heaps upon his work has echoes in Chandler's own self-doubt and uncertainty about his own worth in the writing profession. As Wade says: "You're looking right at a small-time operator in a small-time business, Marlowe. All writers are punks and I am one of the punkest" (*The Long Goodbye* 148–49). Wade does not hold back. He continues:

> I've written twelve best-sellers [. . .] And not a damn one of them worth the powder to blow it to hell. I have a lovely home in a highly restricted residential neighborhood that belongs to a highly restricted multimillionaire. I have a lovely wife who loves me and a lovely publisher who loves me and I love me the best of all. I'm an egotistical son of a bitch, a literary prostitute or pimp—chose your own word—and an all-round heel. (*The Long Goodbye* 149)

Wade's words are an expression of the derision for the style which had made him wealthy and famous and is suggestive of Chandler's own inner dissatisfaction with the genre; as Wade later says, "I could vomit just thinking about the lousy racket" (*The Long Goodbye* 172). It seems as though these insightful extracts are an illuminating window into Chandler's own frame of mind at the time.

While Chandler's self-reflective insights are certainly enlightening, it is his use of suppressed memory, blackouts, and guilt that makes *The Long Goodbye* such a fascinating text. Acknowledging theories of the subconscious by referring to "some Freudian bastard" (*The Long Goodbye* 148) Chandler weaves his plot around a complex psychological theory, a plot that originates before the Second World War in England with the marriage of Paul Marston (Terry Lennox) and Eileen Sampsell (later, Wade). Exploiting both of her husbands' mental frailties, Eileen—as Sylvia Lennox's real murderer—first blames the scarred Lennox and then the traumatized Roger Wade, for Sylvia's death. Although she refers to Lennox as insane, it is for Wade that Eileen saves her most hostile accusation. Seizing upon Marlowe's belief that the source of Wade's troubles originated "a long time ago" (*The Long Goodbye* 91) she puts together a story that dupes the detective into suspecting that Wade's hidden memory is in fact the guilt he harbors for Sylvia's murder. She says later: "Roger didn't know he had killed her. He had blacked out completely. He knew something was wrong and he tried to bring it to the surface, but he couldn't. The shock had destroyed his memory of it" (*The Long Goodbye* 260). Wade is burdened with an enormous guilt complex and starts believing that the police and the media have wrongly blamed Terry Lennox for a crime that he himself committed, and he remorsefully says, "A good man died for me once" (*The Long Goodbye* 157). Although Wade does not disclose the identity of this "good man," the suggestion is that Lennox's flight to Mexico and subsequent "death" mean that in the eyes of the police Sylvia's murder is deemed solved, while in Wade's eyes an innocent man died for his crime.

Wade's reaction to Lennox's death is strikingly similar to the needless shame of survivor guilt that often haunts war veterans as they display a "sense of heightened vulnerability" (Lifton 106), or as Herman says about the condition, "To be spared oneself in the knowledge that others have met a worse fate, creates a severe burden of conscience" (54). While writing the novel Chandler appeared to be similarly vulnerable and fragile, and his erratic emotions appear to be indicative of survivor guilt. Wade's belief that a good man died for him suggests that Chandler subconsciously drew on his own experience of the ailment when penning his work. One of the most common symptoms of survivor guilt is the predisposition toward suicide, which is a disconcerting feature of Wade's character and contextualizes his attempts to take his own life. Dismissing the incident as "Just a wild shot into the ceiling,"[1] Wade's escalation from heavy drinking to attempted suicide would imply that his traumatized mind had gone beyond the need for anesthetizing agents and reached a serious level of instability.

The Long Goodbye is the only novel in which Marlowe develops genuine male friendships, and it is no coincidence that the characters he befriends are both war veterans. Lennox, too, admits to Marlowe that the interdependence is mutual and derived from the shared experience of war that forges close relationships between men: "Randy and I and another fellow were in a jam once. *It made a sort of bond between us*" (*The Long Goodbye* 18. Emphasis added). Similarly, Marlowe's relationship with Lennox suggests, as Freeman notes, "the love of an achingly lonely man for one true buddy, a soul mate of the same sex" (173).

After receiving news of Lennox's supposed death in Mexico, Marlowe carries out the instructions that Lennox had left for him in a letter written shortly before his death: "I did what he asked me to do, sentimental or not. I poured two cups and added some bourbon to his and set it down on the side of the table where he had sat the morning I took him to the plane. I lit a cigarette for him and set it in an ashtray beside the cup. I watched the steam rise from the coffee and the thin thread of smoke rise from the cigarette" (*The Long Goodbye* 73). While many have attributed Marlowe's actions as a symbol of his sentimentality, he is merely displaying a natural human response to the death of a friend. The detective is, after all, human; he is mourning the passing of a fellow veteran who had suffered a particularly harrowing war experience. When later in the novel Marlowe is asked to explain his motives for assisting Lennox and his reluctance to accept any money, Marlowe tries to explain their relationship and his poignant goodbye to Bernie Ohls: "The last time I saw Terry Lennox we had a cup of coffee together that I made myself here in this house, and we smoked a cigarette. So when I heard he was dead I went out to the kitchen and made some coffee and poured a cup for him and lit a cigarette for him, and when the coffee was cold and the cigarette was burned down I said good night to him" (*The Long Goodbye* 237). Chandler proclaimed that his intention in writing the novel was to emphasize the overpowering duplicity that sullies everything in society and which brings an enforced individualism that atomizes any trace of community and compassion. He said: "I wrote this as I wanted [. . .] I didn't care whether the mystery was fairly obvious, but I cared about the people, about this strange corrupt world we live in, and how any man who tried to be honest looks in the end either sentimental or plain foolish" (qtd. in Hiney 315). However, far from being sentimental, Marlowe's actions and emotions toward the departed Lennox highlight something far more fundamental to the detective's state of mind: his loneliness. Later in the novel Marlowe drinks a gimlet in honor of Lennox and meets Linda Loring, the sister of Sylvia Lennox. After he explains his purpose for being in the bar, Linda asks: "A bit of a sentimentalist, aren't you, Mr. Marlowe?" Confused, the detective questions: "Because I came here to drink a gimlet?" (*The Long Goodbye* 138). Marlowe resists the suggestion that he is a sentimentalist and even tells Linda to "Lay off. I came here to drink a gimlet because a man asked me to" (*The Long Goodbye* 143). When provoked further Marlowe questions *her* reasons for drinking gimlets in the same bar that Lennox frequented, raising the possibility that Linda too is sentimentally paying her respects: "You had one and a half, Mrs Loring. Why even that much? Did a man ask you too, or was it all your own idea?" (ibid.).

What is interesting about the continued questioning of Marlowe's sentimentality is that it reflects how society has become the source of alienation, where the misguided virtue of rugged individualism in fact denotes a crushing loneliness, powerlessness, the loss of community and cherished personal bonds, tedious monotony, individualistic competition, and the emergence of hideous urban sprawls that extinguish the very essence of human compassion. By interpreting Marlowe's natural response to the death of a friend as sentimental the characters in the novel (and also critics of Marlowe's actions) have misunderstood the detective's emotions and actions. He displays his grief by honoring his dead friend in a manner that is familiar to the two characters, by drinking a drink that Lennox had introduced him to. When feeling down Marlowe resorts to indulging in self-pity and allowing himself a brief moment of humanity misinterpreted as sentimentality: "I took Terry Lennox's letter of farewell out of the safe and re-read it. It reminded me that I had never gone to Victor's for that gimlet he asked me to drink for him. It was just about the right time of day for the bar to be quiet, the way he would have liked it himself, if he had been around to go with me. I thought of him with a vague sadness and with a puckering bitterness too" (*The Long Goodbye* 136). Marlowe's compassionate actions are further contrasted with an uncaring society when Linda reveals that Harlan Potter, Sylvia's father, has, for self-serving reasons, deliberately allowed the deceased Lennox to take the blame for his daughter's murder, thereby avoiding the publicity of an investigation and trial. Marlowe's reaction is obvious:

> All of a sudden I got mad, for no good reason. I stood up and looked over the booth [. . .] I sat down again with a bump, pushed my glass out of the way and leaned across the table. I had sense enough to keep my voice down.
>
> "For hell's sake, Mrs Loring, what are you trying to sell me? That Harlan Potter is such a sweet, lovely character he wouldn't dream of using his influence on a political D.A. to drop the blanket on a murder investigation so that the murder was never really investigated at all? That he had doubts about Terry's guilt but didn't lift a finger to find out who was really the killer? [. . .] What did your old man say to him? 'Just run on down to Mexico and shoot yourself, old boy. Let's keep this in the family [. . .] You've had it soft and now is the time you pay back [. . .] She married you because she needed a front [. . .] She needs it worse than ever now she's dead [. . .] And you're it [. . .].'" (*The Long Goodbye* 141–42)

John S. Whitely argues that Marlowe's response suggests that "the lack of any moral centre to the California world produces widespread competition and corruption" (24) and that his alleged sentimentalism is in fact demonstrative of a human response in a world devoid of emotion and sympathy. These contrasting views about what society once was and what it has now become are reiterated later in a meeting between Marlowe and Harlan Potter himself, the latter noting: "In our time we have seen a shocking decline in both public and private morals. You can't expect quality from people whose lives are a subjection to a lack of quality. You can't have quality with mass production" (*The Long Goodbye* 198). Marlowe's objections to Potter stem from his conviction that Potter has used his power and wealth to make the Lennox case disappear, but despite this misdemeanor he does not believe Potter to be a crook. It is left instead to Bernie Ohls to point out:

> "There ain't no clean way to make a hundred million bucks," Ohls said. "Maybe the head man thinks his hands are clean but somewhere along the line guys got pushed to the wall, nice little businesses got the ground cut from under them and had to sell out for nickels, decent people lost their jobs, stocks got rigged on the market, proxies got bought up like a pennyweight of old gold, and the five per centers and the big law firms got paid hundred fifty grand fees for beating some law the people wanted but the rich guys didn't, on account of it cut into their profits. Big money is big power and big power gets used wrong. It's the system." (*The Long Goodbye* 234)

The social criticism expounded in *The Long Goodbye* shares a number of parallels with F. Scott Fitzgerald's *The Great Gatsby*. The rich live in a different world, able to dictate how the world is managed and look upon the rest of society as inconsequential and subordinate to their wishes. Nick Carraway's opinions of the Buchanans correspond to Marlowe's view of the Idle Valley rich. Tom and Daisy are "careless people [. . .] they smashed things up [. . .] and then retreat [. . .] back into their money or their vast carelessness, or whatever it was that kept them together, and let other people clean up the mess they had made . . ." (Fitzgerald, *Great Gatsby* 170). Similarly, as Marlowe leaves the scene of Wade's death he ponders with disillusionment the indifferent lives of those who live in the California valley: "A man not unknown to the world had died in a pool of blood in a house in Idle Valley but the lazy quiet had not been disturbed. So far as the newspapers were concerned it might have happened in Tibet" (*The Long Goodbye* 224–25).

In a comparable scene that epitomizes the hedonistic parties of the rich, Marlowe witnesses an incident at Eileen Wade's party when a drunken woman yells at her husband. At first she calls him a rapist and throws her drink over him, but then sobs hysterically before throwing herself into her husband's arms. The party, as Marlowe notes, "was the same old cocktail party, everybody talking too loud, nobody listening, everybody hanging on for dear life to a mug of the juice, eyes very bright, cheeks flushed or pale and sweaty according to the amount of alcohol consumed and the capacity of the individual to handle it" (*The Long Goodbye* 146). The lavish yet monotonous parties thrown by Gatsby are realistically emulated by the dullness of the party thrown by Eileen Wade. As Roger Wade notes, the rich are "the class of the country and they're no better than a bunch of truckdrivers full of cheap whisky" (*The Long Goodbye* 149).

Marlowe's sentimentality, therefore, is an attempt to distance the detective from the opulence and fakery of high society. Marlowe's feelings are real but are continuously challenged by those he encounters. Even Wade notices Marlowe's genuine concern and tells the detective, "Don't go soft on me, Marlowe," to which, in a moment when he shows his true feelings toward Wade, the detective replies, "Soft? [. . .] Or just kind?" (*The Long Goodbye* 150). Marlowe's determination to find justice for Lennox and his continued dogged determination to uncover the connection behind Sylvia's murder and Wade's supposed suicide point toward Marlowe's resolve to reveal the corruption at the heart of society. Jerry Spier notes, "On its most straightforward level, *The Long Goodbye* is a story of friendship established and friendship betrayed. But on a grander scale that story is only the microcosm of a more general social deterioration" (66). Despite continued warnings against doing so, by solving both mysteries Marlowe feels that he will have righted the wrong done to Lennox as well as exposing the deceitfulness of the powerful Potter family. Marlowe is reconciled to the verity that his work will never be fully appreciated and is considered inconsequential in a society that does not care for him. In his own words, he has become "a grain of sand on the desert of oblivion" and as "empty as the spaces between the stars" (*The Long Goodbye* 116, 231). However, for Marlowe, the controlling Potter family represents the personification of American society as a whole, and by achieving justice for his friend, Marlowe attempts to demonstrate that the most insignificant members of society have a greater level of moral superiority. For his part, Chandler's disquiet over social disparity is amply demonstrated in *The Long Goodbye* with the inequitable and arbitrary resolution of moral dilemmas in favor of corporate profit or personal greed. In this setting Chandler places the troubled Lennox as a prism through which we experience a vulnerable man attempting to cope with the corruption and isolation that surround him. Marlowe's behavior is, therefore, indicative of the lonely situation that he feels and the determination to honor the wishes of his "one true buddy," as well as gain the appropriate recognition for all veterans who experience a similarly lonely existence. As Whitely notes: "Marlowe's friendships suggest a more balanced view and a recognition of the detective's need to deny the tough shield and protect himself by breaking out of his deliberately-created loneliness towards some meaningful connections with society" (26). This "meaningful connection" is the empathy he feels toward characters who are similarly troubled by their own past war experiences.

Marlowe identifies himself in both Lennox and Roger Wade because "his idealistic sensibilities draw him spontaneously and sympathetically" (Speir 109) toward them. As Whitely notes, "Compassion often stems from a recognition of compatibility" (28), and in Marlowe's case this compatibility comes from a recognition that both Lennox and Wade have similar distressing backgrounds as the detective. Marlowe demonstrates the extent of his own isolation when, in conversation with lawyer Howard Spender, he says, "I'm a lone wolf [. . .] and when I get knocked off in a dark alley sometime [. . .] nobody will feel that the bottom has dropped out of his or her life" (*The Long Goodbye* 79). Marlowe understands the unenviable position in which both Lennox and Wade find themselves because, like him, they are men suffering from the consequences of an exclusive shared and traumatic experience.

Although Clive James argues that "Chandler in real life was more Lennox than Marlowe" (qtd. in Gross 123), there are aspects of Lennox, Marlowe, and Wade which correspond to the different facets of Chandler's own personality. These characters are a fusion of everything that Chandler both wanted to be and was afraid he had become. As Chandler's "alter egos," Natasha Spender, a close friend of the writer, explains: "All three characters were drinkers, like Raymond himself, two of them disintegrating and despairing [. . .] As with aspects of Raymond's own character, their dominance veered with his mood. Roger Wade his 'bad self,' Philip Marlowe his 'good self' and Terry Lennox his anxious one" (qtd. by Hiney 248–49). As Spender believed, it is likely that Chandler implanted aspects of his own persona into each of his three honorable characters. Philip Marlowe smokes a pipe, displays loyal values, and embodies Chandler's romanticized image of womanhood. So when Lennox tells the detective, "I married her [Sylvia] for her money" (*The Long Goodbye* 13), Marlowe makes his disapproval apparent by showing his irritation and continuously scowling at him for the remainder of his time in Lennox's company. Lennox, in turn, is a representation of Chandler's fierce pride. When Lennox encourages Marlowe to look up his friend Randy

Starr, a Las Vegas thug, the next time he's in town, Marlowe replies, "I don't like hoodlums." To which Lennox responds, "It's just a word, Marlowe. We have that kind of world" (*The Long Goodbye* 18). "My kind of pride is different," says Lennox. "It's the pride of a man who has nothing else" (*The Long Goodbye* 13). And finally Roger Wade represents the anxiety Chandler had about his future as a writer. Although the character Howard Spencer notes in the novel that "[t]he only salvation for a writer is to write. If there is anything good in him, it will come out" (*The Long Goodbye* 81), Wade's (and Chandler's) fear was that alcohol would inhibit him from further meaningful writing. But Marlowe, as if to boost the flagging morale of the author, then proceeds to quash these fears by boldly asserting that if Wade "wants to write the damn book bad enough, he'll lay off the hooch until he does" (*The Long Goodbye* 85).

Interestingly *The Long Goodbye* is told in retrospect, serving to heighten Marlowe's sense of isolation and alienation. The novel begins with the line, "The first time I laid eyes on Terry Lennox he was drunk in a Rolls-Royce Silver Wraith outside the terrace of The Dancers" (5). From here Marlowe charts his relationship with Lennox and also his involvement in the case of Roger Wade, resulting in a complex story that has its origins before the Second World War in England. By writing in retrospect Chandler demonstrates his control over the story and makes it clear that he wishes to utilize Marlowe's first-person narrative to exhibit the wretched loneliness and lack of expectation that permeate the detective's every thought and action. Marlowe's narrative therefore has a weight of insight running through it, and as Marlowe notes in hindsight, "[Lennox] would have told me the story of his life if I had asked him. But I never even asked him how he got his face smashed. If I had and he told me, it just possibly might have saved a couple of lives. Just possibly, no more" (*The Long Goodbye* 21). Although not fully interjecting, we are left in no doubt where Chandler's convictions lie, exposed by the inclusion of his own personality, values, and narrative control over the characters and plot.

Chandler's projection of himself within his work in general, and *The Long Goodbye* in particular, is mirrored by his cameo role in his novel *Playback*. Adding further credibility to Spender's conviction that the writer included aspects of his own character in his novels, Chandler appeared either as he wished to be perceived, as Marlowe and Lennox, or as he perceived himself within his work, as Wade and as Henry Clarendon in the novel *Playback*. In Chandler's final novel Clarendon is a rich, lonely, old man living out his life in hotels, and like Chandler sees himself, he is overintelligent and undernourished. As if to demonstrate Chandler's presence, Clarendon makes the point of refusing to shake hands with Marlowe, saying, "My hands are ugly and painful. I wear gloves for that reason" (*Playback* 114), alluding to the skin complaint that Chandler himself suffered in later life and for which he also wore white cotton gloves. In *Playback* Chandler also allows himself a voice to make social comments, specifically, the dearth of intelligent personnel within the military establishment, again establishing a military link. Clarendon sarcastically says, "Military Intelligence is an expression which contains an interior fallacy" (*Playback* 107).

Marlowe's search for Wade following his disappearance in *The Long Goodbye* provides frequent opportunities for Chandler to speak out on matters related to his own life and his cynicism toward writing. More importantly it discloses two further aspects of the writer's life: first, Chandler's propensity for disappearing for days on drinking binges; and second, Chandler's mistrust of the medical profession. There are certainly parallels to be drawn between Wade's and Chandler's heavy drinking bouts and disappearances, during which Chandler would also threaten suicide. Similarly we see Marlowe call on various physicians of dubious reputation in the novel. Chandler himself was a frequent patient at hospitals and convalescence homes, especially in his later years. His inclusion of three questionable doctors reveals the extent of his skepticism of physicians and medical institutions. Likewise, Wade's attempted suicide, prevented by Eileen, bears an uncanny precursor to the suicide attempts that Chandler made in the year following Cissy's death in 1954. Wade's attempt to take his own life alludes to a combination of alcohol and dramatic exaggeration. This is confirmed by Marlowe's questioning of Wade following the incident.

> "Did I hit right about that shot? It was just a crazy bit of acting?"
> "More or less," he turned his head away. (*The Long Goodbye* 178)

As Chandler candidly admitted after his own fourth attempt: "I couldn't for the life of me tell you whether I really intended to go through with it or whether my subconscious was putting on a cheap dramatic performance" (qtd. in MacShane, *Life* 226). Marlowe corroborates this version of events by admonishing Wade and informing him: "You got up and got the gun and got back into bed and there you were all ready to wipe out the whole messy business. But I don't think you had the nerve. You fired a shot not meant to hit anything. And your wife came running—that's what you wanted. Just pity and sympathy" (*The Long Goodbye* 177). The inclusion of Wade's attempted suicide suggests that suicidal thoughts were foremost in Chandler's mind during the two years that it took to complete the novel. Similarly to Wade, Chandler's antics were lonely cries for help from a deeply troubled man.

As in many of his novels, the crux of Chandler's *The Long Goodbye* is the long-standing acrimony between two women. In the story Eileen Wade suffers the fate of losing her dearest love, Lennox, first to the war and then once again through his marriage to Sylvia upon his return. Eileen similarly realizes that she has lost her second husband, Wade, to Sylvia when she discovers their affair. The war deals Eileen a double blow. Jerry Speir notes that "always, in the background, there is the war, that grand madness beyond [Eileen's] control without which her story would have had a decidedly different ending" (75). Neither of the novel's murders would have happened had Eileen not lost to the war her "wild, mysterious, improbable kind of love that never comes but once" (*The Long Goodbye* 156).

Chandler witnessed firsthand the conflicts between women that were ever present throughout his childhood, an unpleasant memory that undoubtedly found its place in his later story lines. When living in England he would have witnessed the humiliation and insults heaped upon his divorced mother, Florence, often wronged and discriminated against as a consequence of her imperfect social status. As Frank MacShane notes: "In later years Chandler recalled the various petty humiliations imposed on his mother by her sister Ethel and by her own mother: at dinner time, sitting at the head of the table, Chandler's grandmother would offer wine to everyone except Florence. It was a way of reminding her of her dependent position" (MacShane, *Life* 4). Many years later it was Chandler's mother who objected to his relationship with Cissy Pascal. This pattern of female conflicts appears to have ingrained in Chandler a distinctive viewpoint that would reemerge in his later work, exemplified by the belittling relationship between Mrs. Murdock and Merle Davies in *The High Window* and the discord between Orfamay Quest and her mother in *The Little Sister*.

Spender's argument that Chandler created Philip Marlowe, Terry Lennox, and Roger Wade as expressive aspects of his own character is therefore eminently credible, with the inclusion of Clarendon in *Playback*, Wade's attempted suicide, and themes drawn from Chandler's own life experience that illustrate the writer's penchant for including facets of his own persona in the action. Because both Terry Lennox and Roger Wade are portrayed as troubled alcohol-dependent war veterans, it is not unreasonable to consider Marlowe's own background as being very similar to their own, since Marlowe's predilection for alcohol is well documented throughout the novels.

When Chandler moved to La Jolla in 1946, Spender believes that he turned his attention away from the streets and became deeply introspective. In presenting the characters of Lennox, Wade, and Marlowe as equals, Chandler is placing Marlowe alongside two established veteran characters. This association raises the definite prospect that since Chandler routinely incorporated aspects of his own personality into his work and was a veteran himself, he was able to draw from his own traumatic experience to create a profoundly honest and emotionally realistic depiction of veteran behavior. Furthermore, by placing Marlowe so empathetically close to both Lennox and Wade, it suggests that Chandler created Marlowe as a veteran also.

Whitely has noted that many serious writers seek perfection in their work and "will consistently strive to find greater freedom within the confines of a given formula" (32). Chandler was such a writer who consciously, in the interest of realism, introduced his own experiences and, consciously or otherwise, brought his own idiosyncrasies and mental frailties to his unique work. Chandler's novels precisely embody the sentiment expressed by Ross Macdonald when he said that "a novelist lives through his characters" (28). What is particularly noticeable about Chandler's work and especially *The Long Goodbye* is the extent to which his characters are inflicted by the self-same mental frailties that imposed themselves upon Chandler himself. In each of his thirty-one short stories and his seven novels that extol the virtues of a bygone chivalric code, behind the fearlessness and courage lurk the unmistakable symptoms of traumatic psychological injury.

Many writers have been subjectively pigeonholed by assessments that are generally justified by arbitrary demarcation that comes from the narrow interpretation of genre. This categorization is made without sufficient consideration of the ways in which the author has developed and broadened the limits of the genre, and also the ways in which the author blurs the boundaries of a particular style or form.

In the fictional character of Philip Marlowe, Chandler created a unique individual who used the genre as the means of outwardly expressing his own troubled emotions, an individual who was both imaginary and a very real person to whom Chandler could relate. The longevity of Chandler's appeal, as Mark Billingham has so eloquently noted, is because "the Marlowe beneath [. . .] remains so compelling: the lonely, 'shop-soiled Galahad' who plays chess and reads poetry; who keeps the biggest bruises hidden; who, in a world where no one is quite what they seem, is perhaps the greatest faker of all" (qtd. in *The High Window* v). In other words, his lasting appeal is a natural consequence of Chandler's desire to make Marlowe like anyone else, and not super-human or an indestructible champion of justice.

And yet Chandler's work shows something far more significant. As Whitely argues, Chandler's work "prove[s] that the dividing barriers between 'high' and 'low' art are often flimsier than supposed and that many of the preoccupations of 'serious' novelists are theirs, too" (32). Like his creator, Marlowe emerges as a lonely and isolated war veteran suffering troubling posttraumatic symptoms and endeavoring to conceal his troubling injuries and lonely existence behind a chivalric façade. As Terry Lennox unhappily notes in the closing lines of *The Long Goodbye*, for veterans, "[a]n act is all there is. There isn't anything else" (320).

7

AFTERMATH: CHANDLER'S LEGACY

War is stupid. The most terrible thing a man can do to himself.

—CRUMLEY, *ONE TO COUNT CADENCE*

In their efforts to further the genre and create a crime literature, contemporary crime writers have been influenced by Chandler's self-consciousness within the genre, his aspiration to understand the confines of the form, and his desire to push the boundaries (Haut, *Pulp Culture* 72). As LeRoy Lad Panek has noted, "The hard-boiled books of the last quarter of the century repeatedly and clearly pay homage to Raymond Chandler" (205). Since the First World War numerous military veterans have turned their hand to writing in the crime genre, utilizing the hard-boiled style to perfectly embody their disillusionment and cynicism with American society. Elmore Leonard, Charles Willeford, and Robert B. Parker are just some of the veteran writers who have become renowned in the genre for their work. Leonard, a petty officer with the US Navy in the Pacific during the last years of World War Two, was part of the US Naval Construction Forces (the "Seebees")[1] and saw plenty of fighting. Likewise, Parker was a soldier in the US Army Infantry during the Korean War. Although their characters are not specifically identified as veterans, the characteristics of their detectives are the characteristically hard-boiled productions of war.

However, it is Charles Willeford who deserves the closest attention of these three writers. Enlisted with the army between 1935 and 1956, Willeford fought in the Second World War as a tank commander with George S. Patton Jr.'s Third Army in Europe. He participated in the Battle of the Bulge, earning a Silver Star, a Bronze Star for outstanding bravery, a Purple Heart with one oak leaf cluster, and the Luxembourg War Cross. Publishing much of his early work while still enlisted in the army, Willeford developed his writing style, according to Sybil Steinberg, "in dozens of journeymen tasks including dashing off soap operas for the Armed Forces radio station and ghost writing speeches for base commanders" (qtd. in Gorman, Server, and Greenberg 313).

Although Willeford was a decorated war hero by the time of his retirement in the mid-1950s, like Raymond Chandler he was always reticent about his war experiences: "In wartime the opportunities to become a hero come every day" (qtd. in Cochran 41). Yet, although he didn't receive widespread acknowledgment and success until the 1980s with the publication of his Miami series of novels featuring Hoke Moseley,[2] his military background certainly colored his worldview within all of his novels. His characters, in particular, are tainted by war and are frequently veterans who, as David Cochran notes, "often apply wartime morals to their lives" (41). One explicit example of this comes from the character Dover, an American Civil War veteran, in The *Hombre of Sonora* (1971), who notes that "in four years of fighting . . . I learned two important things about men. First, men are more like animals than gods" (56–54). Describing the similarity between men and sheep, in a manner reminiscent of Chandler (see chapter 2), Dover goes on to describe how during battle men will stay close to each other for comfort even when they know that spreading out will be safer. Second, Dover learns "something about victory and defeat. The only men who win in a war are those who are still alive when it's all over . . . The cause—the right and wrong of war—is a notion that don't mean anything, no matter how many fancy words are embroidered around it" (54). And in a manner similar to Ernest Hemingway's Frederic Henry, Willeford was also incredibly suspicious about the intangible reasons used to justify war: "Like most everybody else at the time, I bought the whole bill of goods . . . Now I know better; there are no such things as 'good' wars. Nothing ever changes because of them, 'cept some people make money and lots of good young boys are killed for nothing. It's always for nothing" (qtd. in Sathis 9).

Like the later Vietnam generation, Willeford's military service also provided source material for the shocking figures that populate his fiction. As would later be considered by psychological studies of war's impact, Willeford examines how the skills necessary for survival in wartime simply do not translate to postwar American society. Having witnessed instances in which soldiers cold-bloodedly murdered unarmed prisoners, Willeford said, "I used to wonder, 'What's going to happen to these guys when they go back into civilian life? How are they going to act?' You can't just turn them off and go to work in a 7–11 . . . These guys learned to do all sorts of things in the Army that just weren't considered *normal* by civilian standards" (qtd. in Sathis 10). "A good half of the men you deal with in the Army," Willeford argued, "are psychopaths" (qtd. in Sathis 9). Reinforcing this, R. L. Swank and W. E. Marchand noted in their famous study examining the traumatizing impact of World War II, "Combat Neurosis: Development of Combat Exhaustion" (1946), that after sixty days of continuous combat, 98 percent of all *surviving* soldiers would become psychiatric casualties. However, they also found a common trait among the 2 percent who were able to endure sustained combat: a predisposition toward what they termed "aggressive psychopathic personalities" (236–47). Willeford, therefore, followed the lead of Chandler, Hammett, and other writers in the genre by writing about what he knew.[3] As the character Troy Louden tells us in *Sideswipe* (1987), "[I'm] What the shrinks call a criminal psychopath. What that means is, I know the difference between right and wrong and all that, but I don't give a shit" (48). Willeford declared that during the war he knew "plenty of guys like Junior in *Miami Blues* and Troy in *Sideswipe*. Like, some of these other Tankers I knew used to swap bottles of liquor with infantrymen in exchange for prisoners, and then just shoot 'em for fun . . . So that sort of behaviour became normal to them" (qtd. in Sathis 9–10).

Colorfully describing Willeford's style and characterization, Lou Sathis states, "These are *scary* motherfucking books, lulling you with blandly innocent faces and then sneaking up behind you with exacto knives to open your spine like a puffed-up fish belly. Nasty." But, as Willeford himself noted, "I'm not really breaking the genre, just bending it a bit" (qtd. in Sathis 7, 13).

What is so fascinating about Willeford's work, however, is the obvious influence of the hard-boiled prewar magazine *Black Mask*. In *Wild Wives* (1955) for example it is plain to see the influence of writers like Dashiell Hammett and Raymond Chandler: "I smashed my right fist into his face. His nose crushed noisily and blood spattered and smeared against his skin. His nose would never be termed aristocratic again. I hit him again in the face several times. After each blow he tried to scream, but before he could get it out I would hit him again. I didn't try to knock him out. I wanted him conscious; I wanted him to feel it" (60).

Although Willeford's work—spanning four decades—provides the bridge between the hard-boiled stories of Hammett and Chandler and the post–Second World War consumerist glut, it is predominantly since the Vietnam War that writers have come to view crime fiction as a subversive style that draws upon and conveys the utter distrust and anger of veterans toward the government and society. Both veterans and nonveterans alike—James Crumley,

Robert Stone, Newton Thornburg, James Lee Burke, Jeremiah Healy, Robert Crais, Benjamin M. Shutz, Robert Ray, Geoffrey Norman—have incorporated troubled war-veteran detectives as the protagonists in their war noir fiction.

Like the First World War, the war in Vietnam had a profound effect upon detective fiction, and the novels that emerged were "so authentic as to reinterpret the national narrative" (Haut, *Neon Noir* 2). As Panek observed, "The First World War had about the same chronological relationship to the original generation of hard-boiled writers [. . .] as Vietnam has to the writers of the eighties and nineties [. . .]" (210), and several writers have attempted to emulate Chandler's work and style. For example, the use of chivalric and knightly imagery retains its potency amongst writers in the genre: Richard Hillary's detective Ezell Barnes refers to himself as a "Black Knight" (80) in *Snake in the Grasses* (1987); Robert B. Parker's allusions to Sir Lancelot in *Sudden Mischief* (1999); references to Excalibur in Max Byrd's *California Thriller* (1981), and so on. But one author in particular has succeeded in recreating Philip Marlowe's disillusionment and cynicism for a contemporary audience. In the writings of James Crumley, Chandler's characterization of the war veteran detective is relocated from the interwar urban environment to the post-Vietnam Midwest. As Crumley observed, "We cover some of the same ground, his dark streets in LA, my twisted highways in the mountain west" (*Contemporary Authors* 67). Crumley identified with Chandler's characterization of a troubled detective and incorporated similarly traumatized characters into his own series of novels, admitting that "without [Chandler's] books, my books would be completely different" (ibid.). Because of his experience during the war in Southeast Asia and the incorporation of the era's trauma into his work, Crumley is representative of the contemporary generation of war noir detective fiction. Whereas 1920s and 1930s America had no appetite for novels concerning disenchanted veterans, Crumley used the genre in the 1970s to formulate a crime literature that *forcefully* incorporated a war-traumatized protagonist into the disillusionment of the era. Reinforcing this, Panek notes that the experiences of First World War soldiers "and the ghastly, beastly carnage in the Great War in Europe never directly enter the fiction of the old writers. Not so with current writers [. . .] Indeed, the recent hard-boiled novel presents its readers with a cross-section of images of the ways in which men in this country respond to the war in the jungles of Southeast Asia" (214). Panek explores why the writers of the earlier generation were reluctant to incorporate such forcefulness into their writing, concluding that "[p]erhaps what then carried the generic name of 'shell-shock' had too great a stigma attached to it to be acceptable in mass-market fiction of the twenties and thirties; certainly inherited notions of self-possession and the nature of manliness had yet to begin to accept the value and virtue of emotional self-awareness and revelation; and it certainly was not in the best interest of those in power to broadcast the effects that modern warfare has on all who take part in it" (ibid.).

Pin-pointing the duality of characters created in the post-Vietnam era, which many earlier protagonists fail to capture, Panek observes that they are "at once tough and high-minded, sensitive and humane" (ibid.). Yet if we cast our eyes back over Chandler's works we see that in actual fact Philip Marlowe *does* capture both the toughness and the humanity that Panek refers to; the difference in Marlowe is simply his reluctance to *forcefully* voice his experiences and trauma. So while Marlowe's psychological symptoms are subconscious, Crumley's contemporary detectives openly display their postcombat trauma. Both writers, however, locate their respective wars at the center of the detective fiction they produced.

By taking inspiration from Chandler's novels, as well as taking plot lines directly from them, Crumley's work exhibits one of the most explicit examples of war's traumatic influence upon the crime genre. Describing himself as "a bastard child of Raymond Chandler" (*Contemporary Authors* 67), Crumley developed a brutal representation of the traumatizing effects of warfare, and, in doing so, was instrumental in elevating the crime genre to a new level of authenticity which allowed for the open expression of the anger and trauma of a generation. Arguing that contemporary hard-boiled writers are, without a doubt, the "descendants of [. . .] hardboiled pulp writers," Woody Haut notes, "Emerging from the maelstrom of the 1960s, neon noirists would be deeply affected by the Vietnam War and the political atmosphere surrounding it. Dividing the nation, the war instilled an atmosphere of paranoia, a condition exacerbated by government secrecy, inflexible policies, and the effect of drugs on the political consciousness of numerous dissidents" (*Neon Noir* 4). He continues by saying that "America's involvement in Vietnam made its past crimes appear insignificant" (*Neon Noir* 13). As a result of extended media coverage and continuous exposure even noncombatants became increasingly disturbed as they were confronted by the horror of the conflict. Touching upon why nonveterans similarly began using the motif of the veteran detective, Robert Jay Lifton notes that "Americans who [had] not seen Vietnam, [felt] something of a national descent into existential evil, a sense that the killing and dying done in their name [could not] be placed within a meaningful system of symbols, [could not] be convincingly formulated" (67).

Herbert Hendin and Ann Haas have asserted that American involvement in Vietnam was "the crucible we needed to at long last explore the corrosive effects of war on the combat soldier" (6). In the post-Vietnam period many authors, including Crumley, Walter Mosley, and James Ellroy were able to create imperfect and paranoid characters traumatized by the era's ambiguous war and corrupt politics. As Panek notes, these are writers that brought together "the hard-boiled hero and the complexity and confusion unique to the last quarter of the twentieth century in the United States" and who "participated in the renaissance of hard-boiled fiction" (5). Like the Lost Generation, the literature of the post-Vietnam era similarly depicted a generation that had been lost to war, and the traumatized characterization of the detective became far more perceptible. Detectives in this era were "no longer wise-cracking know-it-alls," but were, as Haut observes, "psychologically scarred inhabitants of a morally ambiguous world in which people are capable of perpetrating any and every outrage" (Ne*on Noir* 4–5). Unlike the detective fiction of Chandler's era, the crime genre since Vietnam has sought to establish a far closer link with the past and confront personal traumas head-on. Although unacknowledged sacrifice and veteran disillusionment were subliminal themes that Chandler incorporated into his personification of Marlowe, it was not until the aftermath of the war in Southeast Asia that such characterization was made openly symbolic of the sheer discontent and psychological trauma of those involved.

Recognizing the traumatic consequences of warfare contemporary writers no longer felt compelled to keep trauma hidden and managed to successfully articulate their anger and resentment. By communicating their pain and suffering in their work and focusing on their traumatic psychological injury, personal expression played a significant role in the development of the genre. A protagonist's psychological trauma became an important feature of post-Vietnam crime fiction, and detectives became more openly flawed and damaged, just as soldiers returning from war are physically and psychologically tormented by their experiences. Writers were eager to make their protagonists flawed individuals because it more accurately portrayed the emotional complexity at the heart of contemporary society. By articulating traumatic suffering through their work, writers reached a new level of authenticity in the same way that Chandler had done less than half a century earlier. Confronting the traumatizing effects of combat, post-Vietnam crime writers used war-veteran protagonists to further develop the detective novel. Even those detectives who were not drafted give reasons and justifications for becoming investigators or law enforcement officers. As the private eye Jake Lomax notes in Michael Allegretto's *Blood Stone* (1990): "I felt guilty about not fighting over there, so I decided to fight the bad guys over here" (64). The war in Southeast Asia forced the American public to recognize that a section of society scarred by war had been largely ignored during the twentieth century. More significantly, however, it also permitted a reevaluation of twentieth-century veteran literature to include crime and genre fiction.

Although the themes of physical violence and brutality have always existed as an essential facet of crime fiction, the early pioneers of the genre created a style of writing in which acts of violence came to symbolize the ugliness and unpredictability of society. Julian Symons believes that contemporary writers have not so much changed the direction of the crime genre as seen a need to take the brutal reconstruction of physical violence and depravity first expounded by Hammett and Chandler to a hitherto unknown level. In his novels Chandler laid bare a world that was depraved and dog-eat-dog by stripping back society's layers to expose its rotten and corrupt core. The key difference in the work of contemporary writers is the explicit and savage articulation of violence that has significantly altered the tone and texture of the genre in the wake of the Vietnam War. As such they have spawned a school of writing that Symons argues "dwell[s] lovingly on the physical details of violence, the blood on the bed and the head battered to bits, the torture done for fun, the women tied-up and gang raped. Their work aspires to a kind of toughness that [. . .] make[s] Hammett's toughest scenes look soft as three-minute eggs" (*Bloody Murder* 313). However, Symons's remark here demonstrates the exact reason why Chandler's work—and the work of those writing in the crime genre—has never been considered highbrow. While contemporary crime writers have indeed sought to further develop the emotional and physical depth of the genre, Symons's overdramatic and exaggerated claims are far from the truth. Rather than dwelling lovingly, almost pornographically as Symons would have readers believe, on the brutality of violence, torture, or rape, contemporary writers attempted instead to dislodge the idea that society was automatically synonymous with decency. While many stories were indeed violent, the focus was shifted onto protagonists that were imperfect and attempting to cope with individual traumatizing experiences that had cultivated in them an unashamed pragmatism and that had fashioned their individual sense of reason.

One of the most explicit examples of contemporary war's traumatic influence on the crime genre exists in James Crumley's work. Crumley acknowledged that, despite not having any original intention of writing crime fiction, Chandler's novels, where characterization and style are of major importance, greatly influenced his decision to alter literary direction. He acknowledged that after reading Chandler's fiction, his own work became heavily influenced and consequently developed into contemporary interpretations of Chandler's novels. Thus, Crumley managed, in the last three decades, to "clear the field for future noir fiction" (Haut, *Neon Noir* 62) by expanding Chandler's hard-boiled style while at the same time dissolving the boundaries that separate the genre from others. By doing this he has made the genre a far more realistic representation of society. Although his work incorporates an increased level of violence which is representative of post-Vietnam society, Crumley's novels are essentially contemporary variations on the themes first established in Chandler's Marlowe stories. In their respective generations Chandler and Crumley broke down the generic boundaries of detective fiction to develop a form of writing that is not "lovingly" violent or lewd as Symons describes, but instead holds an important position in American literary history.

Like Chandler's Marlowe, Crumley's detectives, Milton "Milo" Milodragovich and C. W. Sughrue, suffer what Johannes Bertens and Theo D'Haen refer to as an "alienation that results from the fundamental incompatibility between the private eye's moral ideal and the unruly reality of the world [they] live in" (2). This traumatizing realization is evident in the works of other Vietnam veteran writers including Robert Stone, Newton Thornberg, and George V. Higgins, whose protagonists, alienated by the effects of war, drugs, drink, and oppositional politics do their best to survive in a world that has altered beyond their recognition: "With the line separating perpetrator and investigator having become blurred, they are inevitably drawn into a noir existence. With a live-and-let-live attitude and scant regard for the law, these anti-heroes retreat into a primeval existentialism in which survival and quelling one's demons are what matter, while the heroic quest becomes a matter of getting through the day" (Haut, *Neon Noir* 44). Haut notes, "By taking into account the state of the culture [Crumley] makes one of the most significant revisions of private eye fiction since Chandler's cynical parodies of Hammett and the Black Mask school of writing" (62). Through his brutally honest crime stories Crumley influenced future crime writers and furthered the genre more than any other writer since Chandler himself. By adding elements of witnessed reality to their fictional works, "Contemporary crime writers [. . . sought] to replicate life at street level" (Haut, *Neon Noir* 2) and have consequently made the genre more accessible and also a more accurate representation of life's frustrations and stresses. Haut notes that contemporary writers "have created a genre whose predominant artifice is its apparent lack of artifice; consequently, the line separating fiction and reality has become increasingly blurred" (ibid.).

Writing at a time when crime fiction was suffering a decline in popularity, Crumley's work marked a significant shift in the structure of the genre during the 1970s, representative of an era in which the central crime committed became *the war itself.* Focusing upon corporate greed and blistering wartime anger, Crumley's work confronts the traumatizing effects of the Vietnam War head-on by employing detectives explicitly characterized as Vietnam veterans in order to reveal the disillusionment and frustrations concerning the legality of the war and the subsequent treatment of American veterans. Crumley exposes a society ignorant of his characters' trauma and directs his anger toward a government that abandoned its soldiers upon their return from combat. In his novels Crumley incorporates a brutally explicit level of violence and seething underlying anger.

Along with Newton Thornburg's 1976 novel *Cutter and Bone*, Crumley's hard-boiled and war-traumatized protagonists, combined with the unforgiving social environment, produced a unique convergence of the war (or postwar) story and the crime novel. Representing a distinctive form that embodies war noir, Crumley's style absorbed the anger, discontent, and brutality of both genres, which were then used to attack an unsympathetic society, expose a corrupt state, and reveal the utter despair of his characters. Although he never published a bestseller, Crumley developed a large cult following and received tremendous critical acclaim. Despite receiving little examination in terms of the representations of trauma in his work (probably because the trauma is so obvious), it can be argued that Crumley best represents the balance between crime fiction and the "war-brought-home" novel discussed in chapter 3. The disillusionment and anguish stemming from the war are explicitly represented in his work in the way that he highlights the nation's hypocrisy and the state's corruption. His novels represent a brutal and progressively realistic representation of the American social landscape depicted through the eyes of traumatized war-veteran detectives.

Set in Montana and later Texas, Crumley's novels paint a harsh portrait of American society in the wake of Vietnam. His private eyes trawl a lawless frontier where the authorities are either corrupt or drowning in unsolved crimes. It is a society where, as Milo notes in *The Wrong Case* (1986), "divorce, suicide and alcoholism rates [. . .] embarrass [. . .] the national average," and kids "had begun to kill themselves with pills, speed and needles" (*The Collection* 67). Crumley describes a government that does not care for its citizens, is overrun with crime, ignores the pleas of its veterans, and is rotten to the core; every character we meet is a "wino," a drug addict, a war veteran, or a dubious authority figure. As Milo says in *Bordersnakes* (1996) "all the people I knew were criminals, drunks, and bad-dog lawyers" (169).

By bridging the gap between war and crime, Crumley managed in the 1970s to clear the field for future writers not only by expanding the hard-boiled style, but also by dissolving the boundaries that have kept crime fiction separate from other styles and prevented it receiving prominent literary status. As Cunningham, Davis, and Newsom have noted, Crumley is "a literary novelist whose canvas just happens to be crime fiction" (xii). He made the crime story resonate to a more contemporary generation by making the veteran characterization of his detective far more explicit.

Although Crumley's work incorporates an increased level of violence representative of the chaotic post-Vietnam environment, his novels are essentially contemporary variations on the themes first established in Raymond Chandler's Philip Marlowe stories. But in the 1970s the impact of the war began to explicitly and deliberately blur the generic boundaries, creating a form of writing that now holds an important position in American literary history. The quagmire of Vietnam, escalated between 1963 and 1969 with the deployment of US ground troops in 1965, began to draw attention to the concept of *crime* itself. Consequently, writers angered and confused by media images of the war in Indochina began depicting more explicit representations of crime as well as more overt depictions of war-traumatized protagonists. Newton Thornburg's protagonist Alex Cutter is an example of the type of disillusioned and deeply troubled characters emerging during the 1970s. However, as Robert E. Burkholder noted, it was Crumley who succeeded in "drawing serious critical attention to high quality detective fiction that transcends its genre" (qtd. in *Contemporary Authors* 66).

Both war and social reaction are crucial and influential aspects of Crumley's novels, and both of his detectives, Milo and Sughrue, suffer the catastrophic effects of witnessing and participating in traumatic acts during their time in combat, Milo in Korea and Sughrue in Vietnam. Their troubling experiences have caused drug addiction, alcohol dependency, nightmares, and flashbacks which continue to haunt them explicitly throughout the series of novels. Confronting head-on the traumatizing effects of combat, Crumley uses his war veteran protagonists to develop the genre by making the war the central aspect of the characters' lives, thereby driving the plots. Despite his detective series spanning thirty years, from his first detective novel, *The Wrong Case,* in 1975 to his final novel, *The Right Madness,* in 2005, the social and psychological impact of experiencing war is always what drives the Milo and Sughrue series. War is detailed in every novel, and over time becomes not simply a *place*, but instead adopts a weight of *meaning* that thirty years' worth of trauma and disillusionment has given it.

Crumley himself is also an interesting personality because crime fiction was not his first literary venture; in fact crime fiction did not influence his first work of fiction in any way. In the same way that Chandler attempted his own war prose with the unfinished short story "Trench Raid," Crumley's first novel, *One to Count Cadence* (1969), was in fact a war novel which laid the groundwork for the characterization, style, and themes of his later detective series. Set between the Philippines and Vietnam, the novel bears a greater resemblance to Vietnam literature than to crime fiction. Yet, there is certainly a darkness and cynicism to *One to Count Cadence* that bridge past war novels by the likes of Normal Mailer and Joseph Heller with the Vietnam chroniclers and later crime fiction writers. The manipulation of the truth by those in charge of the war, combined with the inability of soldiers to understand their place within the conflict, results in a dark and paranoid text about the early years of the Vietnam War. As the character Joe Morning says in the novel: "Fucking America off to make the world safe for General Motors and AT&T" (257–58).

Shortly after engaging with the work of Raymond Chandler, Crumley changed his literary direction by incorporating war-traumatized characters into his crime fiction. Consequently, Crumley is worthy of consideration alongside the likes of Michael Herr and other Vietnam War chroniclers because they all similarly write about criminal activities. Taking the war as the ultimate in state-sponsored criminal activity, these writers, as Haut says, "gravitated towards a form—be it memoir or its fictional variant—on which they could overlay their disordered experiences" (*Neon Noir* 44).

Crumley's war noir, therefore, represents a backlash against the state in the wake of Vietnam, and he used the crime genre in the 1970s to formulate a crime literature that takes its place alongside the war novels and chronicles of the time. Forcefully incorporating war-traumatized protagonists into the disillusionment of the postwar era, Crumley's detectives cannot escape their war experience. Describing Crumley's work, Christopher Lehmann-Haupt noted that it depicts "a violently chaotic world that can be seen as a legacy of Vietnam, of which his characters are nightmare-haunted veterans" (15). And as Sughrue states on one occasion, "I was supposed to have come home from the war years ago. But sometimes it follows you home like a bad dog" (*Bordersnakes* 202).

Crumley's novels are a brutal work of literary art. "Time Out Magazine" noted on the front cover of the Collected Edition of Crumley's first three crime novels that it was "One of the finest books of American fiction of *any* sort ever to grace a bookshelf" (emphasis added). And Crumley's editor, Molly Stern, called him "a poet of violence" (qtd. in McLellan). Crumley's detectives, who openly display their postcombat trauma and distrust of the state, burst free from generic classification. As "The Times Literary Supplement" noted on the back of Crumley's collected edition, Crumley "take[s] realism beyond the limits of [. . . his] chosen genre, showing us a darker, more provoking vision." Crumley utilized the war in Vietnam as the major *criminal* inspiration for his novels.

The Vietnam War had a profound effect upon detective fiction, and the novels that emerged were, as Woody Haut notes, "so authentic as to reinterpret the national narrative" (*Neon Noir* 2). His work represents a significant, but rarely studied, example of war's traumatic influence upon crime fiction. Crumley developed a brutal representation of not only the traumatizing effects of warfare but also the impact of society's rejection of the veteran and the veteran's rejection of the state. In this manner he was instrumental in elevating the crime genre to a whole new level of authenticity and brutality which allowed for the open expression of dissatisfaction, anger, and trauma. And yet along with the violence depicted, Crumley's novels capture the utter absurdity of war. As Jacob Krummel, the protagonist of *One to Count Cadence,* pointedly notes: "Anything Fredric Henry can do, I can do better" (16). And in a scene reminiscent of Henry's hospital-bed conversation on the absurdity of war with Captain Rinaldi in *A Farewell to Arms*, in Crumley's *Dancing Bear* the veteran Simmons discusses his wounding with Milo: "I got my Purple Heart when a gook rocket hit the half-track parked in front while I was sitting on the side of the APC reading a Spiderman comic, took a piece of shrapnel no bigger than a pencil eraser" (*The Collection* 606). Summing up the sentiment behind Crumley's work, Haut described how "[e]merging from the maelstrom of the 1960s, neon noirists would be deeply affected by the Vietnam War and the political atmosphere surrounding it. Dividing the nation, the war instilled an atmosphere of paranoia, a condition exacerbated by government secrecy, inflexible policies, and the effect of drugs on the political consciousness of numerous dissidents" (*Neon Noir* 4). It is an era where law enforcement officials are regarded as "turkeys," and the FBI stands for, in Sughrue's words, "Fucking Bureaucratic Idiots" (*The Mexican Tree Duck* 19, 81). The "Vietnam War Games," as the detective describes it, means that war veterans "never get to be civilians" (*The Mexican Tree Duck* 52, 109).

Recounting tales of society's rejection, of being called "baby-killer[s]" (*The Mexican Tree Duck* 113), the level of cynicism and disillusionment is palpable. As Sughrue ponders: "I wondered what had happened to that teenager who couldn't wait to get to war, who had raised his hand to swear allegiance to country and Constitution and commander-in-chief. I also wondered what had happened to said country, Constitution, and president that had left the sullied and aged remains of that teenager feeling as if he possessed some of the last bits of moral integrity in this troubled world" (*The Mexican Tree Duck* 207). In the post-Vietnam period, therefore, Crumley's work is a hard-boiled style born of war, trauma, and criminal activity—a hard-boiled war noir.

Similarly, Thornburg's *Cutter and Bone* displays many of the features that identify his work as war noir. Although not crime fiction in the traditional sense, the protagonists are just as likely to commit suicide as they are homicide. Thornburg's Alex Cutter says in the novel: "Lately I been thinking of killing myself, Rich. You got any advice?" When asked "why" by his friend Richard Bone, Cutter responds:

> "I don't know. It's not the goddamn eye, or the arm and the leg—some list, huh? They don't help, Christ knows. But they're not it, not the real problem. No, that's in here," he said, tapping his head. "And I can't fix it. Can't change it." (Thornburg 54)

Along with Crumley's work, George Pelecanos has observed that "Newton Thornburg's *Cutter and Bone* seemed to challenge the very foundation of the traditional crime novel when it was first published in 1976" ("Introduction" Thornburg). By incorporating the obvious signs of trauma and PTSD Thornburg manages to capture the disillusionment of the era, and the trauma suffered by Vietnam veteran Cutter is explicitly recounted. Noting that Cutter "lived constantly at the edge of rage" (Thornburg 100), Bone (who is not a veteran) is aware of his friend's daily struggle. Recounting how "everyone did his little part" in the atrocities that were committed in Vietnam, Cutter explains how as a consequence of his experiences: "I get out of bed every day like it was Armageddon" (Thornburg 55). No longer does he feel his former patriotism, stating in a manner reminiscent of Hemingway's Krebs: "I hate America" (Thornburg 81).

Both Crumley and Thornburg created imperfect and paranoid characters traumatized by the government's ambiguous war and corrupt politics. As Sughrue scornfully states in Crumley's 1993 novel *The Mexican Tree Duck*: "Thanks to the vested unfairness of the Selective Service Act [and . . .], because the American military and political establishment used the war for their own benefit, then manifestly displayed all the meretricious mendacity of a Mafia don or a Hollywood whore, a huge number of kids ended up on the bush who should never have been allowed to leave their hometowns" (235). Referring to those in charge of the war as "white devils," Sughrue fumes that "they were too often blessed with equal parts of greed for 'career advancement' and simple stupidity" (*The Mexican Tree Duck* 235). Like Milo and Sughrue, Cutter's attitude toward representatives of the state is just as bitter. When asked to justify his certainty in JJ Wolfe's guilt, Cutter's response is once again explicit and full of anger:

> I don't like this motherfucker Wolfe and all the motherfuckers like him, all the movers and shakers of this world, kiddo, because I saw them too many times, and I saw the people they moved and shook. I saw the soft white motherfuckers in their civvies and flak jackets come slicking in from Long Binh to look us over out in the boonies, see that everything was going sweet and smooth, the killing and the cutting and the sewing up, and then they'd grunt and fart and squeeze their way back into their choppers and slick on back to Washington or Wall Street [. . .] and say on with the show, America, a few more bombs will do it, a few more arms and legs [. . .] one fact was always the same, *is* always the same—it's never their ass they lay on the line, man, never theirs, but ours, *mine.* (Thornburg 100–101)

Like Crumley's detectives Milo and Sughrue, Thornburg's Cutter and Bone are not wisecracking know-it-alls in the traditional crime fiction mold. Instead they are psychologically scarred individuals of a morally ambiguous world who realize that people are capable of perpetrating any and every sin. With the aftermath of the war in Southeast Asia such traumatic characterization was made openly symbolic of the discontent and psychological trauma that war could inflict upon the individual and society. Cynicism and anger toward the government is especially noticeable. As Sughrue cynically states in Crumley's *The Mexican Tree Duck* (1993), "Money counts with bureaucrats. When Dan Rather makes more money than the President, who the fuck's really in charge?" (52).

Recognizing the traumatic consequences of warfare, crime writers during and after Vietnam no longer felt compelled to keep trauma hidden and managed to successfully articulate their anger and resentment. Personal expression played a significant role in the development of a style that became ultimately a backlash against the state. This resentment is perfectly summed up by the very last words of *The Mexican Tree Duck*. Accepting a loan to buy a bar, Milo asks Sughrue, "How am I going to explain to the government where this money came from?" Sughrue calmly states, "Fucking lie about it [. . .] They don't mind lying to you" (260). By articulating traumatic suffering and resentment toward the state, Crumley reaches a new level of authenticity in the crime genre in which the protagonist's psychological trauma is crucial. Crumley's portrayal of flawed protagonists exposes the emotional complexity at the heart of contemporary society and also war noir.

While the early pioneers of the crime genre created a style of writing in which acts of violence came to symbolize the ugliness of society and frustration toward a corrupt state, Crumley takes this brutal reconstruction of physical violence and depravity to a far higher level. The key difference in Crumley's work is the explicit and savage *articulation of violence* as well as his *violence of articulation*. The language is harsh, indignant, gritty, and full of expletives that significantly alter the tone and texture of the hard-boiled novel. Milo and Sughrue are imperfect, flawed, hostile, and aggressive, but they are also attempting to cope with individual traumatizing experiences that cultivated in them an unashamed pragmatism and that fashioned their distinctive sense of reason and justice. Their alienation stems from a fundamental incompatibility between their moral ideals and the chaotic reality of the world they live in.

While the impact of war upon culture and society is generally recognized and understood, it is the impact upon the individual that is important to understanding the significance of war noir. With combat-related PTSD only becoming officially recognized in 1980 the reconfiguration of the character of the detective allows us to consider characters that are far more flawed. In this respect Crumley made one of the most significant revisions of crime fiction by notably transforming and furthering the genre in the post-Vietnam era. In doing so he created a hard-boiled noir style deeply entrenched in war that significantly blurs the boundaries between two complementary and popular genres.

While critics have observed that many of Crumley's stories bear a distinct similarity to those of Chandler (so similar, in fact, that many have argued a case for plagiarism), by imbuing his work with certain plot lines and scenes reminiscent from the Philip Marlowe novels Crumley appears to have been building upon the work of his predecessor. Yet it is worth highlighting that Crumley did much more than this. He identified something in Philip Marlowe that had not been recognized before and, as a result, extended Chandler's vision of what the crime genre *could* be. His response to Chandler's work suggests that a subconscious trigger, or subtle indicators in Marlowe's characterization, enabled him to establish the veteran status of his detectives early on and build upon Chandler's work. Crumley made the crime story resonate to a contemporary generation by making the veteran characterization of his detective far more explicit. As Peter Messent observed, what is apparent in Crumley's novels is "the degree to which he is sticking close to the Chandler model at the same time as veering away from it" (156). The reason for this, Crumley argued, was that "because of the events surrounding the Vietnam War, my detectives are not as comfortable with traditional morality as Philip Marlowe seems to be" (qtd. in *Contemporary Authors* 67). The war plays a defining role in the lives of Crumley's detectives, who and both suffer the catastrophic effect of witnessing and participating in traumatic acts during their time in combat which haunt them explicitly throughout the series of novels.

Crumley's admiration of Chandler's style and work unquestionably indicates that he was more of a "Chandler man" than a "Hammett man" when it came to plotting his novels. He remarked that "it seems to me I belong more to the Chandler side of things; what I do is different from what Hammett meant to do . . . [F]or me, the mystery novel, the detective novel, is just something to hang the words on. I don't much care about the mystery itself, I don't like puzzle mysteries, don't write them, and in that way I'm more like Chandler, owe more to Chandler" (qtd. in Messent 152). On the surface Crumley appears to do Chandler an injustice by claiming that the author did not produce elaborate mysteries like the creator of the Continental Op, despite admitting, "I do my plotting in my head as I go along [. . .] and I usually do it wrong and have to do it again" (qtd. in MacShane, *Life* 67). Chandler undoubtedly managed to compose complex mysteries, as is demonstrated by the intricate plot of *The Big Sleep*. But Crumley's assertion that he does not care for plotting has further significance because it draws upon Joseph T. Shaw's belief that mystery and detective stories should not necessarily concentrate on plot but aim to represent genuine characters operating in a realistic world. To do this, character, events, and circumstances need to be authentic in order to convey the level of realism required, while the use of fate or chance would dilute efforts to create an authentic literature. Although Chandler does rely on coincidence on certain occasions, the circumstances of these occurrences can be legitimately justified, adding to the sense of realism. While Marlowe observes on one occasion in *The Big Sleep* that "[f]ate stage-managed the whole thing" (177), Chandler's plots realistically illustrate how the majority of the action in the novels is entirely out of Marlowe's control. Although the notions of fate and coincidence can be interpreted as plot device cheats, they are also realistically reflective of events occurring at that moment in the plot. Rejecting any notion of a ubiquitous narrator which is generally compounded by a third-person narrative, it demonstrates that events are realistically guided by occurrences beyond the detective's influence. These events are not acts of fate as such, but occurrences that can be legitimately rationalized.

Although Crumley makes an obvious distinction between Chandler and Hammett, Chandler himself felt indebted to his predecessor for severing the ties to the traditional mystery story and making the hard-boiled style far more believable. No longer was crime fiction an unimportant genre; instead it became a legitimate and significant form of literature. Chandler famously declared in "The Simple Art of Murder" that Hammett "took murder out of the Venetian vase and dropped it into the alley" (14) and believed that Hammett's writing was comparable to that of more famous writers such as Ernest Hemingway. Chandler also believed that the development of a realistic and believable character and the importance of placing him in authentic surroundings were essential preconditions that allowed the intricacies of the plot to unfold. Chandler once noted that in most crime stories, as the plot thickens, "the people become mere names," so the "idea of being committed in advance to a certain pattern appals me" (qtd. in MacShane, *Life* 67, 68). He said, "With me a plot, if you could call it that, is an organic thing. It grows and often overgrows. I am continually finding myself with scenes that I won't discard and that don't want to fit in. So that my plot problem invariably ends up as a desperate attempt to justify a lot of material that, for me at least, has come alive and insists on staying alive. It's probably a silly way to write, but I seem to know no other way" (qtd. in MacShane, *Life* 68). Chandler's aversion to preplanning his plot-lines and his reluctance to tie up loose ends is typified by his blunt response to a question concerning the film adaptation of *The Big Sleep* in 1946. When asked by the screenwriters who had killed the chauffeur, Owen Taylor, in the novel, Chandler's response was simply, "I don't know" (qtd. in Speir 29). His reply was not intended to be flippant but goes to the very heart of what he was trying to achieve. The use of the first-person narrative means that knowing who actually killed the chauffeur becomes irrelevant because we are meant to only see and understand what Marlowe does. Jerry Speir notes that Chandler's reaction to the question of Owen Taylor's death also "underscores his deep-seated aversion to strictly rational explanations for human actions" (ibid.). Within this framework Marlowe *must* remain ignorant of certain events because being an omnipresent private eye would cause a first-person narrative to lose its sense of realism.

Just as Chandler gave his plots and narrative style a sense of realism, he also took great care to create believable protagonists and to provide his detective with extensive emotional and psychological depth. He argued that the mystery novel in its traditional form was "a dream world which may be entered and left at will, and it leaves no scars" (qtd. in MacShane, *Life* 71). To combat the shallowness of this light-hearted tendency, Chandler's objective "was to bridge the gap between detective fiction and ordinary fiction by imbuing his characters with attitudes and feelings that *do* in fact leave scars" (ibid. Emphasis added.). As well as attempting to direct his stories away from the violence of the era's pulp stories Chandler attempted to maneuver his audience into a position that allowed him to become "a bit more humane" (ibid.) with his characters and style of writing.

Although contemporary crime fiction is increasingly located in the gritty inner cities and aims to "replicate life at street level" (Haut, *Neon Noir* 2) it is not a theme that is new to the crime genre. In fact, the representation of a realistic urban environment is a theme that has existed in the genre since Hammett began writing. However, the traumatizing effects of the Vietnam War and its effects on American culture expand the genre into a far darker representation, which suggests an intense evolution of the original concept of the noir style. Despite this reinterpretation, many post-Vietnam critics note that the style still retains the original principles of the noir form. Haut argues that, by "substituting the language of survival for the phoney street wisdom of past investigative fiction, [Vietnam War chroniclers] set a precedent for future noirists" (*Neon Noir* 52).

However, what is generally disregarded is the precedent that was set by the original hard-boiled noirists. In fact, although war noir reached its zenith with the Vietnam War, it is a style that can be traced back to Chandler and his Philip Marlowe novels. The combination of war themes and the noir style made Chandler's work so subtly different from his contemporaries that critics have failed to recognize its significance within the genre. Commentators in the field have argued that the incorporation of war to the form is exclusively associated with post-Vietnam writers because it starkly represents the trauma of the era. Yet Chandler's work depicts the same themes from an earlier generation. What made Chandler's work so appealing and relevant to the writers of the Vietnam era were exactly the themes and motifs that they themselves would take to heart in their own works.

John Cawelti argued over three decades ago, "The hard-boiled detective has a few scratches, but no deep wounds spoil his function as a fantasy hero. He is a man of who has been able to say the hell with it, yet retain the world's most important benefits—self-esteem, popularity and respect" (161). Yet in a contemporary environment plagued by warfare, the modern popularity of the crime genre and the increasing fragmentation of society have ensured renewed interest and recognition for detectives who, like Philip Marlowe, "cannot simply brush off his or her 'few scratches' and unproblematically retain his or her 'self-esteem, popularity and respect'" (Pepper 168). In an increasingly chaotic and uncertain contemporary America, the growing popularity of uncompromising "Chandleresque" novelists, as well as the furthering of the hard-boiled noir style by filmmakers such as Quentin Tarantino, has expanded Chandler's literary following. This contemporary revival of interest "has pushed attention back to the American roots of hard-boiled fiction" and onto Raymond Chandler in particular (Hiney 282).

The longevity of Chandler's detective reveals a great deal about both his style as a writer and Philip Marlowe's appeal as a character. Haut observes that Marlowe became "a template for private eyes from the pulp era to the present" (*Pulp Culture* 71), and Frank MacShane has noted that Marlowe's "wisecracks create [a] quasi-cynical, quasi-romantic atmosphere" which makes him completely unique. "Most detective-story narrators are colourless," says MacShane, but "Marlowe was something quite different" (*Life* 69). Yet, the detective is more than merely a character; he is a fully formed, fully realized, coherent being who truthfully embodies the pain and distress of a tormented war veteran. He wanders the streets of Los Angeles trying to right wrongs and bring justice to a blighted city while also struggling to locate himself in a society that does not see him. Marlowe's characterization embodies the qualities noted in *Death in the Afternoon*, where Hemingway declares, "When writing a novel a writer should create people; people not characters" (168). Similarly Joseph T. Shaw believed that in the detective story "action is meaningless unless it involves [a] recognizable human character in three-dimensional form" (qtd. in MacShane, *Life* 47). Shaw argued that authentic detective fiction needed to emphasize one thing in particular: "character and the problems inherent in human behaviour" (ibid.). Marlowe is not simply a one-dimensional character; he is encoded with a specific psychology, which, when considered alongside an intimate first-person narrative, reveals him to be much more than simply a generic character. Marlowe is a troubled and multidimensional individual representative of a psychologically complex self.

By reevaluating the significance of Chandler's combat experience it is clear that the First World War had a profound effect upon his emotional stability and, consequently, upon all aspects of his life and work. This shift of focus significantly alters the way in which both Chandler and his work can be viewed because it not only uncovers the depth of trauma suffered by Chandler, but it also shows how the effects of his experiences are reflected in the characters and works he created. The symptoms of PTSD that he suffered intruded into almost every aspect of his life, prompting numerous suicide attempts and other not-so-veiled cries for help. Yet in a society that, at the time, did not recognize or understand the devastating effects that war could wreak upon a person's mind, Chandler's salvation came in the form of writing. Philip Marlowe acted as Chandler's sounding board and someone he could take strength from. The detective became a catharsis to alleviate Chandler's stress and someone he could pour all his thoughts, emotions, and traumas into. Through his protagonist he transferred his trauma onto the page in an attempt to relieve his physical and psychological posttraumatic symptoms. Consequently, Marlowe came to personify the image of an antihero, and Chandler's trauma became his detective's trauma.

Although his stated aim in writing the Marlowe novels was to shift the public mindset regarding the traditional style of the crime story, what Chandler constructed in its place was a far grittier and more realistic representation of American society that incorporated honest emotions and people. As he said in December 1950, his private eye was "an exaggeration of the possible" (qtd. in Gardiner and Walker 60). Chandler's novels were also accurate portrayals of the hypocritical nature of society and the depravity at its heart, as well as truthfully illustrating the invisibility of veterans in a society that refused to acknowledge their sacrifice. D. C. Russell noted that Chandler "writes of a world and order of society in which there is little beauty or serenity" (123). Yet Marlowe refuses to give up. In the article "A Cato of the Cruelties" published in May–June 1947 for the *Partisan Review*, R. W. Flint argues that "Philip Marlowe is as much of [an] existentialist [. . .] as modern America has stomach for." The reason for this, Flint argues, is that "[t]he marks of [Marlowe's] integrity are a searing doubt as to the motives of his countrymen [. . .] and a profound awareness of fate. But the red badge that sets him apart is an almost Biblical faith in the value of decision. He is forever rolling the stone uphill [. . .] a blind inevitable moral energy plowing through the wildest ambiguities always into the heart of insecurity and danger" (Bodleian 58:52). Flint believed that in Marlowe's case an argument could be made for the detective's existentialism because in Chandler's novels, "suspense grows [. . .] out of human rather than a literary situation," the detective "is no longer the wizard, the mental giant, the latter-day Paracelsus; he is not even the intellectual master of the situation." Therefore, in comparison to many of his contemporaries and "because he has no aces up his sleeve," Marlowe "lives by the light of his sentimental but genuine humanity" (Bodleian 58:52–53).

▼▼▼

The fifty-fifth anniversary of Chandler's death, combined with the seventy-fifth anniversary of the publication of *The Big Sleep* in 2014, offers a vantage point from which to reassess Chandler's life and work by reevaluating one of the key influences and experiences in his life. Exploring Chandler's war experience in precise detail has uncovered elements crucial to understanding not only Chandler's troubled character, but also that of his war veteran protagonist Philip Marlowe. Chandler's experience during the First World War is a key aspect of his biography that has lacked critical exploration, yet it raises important questions regarding the accuracy and research of earlier biographies. Previous written accounts of Chandler's life and work have overlooked the importance and influence of his war experience not only in the creation and characterization of his detective, but also in Chandler's literary standing. His war experience and its psychological consequences firmly connect him to the disillusionment and estrangement of the Lost Generation. The theme of disenchantment shared by Hemingway and Chandler is a significant connection that can be found in numerous literary articles and reviews from the midtwentieth century, highlighted here together for the first time, and which, perhaps controversially, make the case for Chandler's firm consideration among the Lost Generation. On a simple level, if, as Cowley argued, the Lost Generation represents the First World War generation then Chandler's place among America's literary icons is undeniable. But the case for Chandler's inclusion is much stronger than that. The themes that he returned to in his work, the disillusionment, the vision of society, and the psychological trauma, make Chandler's inclusion among the Lost Generation inarguable.

Because of his social conscience and stylistic realism, Chandler's intentions of creating a brutal yet honest form of crime story came alive. In a letter to William Campbell Gault, Chandler said, "I believe there is a peculiar kind of satisfaction in taking a type of literature which the pundits regard as below the salt and making of it something which the fairminded among them are forced to treat with a little respect" (UCLA 9:13 p. 3). It was a gamble that paid off. By 1945 D. C. Russell had noted that "Chandler writes [. . .] with an artistry of craftsmanship and a realism that can rank him with many a famous novelist" (123). With his unique combination of style, wit, honesty, and real identifiable emotions, Philip Marlowe became a character to emulate.

Yet it is Chandler's incorporation of personal traumas that make his novels, and Philip Marlowe in particular, so profound and endearing. To understand the detective's distinctive behavior Chandler's work needs to be viewed in a specific traumatic context. Marlowe was created as a flawed individual tormented by his war experiences and suffering the effects of PTSD. Yet this was also Chandler's own personal trauma. Believing that a writer's style should be a "projection of personality," Chandler argued that literature should stem from "emotion and perception; it is the ability to transfer these to paper which makes [. . .] a writer" (qtd. in Gardiner and Walker 76). Like the authors of the Lost Generation who wrote of their physical or psychological experiences of war and its consequences, Chandler similarly presented a sense of disillusionment with postwar American society. As Russell noted, Chandler "removed his work from the realm of merely conventional entertainment to the point where it becomes a serious study of a certain kind of American society" (124). By presenting Marlowe in this imperfect form Chandler provided for himself an emotional and psychological release. Writing became a self-liberating mechanism—a safety net—which gave him solace and catharsis that not only connected him to the disillusionment of the Lost Generation, but also served as a model for future writers to emulate, especially in the traumatic aftermath of the Vietnam War.

By viewing the plight of the war veteran detective through this lens, a realistic rationale for the detective's motivations can be discerned, motivations that are considerably more complex than the chivalric character traits that critics have traditionally recognized. Although many believe him to be "the exemplar of tough masculinity" (Horsley 68), Marlowe's character goes far beyond the traditional chivalric context. Marlowe cannot escape the experience of war and its damaging consequences, and his conception reflects the underlying emotional trauma that not only plagued his creator but also troubled American society after the First World War. In his detective novels Chandler displayed the narrow attitudes of Americans toward those who fought and sacrificed themselves for their country, men who went to war and witnessed unimaginable horrors but who returned to American society only to be disregarded and abandoned. Chandler's work exhibits the recognition and acknowledgment that veterans seek in their attempt to reconcile their sacrifices with the self-centeredness of the environment they have returned to. As a result he transferred to his detective the distinctive behavioral patterns of a psychologically wounded war veteran who mirrored his own insecurities and frailties. Marlowe has therefore become a character who embodies the stresses and frustrations of war's aftermath. With an influence that spanned the entire breadth of his work and goes to the very heart of his existence, Chandler created his detective in his own image: a war veteran traumatized by the ever-present and unyielding symptoms of PTSD. Set against this backdrop, the contention that Philip Marlowe is a traumatized war veteran reconfigures the entire field of academic investigation surrounding Chandler and his detective, and as such neither Chandler nor Marlowe can be viewed in the same light again.

NOTES

PREFACE

1. MacShane's version of events can be found on page 30 in *The Life of Raymond Chandler*, while Hiney's account can be found in *Raymond Chandler: A Biography* on page 43.

2. Carlos Baker was acquainted with Ernest Hemingway and so much of the biographical material he used, especially regarding his war experience, came from Hemingway himself. When writing a biography this is not advisable because he assumes that details are correct when, as in Hemingway's case, they were severely exaggerated. Chandler himself once noted of Budd Schulberg's novel about F.Scott Fitzgerald, "[Schulberg] knew Fitzgerald personally, which is probably a disadvantage, since knowing Fitzgerald as a man probably blinded one to what he was or could be as a writer" ("The Raymond Chandler Papers 1930–1959," The University of California Los Angeles. Collection 638, Charles E. Young Research Library Department of Special Collections, Collection 638, Box 10, File 3: 335).

CHAPTER 1

1. A full discussion of the symptoms associated with war trauma and the resulting PTSDs are given by Grossman on pages 45–48. Herman also discusses the "oscillation" between different emotions and reactions in chapter 3 of her book, and she gives a detailed analysis of the key psychological symptoms of PTSD on pages 35–50.

CHAPTER 2

1. Bodleian, "The Raymond Chandler Papers." Box 75, pages 35–62: 42. This is a different quote to that featured in the preface, a sign that Chandler would use "weathered phrases" to describe his experience.

2. Hemingway chose to spin a heroic tale of fighting with the tough Italian Arditi and of being caught up while fighting in an explosion from a trench mortar shell. Then, according to earlier biographies, "[h]is legs felt as if he were wearing rubber boots filled with warm water. Beside him was a man who made no sound. Just beyond him was another, badly

hurt and crying piteously. Ernest groped for his neck and legs, heaved him up in a fireman's carry, and began to stagger towards the command post. He had covered fifty yards when a round from a heavy machine gun tore into his right leg at the knee. It felt like an icy snowball. He stumbled and fell with the man on his shoulder. He never remembered how he had covered the final hundred yards. But he made it, delivered his man, and lost consciousness." (Baker *Ernest Hemingway A Life Story* 45) While it is true that Hemingway was indeed hit by shellfire and had responded bravely enough to allow more severely injured soldiers to be transported first, certain details regarding the event are entirely fictional, added on later while he was in the hospital for the benefit of his family and friends back home. He was in fact injured while handing out chocolate and cigarettes to Italian soldiers behind the front line. Although he was caught in the shell attack, and his legs were embedded with shrapnel, he was not mown down by a machine gun, and he did not carry anyone to safety as many of his biographers have led us to believe. Ted Brumback notes in a letter dated July 14 that "[o]nly a few of these [shrapnel] pieces [were] large enough to cut deep; the most serious of these being in the knee and two in the right foot." Yet Ernest insisted only days later that he had both shrapnel and bullets in his legs—227 in total—but miraculously none had struck bone, not even the bullet in his kneecap. So the circumstances of Lieutenant Frederick Henry's wounding in *A Farewell to Arms* appears to be a fairly accurate account of what *actually* happened to Hemingway at Fossalta, yet as Lynn notes "his readers would by and large refuse to accept [*A Farewell to Arms*] as a summary of the whole story" (Lynn, 86). Carlos Baker, Jeffrey Meyers, and Michael Reynolds are among those who have perpetuated the myth surrounding Hemingway's wounding.

3. It is rather surprising that Chandler chose the subject of sex in order to "test his ear for English dialogue" (MacShane, *Life* 248). That he titled them "A Routine to Shock the Neighbours" also shows his intent that these sketches were written to "shock." The accent and voice of the sketches are distinctly middle to upper class and may have been designed to shock those he knew. The subject could also represent the time spent receiving an English middle-class education at Dulwich, where boys were given strict instruction on sex and taught that masturbation was "dirty" (MacShane, *Life* 11).

4. Judith Lewis Herman, Dave Grossman, Elaine Scarry, and Edward Tick have all reinforced Freud's original opinion that in most cases psychological trauma during warfare is transferred "passively" through the threat of annihilation.

CHAPTER 3

1. A fact that Douglass herself gets wrong, noting that Chandler was writing for *Black Mask* in the 1920s, when in fact his first *Black Mask* story, "Blackmailers Don't Shoot," was published in December 1933.

2. Cowley, *A Second Flowering,* 240. In *A Second Flowering,* Cowley emphasizes that he has included certain Lost Generation authors in his book based on the eight that best represented the literary scene at the time. These are F. Scott Fitzgerald, Ernest Hemingway, John Dos Passos, e. e. cummings, Thornton Wilder, William Faulkner, Thomas Wolfe, and Hart Crane. Cowley acknowledges that he excludes many other respected Lost Generation

writers, including Katherine Anne Porter, Elizabeth Madox Roberts, Henry Miller, Djuana Barnes, Archibald MacLeish, John Steinbeck, James Gould Cozzens, and Nathanael West. Although he notes that at the time of the First World War the writers he includes were "the right age for soldiering" (3), those who are generally considered part of the Lost Generation were not necessarily war writers. Despite saying that a more accurate description would be the First World War generation, this does not mean that they would have had to witness the war firsthand, only be aware of how it had affected American society. It is in this light that the older or younger members of the "Generation" become relevant. As Cowley has shown, despite being out of the generally accepted age range for the Lost Generation, and not writing war material, it is possible for a writer to be included among this prolific "Generation." Therefore an argument can be made for Raymond Chandler's inclusion among the writers of the Lost Generation.

3. The alienation of veterans is widely discussed by many psychologists. See Herman's *Trauma and Recovery: From Domestic Abuse to Political Terror*, 61–62, 66–67, 70–71; Jonathan Shay's *Odysseus in America: Combat Trauma and the Trials of Homecoming*, 164–79. For specific discussions about Vietnam, see Robert Jay Lifton's *Home from the War: Learning from Vietnam Veterans*, 69–71, 132–33; Herbert Hendin and Anne Pollinger Hass's *Wounds of War: The Psychological Aftermath of Combat in Vietnam*, 233–34.

CHAPTER 4

1. Hemingway repeatedly uses the derogatory word "nigger" to denote black Parisians. For example, in *The Sun Also Rises* Jake Barnes says:"Inside Zelli's it was crowded, smoky, and noisy. The music hit you as you went in. Brett and I danced. It was so crowded we could barely move. The nigger drummer waved at Brett" (69). Similarly, repeated use of the word can be found later when Bill is referring to a "Vienna prize-fight" featuring a "Wonderful nigger" (77).

Likewise, demonstrating the discrimination in American crime fiction, Hammett's Continental Op remarks in *The Dain Curse*: "I couldn't see the hand that was exploring my inside coat-pocket, nor the arm that came down over my shoulder; but they smelled of the kitchen, so I knew they were brown" (372).

2. Speir, *Raymond Chandler*, 112. For example, in *The Big Sleep*, after discovering Carmen Sternwood in his bed and promptly removing her from his apartment, Marlowe tells us, "I walked to the windows and pulled the shades up and opened the windows wide. The night air came drifting in with a kind of stale sweetness that still remembered automobile exhausts and the streets of the city. I reached for my drink and drank it slowly. The apartment house door closed itself down below me . . . I went back to the bed and looked down at it. The imprint of her head was still in the pillow, of her small corrupt body still on the sheets . . . I put my empty glass down and tore the bed to pieces savagely" (*The Big Sleep*, 154–55). During his encounter with Carmen, he says, "It's so hard for women—even nice women—to realize that their bodies are not irresistible" (*The Big Sleep*, 153), and the next morning he comments, "You can have a hangover from other things than alcohol. I had one from women. Women made me sick" (*The Big Sleep*, 156). Yet, if we consider the events preceding these passages they give a far better understanding of Marlowe's feelings at the time. Speir tells us,

> Just prior to his encounter with Carmen, Marlowe has come from one roughly parallel with Carmen's sister Vivian, who has also attempted to use her sexuality on him to extract the information and cooperation she desires. And this is not the first time Marlowe has found Carmen nude and playing games of sexual coercion. She has in fact, been throwing herself at him ever since he walked into the door of the Sternwood mansion in chapter 1. And finally, it is at about this point, halfway through the novel, that Marlowe is beginning to perceive that this sort of sexual gamesmanship was at the root of one of the book's essential puzzles, the disappearance of Rusty Regan." (Speir, 112–13)

So it is no wonder that Marlowe feels "sick" of women, they have been attempting to use him for their own purposes from the first page of the novel.

3. *Poodle Springs* is the eighth Philip Marlowe novel. Upon his death in 1959 Chandler had completed just four chapters. With the permission of the Raymond Chandler Estate, the novel was completed in 1989 by the crime fiction writer Robert B. Parker.

4. For example, *The Big Sleep* was constructed from "Killer in the Rain," "The Curtain," and a small section of "The Man Who Liked Dogs." In *Farewell, My Lovely* Chandler reused "Try the Girl" and "Mandarin's Jade," while in *The Lady in the Lake* Chandler merged "Bay City Blues" and the story "The Lady in the Lake." The remaining novels (*The High Window*, *The Little Sister*, and *The Long Goodbye*) were entirely original pieces of work (although the screenplay *Playback* was later recycled and became Chandler's seventh and final novel).

CHAPTER 5

1. In a contemporary context in the United Kingdom for example, Harry Fletcher of the National Association of Probation Officers has noted that in recent convictions involving former British soldiers who served in either the Gulf or Afghanistan, "In virtually every incidence . . . [they] became involved in excess alcohol or drug-taking, and [were] subsequently convicted of an offence of violence" (Doward, *The Observer*, 2008, 11). This has undoubtedly added to the subconscious belief that those returning from combat are in some way corrupted by their experiences. Andrew Neilson of the Howard League for Penal Reform has said that situations where soldiers return and are unable to function properly in society are common. "An inability to cope with the pressures of civilian life, particularly for those who joined the services immediately after leaving school," says Neilson, "can certainly lead to offending and see someone effectively swapping one institution for another" (Doward, *The Observer*, 11).

2. This actually resonates with a letter Ian Fleming once wrote Chandler, which was addressed "Dear Field Marshal Chandler" and signed "Private Fleming" (qtd in Hiney, 230). It shows not only the close relationship between the two writers, but also Fleming's interpretation of Chandler's character, which is reflected in Marlowe in this scene.

CHAPTER 6

1. Chandler, *The Long Goodbye*, 176. This is an eerily similar scenario to Chandler's own suicide attempt in 1955, which is mentioned in chapter 1.

CHAPTER 7

1. A term which comes from "CB," an abbreviation of "Construction Battalions."

2. *Miami Blues* (1984), *New Hope for the Dead* (1985), *Sideswipe* (1987), and *The Way We Die Now* (1988).

3. Chandler incorporated the psychiatric symptoms of PTSD; Hammett drew upon his experiences with the Pinkerton Detective Agency.

BIBLIOGRAPHY

Aichinger, Peter. *The American Soldier in Fiction 1880–1963: A History of Attitudes towards Warfare and the Military Establishment.* Ames: Iowa State University Press, 1975.

Allegretto, Michael. *Blood Stone.* New York: Avon, 1990.

Appel, J. W., and G. W. Bebbe. "Preventive Psychiatry: An Epidemiological Approach." *Journal of the American Medical Association* 131 (1946): 1468–71.

Baker, Carlos. *Hemingway: A Life Story.* Harmondsworth: Penguin, 1969

Bell, Ian, and Graham Daldry. *Watching the Detectives: Essays on Crime Fiction.* London: Macmillan, 1990.

Bertens, Johannes, and Theo D'haen. *Contemporary American Crime Fiction.* Basingstoke: Palgrave, 2001.

Blair, Walter. "Dashiell Hammett: Themes and Techniques." In Gohodes, Clarence (ed.) *Essays on American Literature in Honour of Jay B. Hubbell.* Duke University Press, 1968.

Bloom, Harold. *The Western Canon: The Books and School of the Ages.* New York: Harcourt Brace, 1994.

The Blue Dahlia. Dir. George Marshall. Universal, 1946.

The Bodleian Library, Oxford. "The Raymond Chandler Papers." Department of Special Collections and Western Manuscripts. Accessed May 2008.

Bracken, Patrick. *Trauma: Culture, Meaning & Philosophy.* London: Whurr, 2003.

Bruccoli, Matthew J. *Chandler before Marlowe: Raymond Chandler's Early Prose and Poetry, 1908–1912.* Columbia: University of South Carolina Press, 1973.

Cather, Willa. *One of Ours.* New York: Knopf, 1922.

Cawelti, John G. *Adventure, Mystery, Romance: Formula Stories as Art and Popular Culture.* Chicago: University of Chicago Press, 1976.

Chandler, Raymond. *The Big Sleep.* London: Penguin Books, 1939.

———. *Farewell, My Lovely.* London: Penguin Books, 1940.

———. *The High Window.* London: Penguin Books, 2005.

———. *Killer in the Rain.* London: Penguin Books, 1966.

———. *The Lady in the Lake.* London: Penguin Books, 1952.

———. *The Little Sister.* London: Penguin Books, 1955.

———. *The Long Goodbye.* London: Penguin Books, 1959.

———. *Playback.* London: Penguin Books, 1961.

———. *The Simple Art of Murder.* New York: Vintage Books, 1988.

———. *The Smell of Fear*. Trowbridge, UK: Book Club Associates, 1983.

Cobley, Paul. *The American Thriller: Generic Innovation and Social Change in the 1970s*. New York: Palgrave, 2000.

Cochran, David. *American Noir: Underground Writers and Filmmakers of the Postwar Era*. Washington: Smithsonian Institution Press, 2000.

Contemporary Authors. Vol. 121, 2004: 65–68. Detroit: Gale Group.

Cooper, David E. *Existentialism: A Reconstruction*. Oxford: Blackwell, 1999.

Cooper, John Milton, Jr. *Pivotal Decades: The United States, 1900–1920*. London: W. W. Norton, 1990.

Cooperman, Stanley. *World War I and the American Novel*. London: Johns Hopkins University Press, 1967.

Cowley, Malcolm. *A Second Flowering: Works and Days of the Lost Generation*. New York: Viking Compass, 1973.

Craig, H. A. L. "The Whiskey of Affliction." *The Listener* (27 September 1951): 513–15. Crais, Robert. *The Monkey's Raincoat*. London: Orion, 2003.

Crumley, James. *The Collection: The Wrong Case, The Last Good Kiss, Dancing Bear*. London: Picador, 1991.

———. *Bordersnakes*. New York: Warner Books, 1996.

———. *Dancing Bear*. New York: Vintage, 1984.

———. *The Final Country*. London: HarperCollins, 2003.

———. *The Last Good Kiss*. New York: Vintage, 1991.

———. *The Mexican Tree Duck*. New York: Mysterious, 1993.

———. *One to Count Cadence*. New York: Vintage, 1969.

———. *The Right Madness*. London: HarperCollins, 2005.

———. *The Wrong Case*. New York: Vintage Books, 1986.

Cunningham, Bill, Steven L. Davis, Rollo K. Newsom. *Lone Star Sleuths: An Anthology of Texas Crime Fiction*. Austin: University of Texas Press, 2007.

Dos Passos, John. *Three Soldiers*. London: Penguin Books, 1921.

Diggins, John Patrick. *The Proud Decades: America in War and Peace, 1941–1960*. London: W. W. Norton, 1988.

Dinter, Elmar. *Hero or Coward: Pressures Facing the Soldier in Battle*. London: Frank Cass, 1985.

Directorate of History and Heritage. "Battalion Orders." 7th Canadian Infantry Brigade. 23 March 1918. Confidential War Diary of 7th Canadian Infantry Brigade. Collections Canada. Web. 27 May 2008. http://data2.collectionscanada.ca/e/e044/e001083875.jpg.

———. "Battalion Orders. Confidential War Diary of 7th Canadian Infantry Brigade." June 1918. Web. 27 May 2008. http://data2.collectionscanada.ca/e/e044/e001084152.jpg to http://data2.collectionscanada.ca/e/e044/e001084155.jpg.

———. "Battalion Orders." 7th Canadian Infantry Brigade. 3 June 1918. Confidential War Diary of 7th Canadian Infantry Brigade. June 1918. Web. 27 May 2008. http://data2.collectionscanada.ca/e/e044/e001084156.jpg.

———. "Battalion Orders." 7th Canadian Infantry Brigade. 9 June 1918. Confidential War Diary of 7th Canadian Infantry Brigade. June 1918. Web. 27 May 2008. http://data2.

collectionscanada.ca/e/e044/e001084157.jpg and http://data2.collectio nscanada.ca/e/e044/e044/e001084158.jpg.

———. "Battalion Orders." 7th Canadian Infantry Brigade. 12 June 1918. Confidential War Diary of 7th Canadian Infantry Brigade. June 1918. Web. 27 May 2008. http://data2 .collrctionscanada.ca/e/e04/e001084159.jpg.

———. "Casualty Form-Active Service." Raymond Thornton Chandler. 1917–1919. Canadian Archives (photocopy). Correspondence. 6 March 2008.

———. "Confidential War Diary of 7th Canadian Infantry Brigade." March—May 1918. Collections Canada. Web. 27 May 2008:

1–13 March 1918 http://data2.collectionscanada.ca/e/e044/e001083865.jpg.

14–25 March 1918 http://data2.collectionscanada.ca/e/e044/e001083866.jpg.

26–31 March 1918 http://data2.collectionscanada.ca/e/e044/e001083867.jpg.

31 March–4 April 1918 http://data2.collectionscanada.ca/e/e044/e001083914.jpg.

5–8 April 1918 http://data2.collectionscanada.ca/e/e044/e001083915.jpg.

9–13 April 1918 http://data2.collectionscanada.ca/e/e044/e001083916.jpg.

13–19 April 1918 http://data2.collectionscanada.ca/e/e044/e001083917.jpg.

20–27 April 1918 http://data2.collectionscanada.ca/e/e044/e001083918.jpg.

28–30 April 1918 http://data2.collectionscanada.ca/e/e044/e001083919.jpg.

30 April–7 May 1918 http://data2.collectionscanada.ca/e/e044/e001084023.jpg.

8–17 May 1918 http://data2.collectionscanada.ca/e/e044/e001084024.jpg.

18–26 May 1918 http://data2.collectionscanada.ca/e/e044/e001084025.jpg.

27–31 May 1918 http://data2.collectionscanada.ca/e/e044/e001084026.jpg.

———. "Confidential War Diary of 7th Canadian Infantry Brigade." 1–8 June 1918. Canadian Archives (photocopy) Correspondence. 6 March 2008.

———. "Confidential War Diary of 7th Canadian Infantry Brigade." May 1918. Web. 27 May 2008. http://data2.collectionscanada.ca/e/e044/e001084023.jpg to http://data2.collec tions canada.ca/e/e044/e001084026.jpg.

———. "7th Canadian Infantry Battalion (7th British Columbia) Battalion Orders." Collections Canada. Web. 27 May 2008. http://data2.collectionscanada.ca/e/e044/e001084159.jpg.

———. "Department of Veteran Affairs Statement of service in the Canadian Armed Forces." Raymond Thornton Chandler. 1917–1919. Canadian Archives (photocopy). Correspondence. 6 March 2008.

———. "Pay Documents." Raymond Thornton Chandler. 1917–1919. Canadian Archives (photocopy). Correspondence. 6 March 2008.

Douglas, Ann. *Terrible Honesty: Mongrel Manhattan in the 1920s*. New York: Noonday, 1996.

Doward, Jamie. "Record Numbers of Ex-Combat Soldiers in UK Jails as Combat Trauma Blamed." *The Observer*, 31 August 2008: 11.

Durham, Philip. *Down These Mean Streets a Man Must Go: Raymond Chandler's Knight*. Chapel Hill: University of North Carolina Press, 1963.

———. "Introduction," in Nolan, William F., *Dashiell Hammett; A Casebook*. Santa Barbara: McNally & Loftin Publishers, 1969.

Evans, Martin Marix. *The Battles of the Somme*. London: Weidenfeld and Nicolson, 1996.

Fagin, James A. *Criminal Justice*. New York: Allyn and Bacon, 2003.

Faulkner, William. *Soldier's Pay.* London: Penguin, 1926.

Fitzgerald, F. Scott. *The Great Gatsby.* Penguin Books: London, 1925.

———. *This Side of Paradise.* London: Bodley Head, 1971.

Freeman, Judith. *The Long Embrace: Raymond Chandler and the Woman He Loved.* New York: Vintage, 2007.

Freidel, Frank. *Over There: The American Experience in World War I.* Short Hills, NJ: Burford Books, 2003.

Freud, Sigmund. *Beyond the Pleasure Principle and Other Writing.* London: Penguin, 2003.

Fussell, Paul. *The Great War and Modern Memory.* Oxford: Oxford University Press, 2000.

Gabriel, Richard. *Military Psychiatry: A Comparative Perspective.* New York: Greenport, 1986.

Gardiner, Dorthy, and Katherine Sorley Walker, eds. *Raymond Chandler Speaking.* New York: Houghton Mifflin, 1971.

Gay, Peter. *The Freud Reader.* London: Vintage, 1995.

Gohodes, Clarence, ed. *Essays on American Literature in Honour of Jay B. Hubbell.* Duke University Press, 1968.

Gorman, Ed, Lee Server, and Martin Greenberg, eds. *The Big Book of Noir.* New York: Carroll and Graff, 1998.

Graves, Robert. *Goodbye to All That.* New York: Doubleday, 1957.

Grinker, Roy, and John Speigel. *Men under Stress.* Philadelphia: Blakeston, 1945.

Gross, Miriam, ed. *The World of Raymond Chandler.* London: Weidenfeld and Nicholson, 1977.

Grossman, Dave. *On Killing: The Psychological Cost of Learning to Kill in War and Society.* New York: Back Bay Books, 1996.

Hammett, Dashiell. *The Continental Op.* London: Vintage, 1992.

———. *The Maltese Falcon*, London: Orion, 2002.

Hartmann, Geoffrey. *The Fate of Reading and Other Essays.* London: University of Chicago Press, 1975.

Haut, Woody. *Neon Noir: Contemporary American Crime Fiction.* London: Serpent's Tail, 1999.

———. *Pulp Culture: Hard-boiled Fiction and the Cold War.* London: Serpent's Tail, 1995.

Hemingway, Ernest. *Death in the Afternoon*, London: Jonathan Cape, 1932.

———. *A Farewell to Arms.* London: Arrow Classics, 1929.

———. *The First Forty-Nine Stories.* London: Random House, 1939.

———. *In Our Time.* New York: Scribner, 1925.

———. *The Sun Also Rises.* New York: Scribner, 1926.

Hendin, Herbert, and Ann Pollinger Haas. "Suicide and Guilt as Manifestations of PTSD in Vietnam Combat Veterans." *American Journal of Psychiatry* 148 (1991): 586–91.

———. *Wounds of War: The Psychological Aftermath of Combat in Vietnam.* New York: Basic Books, 1984.

Herman, Judith Lewis. *Trauma and Recovery: From Domestic Abuse to Political Terror.* London: Pandora, 2001.

Herr, Michael. *Dispatches*. London: Picador, 1979.

Hilary, Richard. *Snake in the Grasses*. New York: Bantam Books, 1987.

Hilgard, Ernest. *Divided Consciousness: Multiple Controls in Human Thought and Action*. New York: John Wiley, 1977.

Hiney, Tom. *Raymond Chandler: A Biography*. New York: Grove, 1997.

Hiney, Tom, and Frank MacShane, eds. *The Raymond Chandler Papers: Selected Letters and Notification. 1909–1959*, New York: Grove, 2000.

Horowitz, Mardi. *Stress Response Syndromes*. Northvale, NJ: Jason Aronson, 1986.

Horsley, Lee. *Twentieth Century Crime Fiction*. Oxford: Oxford University Press, 2005.

Jacobs, Joesph, and A. Porter. "Chess." The Jewish Encyclopedia. Web. 24 February 2009. www.jewishencyclopedia.com/view.jsp?artid=437&letter=C.

Jameson, Fredric, *The Political Unconscious: Narrative as a Socially Symbolic Art*. Ithaca, NY: Cornell University Press, 1981.

Joiner, Ann Levington. *A Myth in Action: The Heroic Life of Audie Murphy*. Baltimore: PublishAmerica, 2006.

Kardiner. A., and H. Spiegel. *War, Stress, and Neurotic Illness*. New York: Hoeber, 1947.

Kennedy, David. M. *Over Here: The First World War and American Society*. Oxford: Oxford University Press, 1980.

Kiszely, Philip. *Hollywood through Private Eyes. The Screen Adaptation of the Hard-Boiled Private Detective Novel in the Studio Era* Frankfurt: Peter Lang, 2006.

Knight, Stephen. *Crime Fiction 1800–2000: Detection, Death, Diversity*. London: Palgrave Macmillan, 2004.

Lasker, Edward. *Chess*. London: B. T. Batsford, 1973.

Layman, Richard. *Shadow Man: The Life of Dashiell Hammett*. New York: Harcourt Brace Jovanovich, 1981.

Leese, Peter. *Shell Shock: Traumatic Neurosis and the British Soldiers of the First World War*. London: Palgrave Macmillan, 2002.

Legman, Gershon. *Love and Death: Study in Censorship*, New York: Breaking Point, 1949.

Lehmann-Haupt, Christopher. "Mystery and Suspense from Three Old Hands." *New York Times*, December 20, 1993.

Lifton, Robert Jay. *Home from the War: Learning from Vietnam Veterans*. New York: Other, 2005.

Lucy, Calista. Archive manager, Dulwich Collage. Letter. 7 January 2009.

Lynn, Kenneth. *Hemingway*. London: Harvard University Press, 1995.

Macdonald, Ross. *The Moving Target*. New York: Warner, 1949.

MacShane, Frank. *The Life of Raymond Chandler*. London: Jonathan Cape, 1976.

———. *The Notebooks of Raymond Chandler*. New York: Harper Perennial, 2006.

———. *Selected Letters of Raymond Chandler*. New York: Delta, 1987.

———. Chandler before Marlowe. Columbia: University of South Carolina Press, 1973.

Mailer, Norman. *The Naked and the Dead*. London: Flamingo, 1993.

March, William. *Company K*. Tuscaloosa: University of Alabama Press, 1989.

McCann, Sean. *Gumshoe America: Hard Boiled Fiction and the Rise and Fall of New Deal Liberalism*. Durham, NC: Duke University Press, 2000.

McCracken, Scott. *Pulp: Reading Popular Fiction.* Manchester: Manchester University Press, 1998.

McLellan, Dennis. "James Crumely, 1939–2008: Author of Gritty but Poetic Crime Novels." *Los Angles Times*, September 20, 2008 http://articles.latimes.com/2008/sep/20/local/me-crumley20.

Meador, Roy, "Chandler in the Thirties: Apprenticeship of an Angry Man." *Forum* 6, no. 2 (1982): 143–53.

Messent, Peter, ed. *Criminal Proceedings: The Contemporary American Crime Novel.* London: Pluto, 1997.

Meyers, Jeffrey. *Hemingway: A Biography*. New York: Da Capo, 1999.

———. *Scott Fitzgerald: A Biography.* London: Macmillan, 1994.

Mosley, Walter. *Devil in a Blue Dress.* London: Serpent Tail, 1990.

Moss, Robert F. *Raymond Chandler: A Literary Reference.* New York: Carroll and Graff, 2003.

"Murder Business." *Newsweek* (31 October 1949): 69–70.

Murphy, Audie. *To Hell and Back.* London: Corgi Books, 1968.

New York Times. "Blames Superiors for Army Cruelty—'Hard-Boiled' Smith Testifies He Obeyed Orders in Treatment of Prisoners." 30 July 1919 (unknown author). http://query.nytimes.com/mem/archive-free/pdf?res=F10A13F73D5C147A93C2AA178CD85F4D818 5F9. 4 July 2013.

Nicholson, Colonel G. W. L. *Canadian Expeditionary Force 1914–1919.* Published by authority of the Honourable Douglas S. Harkness, P.C., G.M., M.P., Minister of National Defence, and printed by Roger Duhamel F.R.S.C. Queen's Printer and Controller of Stationary: Ottawa, 1962.

Nolan, William F., *Dashiell Hammett; A Casebook.* Santa Barbara: McNally & Loftin Publishers, 1969.

Nyman, Jopi. *Men Alone: Masculinity, Individualism, and Hard-boiled Fiction.* Atlanta, GA: Rodopi, 1997.

Panek, LeRoy Lad. *New Hard-Boiled Writers 1970s—1990s.* Bowling Green, OH: Bowling Green State University Popular Press, 2000.

Parish, Michael E. *Anxious Decades: American Prosperity and Depression, 1920–1941.* New York: W.W. Norton, 1994.

Parsons, I. M., ed. *Men Who March Away: Poems of the First World War.* London: Heinemann Educational Books: 1979.

Pendry, E. D. ed. *Christopher Marlowe, Complete Plays and Poems.* London: J. M. Dent and Sons, 1976.

Pepper, Andrew. *The Contemporary American Crime Novel: Race, Ethnicity, Gender, Class.* Edinburgh: Edinburgh University Press, 2000.

Piep, Karsten H. *Embattled Home Fronts: Domestic Politics and the American Novel of World War I.* Amsterdam, NY: Rodopi B.V., 2009.

Pollock, Wilson. "Man with a Toy Gun." *The New Republic* 146, no. 19 (1962): 21–22.

Prigozy, Ruth, ed. *F. Scott Fitzgerald.* Cambridge: Cambridge University Press, 2002.

Rabinowitz, Peter J. "Rats behind the Wainscotting: Politics, Convention and Chandler's *The Big Sleep.*" *Texas Studies in Language and Literature* 22 (1980): 224–48.

Rawling, Bill. Directorate of History and Heritage. Canadian Archives, Ottawa, Canada. Letter. 17 April 2008.

Rickman, John, ed. *Civilization, War and Death: Selections from Three Works by Sigmund Freud*. London: Hogarth, 1939.

Rottman, Larry, Jan Barry, and Basil T. Paquet. *Winning Hearts and Minds: War Poems by Vietnam Veterans*. New York: McGraw-Hill, 1972.

Ruehlmann, William. *Saint with a Gun: The Unlawful American Private Eye*. New York: New York University Press, 1974.

The Rules of Film Noir. Narr. Matthew Sweet. Dir. Elaine Donnelly Pieper. BBC, 24 December 2009. Television.

Russell, D. C. "The Chandler Books." *Atlantic Monthly* 173, no. 3 (1945).

Sathis, Lou, "Charles Willeford: New Hope for the Living," introduction to Willeford, Charles, *High Priest of California* and *Wild Wives*. San Francisco: Re/Search, 1987.

Saunders, Nicholas J. *Killing Time: Archaeology and the First World War*. Stroud, Gloucestershire: Sutton, 2007.

Scarry, Elaine. *The Body in Pain: The Making and Unmaking of the World*. London: Oxford Paperbacks, 1998.

Scudamore, Major T. V. *A Short History of the 7th Battalion C.E.F.* Vancouver, Canada: Anderson and Odlum, 1930.

Seeger, Alan, and William Archer, *Poems by Alan Seeger*. New York: Charles Scribner's Sons, 1917.

Server, Lee. *Danger Is My Business: An Illustrated History of the Fabulous Pulp Magazines*. San Francisco: Chronicle Books, 1993.

Shay, Jonathan. *Achilles in Vietnam: Combat Trauma and the Undoing of Character*. New York: Scribner, 2003.

———. *Odysseus in America: Combat Trauma and the Trials of Homecoming*. New York: Scribner, 2002.

Shenk, David. *The Immortal Game: A History of Chess, or, How 32 Carved Pieces on a Board Illuminated Our Understanding of War, Science, and the Human Brain*. New York: Anchor Books, 2006.

Shepherd, Ben. *A War of Nerves: Soldiers and Psychiatrists 1914–1994*. London: Pimlico, 2002.

Shepherd, Stephen H. A., ed. *Le Mort Darthur, Sir Thomas Malory*. New York: W. W. Norton, 2004.

Slotkin, Richard. *Gunfighter Nation: The Myth of the Frontier in Twentieth-Century America*. Norman: University of Oklahoma Press, 1998.

Speir, Jerry. *Raymond Chandler*. New York: Frederick Ungar, 1981.

Steinburg, Sybil. "Charles Willeford: An Interview." In Ed Gorman, Lee Server, and Martin Greenberg (eds.), *The Big Book of Noir*. New York: Carroll and Graff, 1998.

Stevenson, Berton Egbert. *Poems of American History*. Boston: Houghton Mifflin.

Sublett, Jesse. *You Can't Go Home Again, James Crumley's Brilliant Ambivalence about Texas, The Austin Chronicle*. Oct. 26, 2001. Web. 21 March 2009. http://www.austinchronicle.com/books/2001-10-26/83407/.

Swank, Roy L., and Walter E. Marchand. "Combat Neurosis: Development of Combat Exhaustion." *Archives of Neurology and Psychology* 55 (1946): 236–47.

Symonds, W. S. *Malvern Chase*. London: Simpkin, Marshall, Hamilton, Kent, 1913.

Symons, Julian. *Bloody Murder: The Classic Crime Fiction Reference*. London: Pan Books, 1992.

———. *Dashiell Hammett*. Florida: Harcourt Brace Jovanovich, 1985.

Tal, Kali. *Worlds of Hurt: Reading the Literatures of Trauma*. Cambridge: Cambridge University Press, 2004.

Tamony, Peter. "The Origins of 'Hard-Boiled.'" *American Speech* 12, no. 4 (December 1937): 258–61.

Thornburg, Newton. *Cutter and Bone*. London: Serpent's Tail, 1976.

Tick, Edward. *War and the Soul: Healing Our Nation's Veterans and Their Families*. Wheaton, IL: Quest Books, 2005.

Tremblay, Yves. *Directorate of History and Heritage*. Canadian Archives, Ottawa, Canada. Letter. 6 March 2008.

The University of California Los Angeles. "The Raymond Chandler Papers 1930–1959." Collection 638, Charles E. Young Research Library Department of Special Collections. 9–12 October 2008.

van der Kolk, B. A. "The Trauma Spectrum: The Interaction of Biological and Social Events in the Genesis of the Trauma Response." *Journal of Traumatic Stress* (1988): 273–90.

Vinevar, Eugene. *Malory: Works*. London: Oxford University Press, 1971.

Walsh, Jeffrey. *American War Literature 1914 to Vietnam*. London: Macmillan, 1983.

Wharton, Edith. *A Son at the Front*. New York: Scribner, 1923.

Whitely, John S. "Detectives and *Friends: Dashiell Hammett's The Glass Key and Raymond Chandler's The* Long Goodbye." University of Exeter, American Arts Documentation Centre: 1981.

Willeford, Charles, *High Priest of California and Wild Wives*. San Francisco: Re/Search, 1987.

——— *The Hombre from Sonora*. New York: Lennox Hill, 1971.

———. *Sideswipe*. New York: Ballantine, 1988.

Willett, Ralph. *The Naked City: Urban Crime Fiction in the USA*. Manchester: Manchester University Press, 1996.

Williams, John. *Into the Badlands: Travels through Urban America*. London: Flamingo, 1991.

Williams, Tom. *A Mysterious Kind of Light: Raymond Chandler, a Life*. London: Aurum, 2012.

Wilson, Edmund. *The Shores of Light: A Literary Chronicle of the Twenties and Thirties*. New York: Farrar, Straus and Young, 1961.

Winks, Robin W., ed. *Detective Fiction: A Collection of Critical Essays*. Vermont: Countryman.

Winn, Merrick. "A Confession by Raymond Chandler." *London Daily Express*, 14 January 1956.

The Witliff Collections, Texas State University. "James Crumley Biographical Sketch." *A Guide to the James Crumley Papers*. Web. 6 October 2007. http://www.library.txstate .edu/swwc/ archives/writers/crumley.html.

Young, Philip, *Ernest Hemingway: A Reconsideration* [Rev. ed.]. University Park; London: Pennsylvania State University Press 1966.

INDEX

Kolibri 360 GmbH
Ferdinand-Jühlke-Straße 7
99095 Erfurt, Deutschland
produktsicherheit@kolibri360.de